REVIEW FOR THE CLEP* GENERAL SOCIAL SCIENCE & HISTORY EXAMINATION

Complete review of skills

By
Ann Garvin
&
Eileen Curristine

This book is correlated to the video tapes produced by
COMEX Systems, Inc., Review for The
CLEP* General Social Science Examination ©1994
they may be obtained from

 *comex* systems, inc.
5 Cold Hill Rd.
Suite 24
Mendham, NJ 07945

© Copyright 1978, 1980, 1981, 1982, 1987, 1990, 1991, 1993, 1995, 1996, 1997, 1998, 1999, 2000, 2002, 2006

Published by

comex systems, inc.
5 COLD HILL RD. SOUTH
SUITE 24
Mendham, NJ 07945

ISBN 1-56030-150-3

CLEP* (College Level Examination Program)

CLEP provides a way to determine the level of knowledge you now have in relation to college level material. CLEP does **not** determine your ability to **learn** a subject. People tend to have a **low** evaluation of their ability. There is no way **you** can determine your present level unless **you** take the examination. You can save time and money taking these examinations to earn credit. Others have. Why not YOU?

WHY DID WE WRITE THIS BOOK?

Our firm has conducted many classroom reviews for CLEP General Examinations. Our instructors have assisted thousands of candidates to do their best on them. From this experience we have learned that:

1. In each area there is specific material beneficial for candidates to know.

2. There is a need for a simple-to-follow review book which would help students improve their ability to achieve.

3. It is important for the students to become accustomed to the specific directions found on the examination before they take an examination.

4. It is beneficial for students to develop a systematic approach to taking an objective examination.

5. Many people have been misinformed about CLEP.

This books will help you, a candidate, perform at your highest potential so that you can receive your best scores.

The flyers "CLEP COLLEGES" (Listing where you can take the CLEP tests and the colleges that accept credit) and "CLEP INFORMATION FOR CANDIDATES" are available free by calling (609) 771-7865 or writing to: CLEP, PO Box 6600, Princeton, NJ 08541-6600.

EXTERNAL DEGREE PROGRAMS

Four states, Connecticut, Illinois, New Jersey, and New York, offer external degree programs that enable individuals to earn degrees by passing examinations, including CLEP tests, and demonstrating in other ways that they have satisfied the educational requirements. No classroom attendance is required. Out-of-state as well as in-state residents are eligible.

Prospective candidates for these degree programs should write for full information, before taking the examinations to the following addresses:

Board for State Academic Awards, 340 Capitol Avenue, Hartford, CT 06115

Board of Governors BA Program, 544 Iles Park Place, Springfield, IL 62706

Thomas A. Edison College, Kelsey Building, 101 W. State Street, Trenton, NJ 08608

Regents External Degrees, 99 Washington Avenue, Albany, NY 12210

CLEP INFORMATION

In our reviews, we have found these were the questions most frequently asked by our students.

WHAT IS CLEP GENERAL?

CLEP is a nation-wide program of testing which began in 1965. Today, over 2900 colleges recognize CLEP as a way students can earn college credit. Each year over 200,000 persons take CLEP examinations. The testing program is based on the theory that "**what** a person knows is more important than **how** he has learned it." All examinations are designed and scored by the College Entrance Examination Board (CEEB). the purpose of each examination is to determine whether your current knowledge in a subject can qualify you for credit in that area at a particular college.

There are five general examinations. The subject areas are:

1. **English Composition**
2. **Mathematics**
3. **Social Science**
4. **Natural Science**
5. **Humanities**

Credits earned by achieving on these examinations replace basic liberal arts credits which are required by many colleges for all types of degrees. Each of these general examinations is very broad in coverage. Questions are from the wide range of subjects included in each of the major disciplines. For example, questions in history (ancient, modern, American, European, Black), sociology, psychology, economics and political science could be included on the General CLEP Social Science Examination. The General CLEP Natural Science Examination might include questions related to biology, astronomy, physics, earth science and chemistry. Because of the broad coverage in each examination, you are not expected to be knowledgeable in all areas. There will be some questions on **all** the tests you will not be able to answer.

HOW LONG ARE THE EXAMINATIONS?

Each CLEP General Examination is 1½ hours in length. Each examination is divided into separate timed portions. For a breakdown of each, check with the specific review book for that examination.

HOW MUCH DO THE EXAMINATIONS COST?

Currently, the fee to take each examination is $46.00. They may be taken one at a time or in any combination. (NOTE: Fees change periodically.)

WHERE CAN THE EXAMINATIONS BE TAKEN?

The CEEB (College Entrance Examination Board) has designated certain schools in every state to serve as test centers for CLEP examinations. The flyers "CLEP COLLEGES" (Listing where you can take the CLEP tests and the colleges that accept credit) and "CLEP INFORMATION FOR CANDIDATES" are available free by calling (800) 257-9558 or writing to: CLEP, PO Box 6600, Princeton, NJ 08541-6600. If you are a member of the armed forces, check with the education officer at your base. Special testings are set up for military personnel.

WHEN ARE THE TESTS GIVEN?

Most CLEP examinations are administered during the third week of every month except December and February. The test center chooses the day of the week. A few test centers administer the tests by appointment only. Check with the center where you will take the test for specific information. If you are serving with the United States Military, check with the Education Services Officer at your base to find out about the DANTES testing program. You will be given information about testing as applicable to military personnel.

HOW DO YOU REGISTER FOR AN EXAMINATION?

A standard registration form can be obtained from the test center where you plan to take the examination. Many centers require that you register (send registration form and fee for examinations to be taken) a month prior to your selected date.

WHEN WILL SCORES BE RECEIVED?

You will receive a copy of your scores approximately six weeks after you take an examination. You can also request that a copy be sent to a college for evaluation. The score you receive will be a scaled score. This score can be correlated to a percentile level. These scores **remain** scores until you become matriculated with a college. CEEB keeps a record of your scores on file for 20 years. You can obtain an additional copy or have a copy sent to a college if you contact:

> College Board
> ATTN: Transcript Service
> PO Box 6600
> Princeton, NJ 08541

Include the date you took the test, the name of the center where you took the test, your date of birth and your social security number. Contact CEEB to find out the current fee for this service.

IS IT NECESSARY TO BE ENROLLED IN A COLLEGE BEFORE YOU TAKE AN EXAMINATION?

That depends. Each college has established policy regarding CLEP. You should check with the school you wish to attend. Many schools do not require you be enrolled before you take CLEP examinations.

HOW MANY CREDITS CAN BE EARNED?

Each college determines the number of credits that can be earned by achieving on an examination. Most award six credits if you achieve on a CLEP General Examination.

HOW ARE THE SCORES EVALUATED?

Before you, a candidate, take an examination, it is administered to college students who are taking a course the examination credits will replace. These students do not take the examination for credit. They take it to establish a standard by which your score can be evaluated. From this testing, percentile levels of achievement can be determined. For example, if you score at the 25th percentile, this would indicate that you achieved as well as the **bottom** 25 percent of those students who took that examination to set a standard.

There is no correlation between the number of questions you answer correctly and the percentile level you achieve. The number would vary from test to test.

CAN THE SAME SCORES EARN A DIFFERENT NUMBER OF CREDITS AT DIFFERENT SCHOOLS?

Yes, because different schools may require different levels of achievement. Your scores may earn you more credit at one institution than at another. For example: if you achieve at the 25th percentile level, you could earn credit at a school which required the 25th percentile level; you could not earn credit at a school which required a higher level of achievement.

CAN CLEP CREDITS BE TRANSFERRED?

Yes, provided the school to which you transfer recognizes CLEP as a way to earn credit. Your scores will be evaluated according to the new school's policy.

CAN AN EXAMINATION BE RETAKEN?

Many schools allow you to retake an examination if you did not achieve the first time. Some do not. Check your particular school's policy before you retake an examination. Also, be **realistic**. If you almost achieved the level at which you could earn credit, do retake the examination. If your score was quite low, take the course it was designed to replace.

IF YOU DECIDE TO RETAKE AN EXAMINATION, six months must elapse before you do so. Scores on tests repeated earlier than six months will be canceled.

HOW CAN I FIND OUT WHAT SCHOOLS ACCEPT CLEP?

In addition to the test centers listed in the back of this text, there are many other schools that recognize CLEP as a way to earn credit. For a free booklet, CLEP Test Centers and Other Participating Institutions, which lists most of them, send your request, name, and address to:

The College Board, PO Box 6600, Princeton, NJ 08541

If the school you wish to attend is not listed, call the admissions office and ask for information. Not all participating schools are included in the booklet.

HOW CAN YOU USE THIS BOOK TO IMPROVE YOUR ABILITY?

We recommend the following procedure:

1. Complete the review material. Take the short tests included at the end of the lessons.
2. If you do well on the tests, continue. If you do not, review the explanatory information.
3. After you have completed the review material, take the practice examination at the back of the book. When you take this sample test, try to simulate the test situation as nearly as possible. That is:
   a. Find a quiet spot where you will not be disturbed.
   b. Time yourself accurately.
4. Correct the tests. Determine where your weaknesses are. Go back and review those areas in which you had difficulty.

HOW THE EXAMINATIONS ARE SCORED

There is no penalty for wrong answers. Your score is computed based on the number of correct answers. When you are finished with the test, make sure that every question is answered. You don't have to answer the question the first time you see it. If you use the coding system you will greatly increase your score.

THE CODING SYSTEM

Over the years COMEX has perfected a systematic approach to taking a multiple choice examination. This is called the coding system. It is designed to:

1. get you through the examination as quickly as possible.

2. have you quickly answer those questions that are easy for you.

3. have you not waste time on those questions that are too difficult for you.

4. take advantage of all your knowledge of a particular subject. Most people think they can get credit only by knowing an answer is correct. You can also prove your knowledge by knowing an answer is incorrect. The coding system will show you how to accomplish this.

5. get all the help possible by using the recall factor. Because you are going to read the total examination, it is possible that something in question 50 will trigger a thought that will help you answer question 3 the second time you read it.

6. have your questions organized for the second reading so you know what questions offer you the best use of your time.

HERE IS HOW THE CODING SYSTEM WORKS*

We are going to make you a better test-taker by showing all of your knowledge and using your time to the greatest advantage. Managing your time on the exam can be as important as knowing the correct answers. If you spend too much time working on difficult questions that you have no knowledge about, you might not get to some easy questions later that you would have gotten correct. This causes a significant decrease in your score. It also makes test taking a very frustrating experience.

Let us attack some sample questions:

1. **George Washington was:**
    a.   the father of King George Washington
    b.   the father of Farah Washington
    c.   the father of the Washington Laundry
    d.   the father of Washington State
    e.   the father of our country

As you read the questions you will eliminate all **wrong** answers:

  a. father of King George Washington NO!
  b. father of Farah Washington   NO!
  c. father of the Washington Laundry NO!
  d. father of Washington State   NO!
  e. the father of our country   YES. LEAVE IT ALONE.

The question now looks like this:

1. George Washington was:

  a. ~~the father of King George Washington~~
  b. ~~the father of Farah Washington~~
  c. ~~the father of the Washington Laundry~~
  d. ~~the father of Washington State~~
  e. the father of our country

Click on the button next to the correct answer and click next.

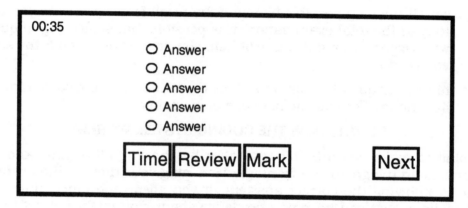

These are the buttons you must know how to use!

You are now finished with this question. Later when we get to the review process this question will be sorted as answered. This will be your signal to not spend any more time with this question. Any time spent will be wasted.

2. Abraham Lincoln was responsible for:

  a. freeing the 495 freeway
  b. freeing the slaves
  c. freeing the Lincoln Memorial
  d. freeing the south for industrialization
  e. freeing the Potomac River

Go through the answers.

a. freeing the 495 freeway	NO!
b. freeing the slaves	MAYBE. ALWAYS READ FULL QUESTION.
c. freeing the Lincoln Memorial	NO!
d. freeing the south for industrialization	MAYBE.
e. freeing the Potomac River	NO!

The question now looks like this:

2.   Abraham Lincoln was responsible for:

a.   ~~freeing the 495 freeway~~
b.   freeing the slaves
c.   ~~freeing the Lincoln Memorial~~
d.   freeing the south for industrialization
e.   ~~freeing the Potomac River~~

Should you guess? You have very good odds of getting this question correct. Pick the choice that you feel is the best answer. Often your first guess will be the best. Before clicking the next button click on the mark box. This will tell you later that you were able to eliminate 3 answers before guessing. Now click on next to go on to the next question.

3.   Franklin Roosevelt's greatest accomplishment was:

a.   building the Panama Canal
b.   solving the Great Depression
c.   putting America to work
d.   organizing the CCC Corps
e.   instituting the income tax

Go through the answers:

a. building the Panama Canal	NO! THAT WAS A DIFFERENT ROOSEVELT.
b. solving the Great Depression	MAYBE. GO ON TO THE NEXT ANSWER.
c. putting America to work	MAYBE. ON TO THE NEXT ANSWER.
d. organizing the CCC Corps	MAYBE. ON TO THE NEXT ANSWER.
e. instituting the income tax	MAYBE. LEAVE IT ALONE!

The question now looks like this:

3.   Franklin Roosevelt's greatest accomplishment was:

a.   ~~building the Panama Canal~~
b.   solving the Great Depression
c.   putting America to work
d.   organizing the CCC Corps
e.   instituting the income tax

Should you answer this question now? Not yet. There might be a question later that contains information that would help you eliminate more of the answers. When you can only eliminate one answer, or none at all, your best course of action is to simply click on next. This will bring up the next question.

Now look at another question:

4. **Casper P. Phudd III was noted for:**
    a.   rowing a boat
    b.   sailing a boat
    c.   building a boat
    d.   designing a boat
    e.   navigating a boat

Even if you have no idea of who Casper P. Phudd III is, read the answers:

a.	rowing a boat	I DO NOT KNOW.
b.	sailing a boat	I DO NOT KNOW.
c.	building a boat	I DO NOT KNOW.
d.	designing a boat	I DO NOT KNOW.
e.	navigating a boat	I DO NOT KNOW.

Since you cannot eliminate any of the answers, simply go on to the next question.

Try another question:

5. **Clarence Q. Jerkwater III**
    a.   sailed the Atlantic Ocean
    b.   drained the Atlantic Ocean
    c.   flew over the Atlantic Ocean
    d.   colored the Atlantic Ocean orange
    e.   swam in the Atlantic Ocean

Even though you know nothing of Clarence Q. Jerkwater III, you read the answers.

a.	sailed the Atlantic Ocean	POSSIBLE.
b.	drained the Atlantic Ocean	NO WAY!
c.	flew over the Atlantic Ocean	MAYBE.
d.	colored the Atlantic Ocean orange	NO WAY!
e.	swam in the Atlantic Ocean	MAYBE.

The question now looks like this:

5. Clarence Q. Jerkwater III
   a.   sailed the Atlantic Ocean
   b.   ~~drained the Atlantic Ocean~~
   c.   flew over the Atlantic Ocean
   d.   ~~colored the Atlantic Ocean orange~~
   e.   swam in the Atlantic Ocean

Do you take a guess? Not on the first reading of the answers. Let us wait to see if the recall factor will help. Do not click on an answer, but do click on mark. Then click on next to get the next question.

Continue in this manner until you finish all the questions in the section. By working in this manner you have organized the questions in a way to maximize your efficiency. When you finish with the last question click on review. This brings up the listing of all the questions. They will be listed in numerical order. This in not the way you want to view them. You sorted the questions as you went through them. You want to view the questions sorted. Click on status. Now the questions are sorted for you. Let's review what each type means:

Answered without a check mark.
You knew the correct answer.

Answered with a check mark.
You eliminated three answers.

Not answered with a check mark.
You eliminated two answers.

Not answered without a check mark.
You could not eliminate more than one answer.

THE SECOND TIME THROUGH

Now you are ready to start your way through the test the second time. Where do you have the best chance of increasing your score? This question should always be at the top of your mind. "How do I show the testing people the maximum amount of information I know?" The best place to start is with the questions that you had some idea about, but not enough to answer. These are the questions where you could eliminate two answers. They are marked with a check mark. Clicking on review, and then status will sort the questions for you. All of the questions that are marked but have not been answered are grouped together for you.

Click on the first one in the group. Reread the question and the answers. Did anything in any of the other questions give you information to allow you to eliminate any answers? If the answer is yes that is great! The coding system has worked. If you eliminated one more answer make your guess between the remaining two. Leave the mark box checked and click on review to go back to the question list to choose your next question. What if you now know the correct answer? Mark it, and **remove** the check from the mark box. This question will now be listed as answered. You will not spend any more time on this question. Click on review to go back to your list of questions.

What should you do if you were unable to eliminate any more answers. Now you still need to guess. While your odds are not as good as if you had eliminated three answers, you will have a better chance than if you had eliminated no answers. Any time you eliminate answers before guessing means you are making an educated guess. Every educated guess you make has a higher chance of being correct than a random guess. More educated guesses means a higher score. Leave the mark box checked. This indicates that you were not sure of your answer.

Continue with this process until you finish all the questions in the group with a check mark that were not answered. Which questions should you work on next? It is now time to work on the questions you had the least knowledge about. These are the questions without a check mark that are not answered. Use the same process that you used for the previous set of questions. Can you now figure out the correct answer? If so mark it and check the box. If not eliminate as many answers as you can and then choose your best answer. If you guess, make sure you check the mark box. Every time you reread a question there is a chance that it will trigger something in your memory that will help you with this question, or with one of the others.

Be very careful to keep track of time. If it is not diplayed at the top of the screen, make sure you click on the box so that it will be displayed. Do not think of the clock as your enemy. It is your friend. It keeps you on your task and keeps you moving efficiently through the test.

When you only have 5 minutes left, be sure that you have every question answered. Remember a blank space counts the same as a wrong answer. If you go through and make an educated guess on all the questions, you will get a better score than if the questions were left blank. Even if you randomly guess you should end up with one correct answer out of every five. Every correct answer will increase your score. While you are guessing, make sure you check the mark box, so that you know you guessed on that question this will allow you to review that question later if time permits.

You are now finally at the point that you only have two types of questions left, those that you knew the correct answer and those that you guessed at the answer. All of the questions are now answered, so does this mean it is time to stop? Not if you want to get your highest score. All of the questions on which you took educated guess have a check mark. Keep working on those problems. Do not waste time looking at any questions that do not have a check. You knew the correct answer and are done with them.

By using the coding system you will move quickly through the test and be sure that you see every question. It also allows you to concentrate your efforts on your strongest areas.

We purposely used ludicrous questions to emphasize how the system works. Practice the system while you are doing your practice quizzes and tests. You can use a similar system with a piece of scratch paper. Put an "A" next to questions as you answer them. Put a check mark next to a question to refer back to it. Then use the system to go back through the test. The system is easy to master and can be an invaluable tool in your test-taking arsenal.

You have now completed the portion of the book which was designed to improve your test-taking ability. When you work the practice exercises and take the sample test, use these techniques you have just learned.

You can also use the coding system on any other multiple choice test. This will not only increase your score on that test, but it will also make you more comfortable with using the system. It has been demonstrated many times that the more comfortable you are when you are taking a test, the higher your score will be.

SOME BASICS FOR THE TEST DAY

1. Get to the examination location early. If you are taking the examination at a new location - check out how to get there **before** the day of the examination.

2. Choose a seat carefully.

    a. In a large room, choose a quiet corner. If possible, sit facing a wall.

    b. If you go with a friend, do not sit together.

3. Stay with your usual routine. If you normally skip breakfast, do so on the test day also, etc.

4. If you do not understand the proctor's directions, ask questions.

5. Do not be afraid to ask for a seat change if the person beside you keeps coughing, talking to himself, or doing anything which you find is distracting.

6. Do not quit. Keep going over questions you were not able to answer the first time. You may work anywhere in each section. Beat the examination, do not let it beat you!

7. If you cannot answer a question, code it and go on to the next. Do not spend a lot of time on one question unless you have already finished the rest of that section of the examination. Go through each section and do the easiest questions first, then go back to the difficult ones.

8. **Be sure** you understand the directions for **each** type of test **BEFORE you take the examination**. Not understanding the directions can cause you to lose valuable time when you are taking the actual test.

9. Remember to use the coding system.

10. If you are unfamiliar with how to use a mouse, try to get some practice. Most libraries have computers where you can practice. If you have to learn how to use the mouse at the test site you are putting yourself at a severe disadvantage.

The CLEP General Examination In Social Sciences and History: Official Description

The CLEP General Examination in Social Sciences and History covers a wide range of topics from the social sciences and history. While based on no specific course, its content comes from sociology, social psychology, United States history, Western civilization and African-Asian civilizations. The objective of the examination is to measure the level of knowledge and understanding expected of college students who have met a distributional or general education requirement in social sciences-history. It measures knowledge and basic concepts that should be familiar to students with a general background in these areas. The use of the examination to award credit-by-examination should be tied to this objective.

This examination is designed to meet general education requirements. It may also be used to satisfy a distribution requirement, or to grant course credit for any multidisciplinary survey course that closely matches the examination. It is not appropriate for use in granting course credit for an introductory course in any one of the subjects covered by the examination. The use of the history subscore to grant credit for a history course requirement is not appropriate. A number of other CLEP Subject examinations may be more appropriate for awarding course credit, e.g., American History, Introductory Sociology. The examination is so broad in its coverage that no one should expect to make a perfect score. Reading introductory texts in the various fields would assist one in preparing for this examination.

The examination is 90 minutes long and includes 125 multiple-choice questions. Approximately 60% of the questions deal with the social sciences and 40% deal with history. These percentages may vary slightly from time to time. A total score is reported. In addition to the total score, separate subscores are reported for history and the social sciences. The purpose for reporting subscores is to serve those colleges which have established minimum acceptable levels of performance both for the social sciences and history.

The division of subject matter on the examination is as follows:

HISTORY	40%
United States History Requires a general understanding of historical issues associated with the following periods in United States history: colonial, revolutionary, late eighteenth and early nineteenth centuries, Civil War and Reconstruction, and late nineteenth and twentieth centuries	17%
Western Civilization Requires familiarity with three broad historical periods: ancient, medieval, and modern	15%
World History Requires knowledge of topics in six broad time periods: Prehistory, Ancient History to 500BCE, 500BCE to 1500 CE, 1500CE to 1900 CE and the 20th century in Africa, Asia, North America and South America	8%

SOCIAL SCIENCES	60%

Sociology, including topics such as
    Methods and statistics
    Demography
    Ecology
    Social stratification
    Deviance and criminology
    Social organization
	11%

Economics, with emphasis on microeconomics topics such as
    Consumer theory
    Production theory
    Investment function
    Fiscal policy
    Monetary policy
    Money and banking
    Business cycles
	10%

Political Science, including topics such as
    Constitutional government
    Voting and political behavior
    International relations and comparative government
	13%

Social Psychology, including topics such as
    Aggression
    Socialization
    Conformity
    Methodology
    Group formation
    Performance
	10%

Geography, including topics such as
    Weather and climate
    Ecology
    Regional geography
    Distance and location
    Space accessibility
	10%

Anthropology, including topics such as Cultural anthropology and ethnography	6%

Questions on the examination require you to demonstrate the following abilities. A single question may require more than one ability.

- Familiarity with terminology, facts, conventions, methodology, concepts, principles, generalization, and theories.
- Ability to understand, interpret, and analyze graphic, pictorial, or written material.
- Ability to apply abstractions to particulars, and to apply hypotheses, concepts, theories, or principles to given data.

Western Civilization

INTRODUCTION

The Roman orator, Cicero, once said of history, "Not to know what took place before you were born is forever to remain a child." In this overview of the development of Western civilization, we will present the broad social, cultural, political, and economic trends that have brought the Western world from its beginnings in the Middle East to its present state.

The study of Western history is usually divided into three broad time periods: the **Ancient World** (from the time of recorded history, about 5,000 BC, until the fall of the Roman Empire in 476 AD); the **Middle Ages** (from 476 to 1492 AD); and the **Modern World** (from 1492 to the present). Although mankind has been on the earth for at least 500,000 years and perhaps for as long as 2 million years, this long period of prehistory had little effect on Western civilization. Only after the development of written languages and records did one civilization or one era have a significant effect on another.

As you study this section for the CLEP examination, try to gain an overall understanding of the main concepts—how nations grow, how governments develop, why there are many different societies and cultures, and how one age or civilization influences the next. This type of broad knowledge will serve you far better than will extensive memorization of dates, facts and names.

THE ANCIENT WORLD

Before the advent of farming everyone was concerned with gathering food.

About 10,000 years ago, mankind learned to do something that would forever change his condition and his future: the cultivation of crops. When man learned to farm, he was no longer forced to search the earth for food. Also, not every person within the group had to be involved with food production or gathering. Once mankind settled down to one spot, some members of the society could then become craftsmen, or merchants, or teachers, or soldiers, or religious leaders—thus the beginnings of civilization and cities.

At approximately the same time, this cultivation of crops and civilization occurred in four areas along four rivers: the **Nile** in Egypt and the **Tigris-Euphrates** in the Middle East, which together provided the foundations for what later became Western civilization; the **Indus**, in what now is Pakistan, which is the basis of the Indian civilization; and the **Hwang Ho**, or Yellow River in China, which is the origin of the Far Eastern civilizations. These river valleys are often called the **cradles of civilization**.

Civilizations initially developed along rivers for two reasons. The valleys were often fertile and allowed a large amount of food to be grown by farming. The second reason was that the rivers let the civilizations transport their goods cheaply. There were no roads at this time for trading, so being able to transport large quantities of material by boat along the rivers was very important.

Recorded history began when writing began—about 5,000 BC The Sumerians were one of the first to develop writing. They poked sharp reeds into clay. They are also one of the first civilizations to use irrigation. This allowed them to farm even more land along the Tigris and Euphrates Rivers. Sumerian Kings were believed to be gods. Even though the Sumerians lacked stone they were able to build temples to their gods. **Ziggurats**, Sumerian temples, were made of bricks. The bricks were made from river mud mixed with straw. The actual temple was always placed at the top of the ziggurat. Some ziggurats were six stories high. The earliest evidence of a wheeled vehicle was found in Sumerian ruins.

About 2000 BC invaders from the Syrian desert conquered both Sumer and its sister state Akkad. They merged their conquered territory to form Babylon. Babylon is probably most famous for its King Hammurabi (1728-1686 BC). Not only did he conquer large amounts of territory (Syria, Assyria and Elam), but he also centralized the government and put governors in place of the former princes. He also developed a code of laws (**Hammurabi's Code**) to help him govern such a vast area. The code recognized three classes of people; the rich land owners, the other freemen who might own a small amount of land or property, and the slaves. The slaves were often prisoners of war. In the code, the rights of each person were spelled out. For instance, if a slave married a woman who was free, his children would be free. His progeny were not locked into slavery for all eternity. The Babylonians were great traders and developed standard weights and measures to facilitate trade.

The Babylonian Empire was conquered many times, most notably by the Assyrians. The Assyrians lived in the northern Tigris Valley. The land was not as fertile as the southern part of the valley. Over time the Assyrians specialized in warfare. The organization started with the squad that consisted of 10 men. All men were required to do military service. The squads were formed into companies. When the Assyrians went to war it was well planned out. They relied heavily on reconnaissance. Once they knew the positioning of the opposing troops they out flanked and destroyed them. They also relied heavily on the chariot for mobility to help them quickly capitalize on advantages in battle. The Assyrians were one of the first people to use iron in their weapons. It offered many advantages over the bronze weapons of their opponents. Most of their opponents lived in walled cities so the Assyrians needed to develop the means to breach the walls. They developed iron-capped rams to break the walls. They also used rolling, armored platforms to allow their archers to shoot down defenders on the walls.

Babylon rose again in the year 626 BC it would last only 87 years before being conquered by Persia, but during this time they were able to make great advances in astronomy. They made a star map, and were able to accurately predict eclipses of not only the moon, but also the sun.

The Hebrews moved out of the desert and settled in Canaan around 3000 BC. Their major contribution to Western Civilization was their belief in one God. They also produced the first great work of Western Literature, the Jewish Torah and the Old Testament of the Christian Bible.

The Persians were located at the crossroads between the Far Eastern and the Western Civilizations. They migrated out of Central Asia and Russia around 2000 BC and their rule lasted until they were conquered by Alexander the Great in 331 BC They had a series of laws that were uniform throughout their empire and a very good banking system. Around 500 BC they also developed a monotheistic (one god) religion. The lead prophet was Zoroaster and he preached that the world consisted of a conflict between good and evil. The good god was Ahura Mazda.

The Persian Empire rose again in 226 AD Trade once again flourished between Eastern and Western Civilizations. They also tried to mold their three main religions: Christianity, Buddhism and Zoarastrianism into a new religion Manichaeism. The Persian culture spread from China to Egypt.

The Phoenicians were the first to build a seafaring trade empire along the Mediterranean Sea. Later one of the cities they founded, Carthage would challenge Rome for supremacy.

These early civilizations laid the foundation for Western culture. Their important contributions were written language and literature, a code of laws, an alphabet, and the idea of one God.

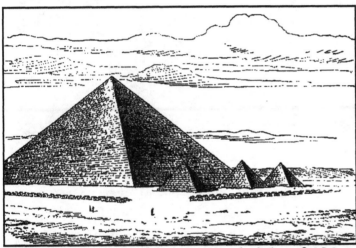

The Egyptians developed their culture at the same time as the others. However they were spared many of the invasions that the other cultures had to endure. Both mountains and deserts separated them from the others. They contributed architecture, engineering skills, and a type of paper (papyrus) to the future civilizations. Their engineering skills had surpassed their contemporaries.

The great pyramid rises to a height of 481 feet and its base is less than one inch short of being a square.

Because there was a great deal of trade and commerce, in addition to wars, among all of these developing civilizations, there was an extensive sharing of ideas and knowledge. This spreading of information, called **cultural diffusion**, brought civilization to such previously uncivilized areas as Crete (the Aegean civilization) and then on to **Greece**, the first civilization in Europe. Cultural diffusion did not only happen in the ancient past. It has occurred constantly throughout human history, for example, the popularity of baseball in Japan after watching American soldiers playing during the occupation after World War II.

During the thousand-year period preceding the birth of Christ, on a small, rocky land, a way of life developed which was to be the beginning of Western civilization. Although drawing from earlier groups, the Greeks contributed many advances to our civilization in such areas as:

1. **architecture and art**—the ideas of beauty, harmony and the standard called classical. Artists made significant strides toward more realistic representations of the real world. Compare this sample of Egyptian art that seems two-dimensional to this sample of Greek art.

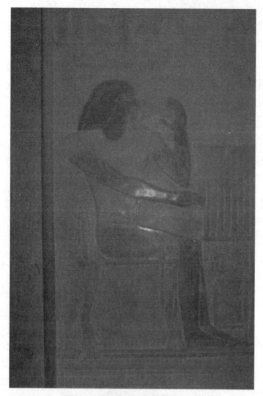

Egyptian   **Greek**

2. **language and literature**—tragedy, comedy, lyric, epic (Homer wrote both the <u>Illiad</u> and the <u>Odyssey</u> the first two great epics) were Greek contributions.

3. **philosophy**—Socrates, Plato and Aristotle with their systems of logic and concepts of ethics contributed greatly to civilization.

4. **science**—the contributions of Pythagoras, Archimedes, and Euclid in mathematics; Hippocrates and Galen in medicine; other contributions in the fields of astronomy, geography, zoology, education and military tactics were made by the Greeks.

5. **sports**—the striving for beauty and perfection of the human body. Started the Olympics where ever four years the greatest atheletes from the city-states met in peaceful contests. The games were held even when some of the city-states were warring against each other.

6. **statecraft**—at least in Athens, the desire for freedom for both the individual and the city-state led to experimentation with monarchy, aristocracy, oligarchy, democracy and even tyranny. Perhaps the most important contribution of the Greeks to what is now the Western World was their conclusion that, while imperfect, democracy is the best form of government.

Although the Greeks once ruled the known world, their civilization declined, mainly because of a series of wars, the **Peloponnesian**, between Sparta and Athens. This infighting left Greece vulnerable to a stronger invader—the Romans, in 146 BC

Rome (753 BC to 476 AD), first a republic and then an empire, produced a civilization noted primarily for its practical usefulness. In some fields (art, literature, and architecture) the Romans are remembered more for adaptation of Greek styles, rather than for their originality. On the other hand, the Romans built well-planned cities, roads that are still in use, aqueducts, public baths, and stadiums. But perhaps the most notable achievement was the political genius of Rome, which ruled a world empire with, for the most part, justice and order. The Romans left an everlasting influence on the fields of law and politics.

The Roman introduction of the **arch** allowed them to build structures to an unprecedented size. Arches were able to hold up huge amounts of weight and allowed for open space below. Until the development of the arch structures were held up by posts and lintels. The size of the beams across the tops of the posts had to increase dramatically in order to span a larger area.

After a relatively short period of persecution of the early Christians, **Christianity** was adopted by the Roman emperors and became the official religion of the empire. It spread throughout the known world to become the key ingredient in Western civilization in the next era.

The Roman government was divided into two branches. The Patricians were descended from the aristocracy when Rome was founded. The Patricians served in the Senate. The other branch was the Plebians. It consisted of the other free citizens.

Initially the Patricians had more power but over time the Plebians demanded equal power. Unfortunately most Plebians lacked the financial resources to get a law passed through the Senate which had to approve all laws proposed by the people.

The Republic era of Rome came to an end in 54 BC when Julius Caesar after defeating the Gauls and the Britains turned his army toward Rome. Pompey, his main rival fled and Caesar became Emperor.

The decline and fall of the **Roman Empire** is a complex subject, but it has some similarities to our own age. The empire became too large and too unwieldy to be governed effectively from the central city. Prolonged wars, plus a corrupt and inefficient government, led to economic decline and persistent inflation of the currency. Economic exhaustion brought deurbanization and the end of the urban-oriented Greco-Roman culture, as most of the population fled the cities and became an agrarian class for the next one thousand years.

In 395 AD, before the fall of Rome, the empire split. The eastern part became known as the **Byzantine Empire**, with its center in **Constantinople**, or Istanbul, Turkey as we know it today. This empire lasted until 1453 AD While it may not be known for any great advances in culture, it was responsible for keeping much of the previous knowledge from earlier civilizations from being lost.

But in the west, the decline accelerated until 476 AD, when the last emperor was deposed by the Germanic invaders. In many ways the Greco-Roman civilization, with its rational, humanistic outlook, had long before given way to the mystical and spiritual world of the Middle Ages.

Before going on with the review, try these sample CLEP questions. Cover the correct answers to the right.

1. **The populations of the cradles of civilization were primarily:**

   (A) merchants
   (B) hunters
   (C) food gatherers
   (D) craftsmen
   (E) farmers

ANSWERS:

1. (E) The word "cradles" indicates beginnings, and therefore farmers, not merchants or craftsmen allowed for great numbers of people to settle in one place. The hunting and gathering periods were before the dawn of civilizations.

2. **The process by which one civilization shares knowledge and ideas with another civilization is called:**

   (A) cultural assimilation
   (B) cultural diffusion
   (C) imperialism
   (D) militarism
   (E) manorialism

2. **(B)** Since the word "diffusion" means "to spread," this is the best answer. "Assimilation" means "to absorb," not "to share." Imperialism and militarism would be more concerned with conquering another culture.

3. **Ancient Greece was primarily a:**

   (A) great empire ruled by a monarch
   (B) great nation ruled by a democratic system
   (C) number of independent city-states
   (D) primitive civilization
   (E) large agricultural area

3. **(C)** Greece was never a nation in the modern sense, but rather a series of city-states such as Sparta and Athens. This rules out choices A and B. D can be ruled out because much of our politacal system, and philosophical roots can be traced back to Greece.

4. **Socrates, Plato, and Aristotle are noted primarily for their contribution in the field of:**

   (A) science
   (B) political science
   (C) literature
   (D) philosophy
   (E) art

4. **(D)** While they may have made contributions in other areas, they were primarily philosophers.

5. **The most important contribution made by the Romans to Western civilization was:**

   (A) their art, architecture, and literature
   (B) the cities and roads they built
   (C) the Latin language
   (D) their economic system
   (E) their political system, with its influence on law and politics

5. **(E)** This question asks for the longest-lasting effect of the Romans on Western civilization. This type of question asks for the BEST answer, not just a correct one. For this reason, even though the Romans affected Western culture in all five areas, the fact that many of our laws are still based on the Roman justice system would lead you to the correct answer.

6. **Which of the following caused explosive growth in the Christian religion during the 4ᵗʰ century?**

(A) the emperors who made it the state religion of the Roman Empire
(B) the Germanic tribes who spread Christianity to Western Europe
(C) the persistence of the early Christians
(D) the adoption of Christianity by the Byzantine Empire
(E) the rejection of Christianity by the Greeks

7. **Constantinople became the center of:**

(A) the Greco-Roman civilization
(B) the western region of the Roman Empire
(C) the Byzantine culture
(D) the Catholic Church
(E) Western civilization

8. **The deurbanization which took place during the decline of the Roman Empire resulted in:**

(A) cities becoming the centers of government
(B) industrial expansion of the empire
(C) an agrarian society during the Middle Ages
(D) the revitalization of the Greco-Roman Civilization
(E) the end of Western civilization

6. (A) This type of question requires that you make an evaluation and draw a conclusion. The fact that the emperors adopted it allowed Christianity to spread throughout the empire. Chrisitianity had already been spread before Rome was conquered by the Germans or the Byzantine empire split off.

7. (C) Rome was the center for the other answers. Remember the Byzantine empire was formed when the Roman empire was split in two. It was initially responsible for the eastern section of the Roman empire.

8. (C) This deurbanization led to the feudal system in the Middle Ages. People moved away from the larger cities to the countryside where they became farmers

THE MIDDLE AGES

While not totally accurate, the term **Dark Ages** (approximately 476 AD to 1492) has often been applied to the first half and sometimes the whole period of the Middle Ages. While it was a time of superstitions, intolerance, ignorance and general misery, the era was not an age of stagnation. The Medieval contributions in religion, philosophy, art and literature have enriched the Modern World as much as have the highest achievements of the Ancient World.

In the centuries after the decline of the Romans, trade came to a standstill and money almost entirely disappeared from use. As people fled the cities, they turned to farming for survival. This led to the political-economic system know as **feudalism**, with most of the population becoming peasants, or serfs, on land owned by a few privileged lords or nobles. In return for a large percentage of their produce, the serfs received protection, as well as health care and a church. Without a strong central government, many nobles set up their own kingdoms and would reward other nobles who promised support during times of war. By the beginning of the eleventh century, feudalism, with all of its excesses, did bring peace and security to Europe.

Feudalism fragmented the population of Europe; the only unifying factor was the **Christian church**. Throughout the Medieval period, the church remained the single most important social, economic and political influence. Not only did the church become the center of learning and a large landowner, it also took over many civic duties: taxation, justice and social services such as schools and hospitals. Even though the church, by the end of this period, had become very powerful (and corrupt in the process), the Christian ethics set the ideal toward which the Western World is still striving.

Around 480 AD a new empire started arising to fill the power vacuum left by the collapse of the western portion of the Roman empire. Based in present day France, or the old Roman province of Gaul, the Franks offered stability to the tribes that Rome had conquered. The Franks were closely tied to the Pope and stressed religious conversion from the pagan religions practiced by the tribes. The greatest Frankish ruler was **Charlemagne**. Pope Leo III crowned him Emperor at St. Peter's Cathedral on Christmas 800 AD Although he could not read and write he saw the value of an education for helping him run his empire and he set up schools to help train clerics. His successors unfortunately were not able to hold the empire together and this rebirth of culture and learning was short-lived.

The Vikings attacked the Corolingian, Frankish Empire. The Vikings were based in Scandinavia. The Viking's contribution to Western Civilization was in the building of ocean going sea vessels. While the Romans and the Phonecians rarely traveled beyond the sight of land, the Vikings traveled hundreds of miles out to sea. They traveled to Greenland and then on to North America. They were excellent traders with trade routes in Africa and down into Arabia. They were also known for lightning raids throughout Europe. When they went raiding, they would often sail up rivers and loot the countryside. They left before the local lord could organize a response. In this way they were able to avoid large-scale warfare that favored the local inhabitants.

The largest feature of the Medieval World, the Gothic cathedral, was a symbol of the power and the strength of religion during the Middle Ages.

While Western Europe was under a "dark cloud" for the first half of the Middle Ages, two other cultures flourished: the Byzantine and the Moslem. The **Byzantine Empire**, a continuation of the Greco-Roman civilization with a heavy oriental influence, became the chief civilizing force of the Slavic people. The Eastern Orthodox Church has its center in Constantinople. Emperor Justinian came to power and he brought Roman law up to date with the Corpus, a collection of civil laws. Many of which are the basis of our current laws.

Notice the difference in architectural style between this Byzantine Empire building and the gothic cathedral above.

The **Moslem Empire** (about 700 AD to the 1200's AD) was composed of the followers of the prophet Mohammed. He developed the religion of Islam. A Moslem must declare that there is only one God and follow God's will. The Moslems set about holy wars of conquest in order to establish their religion. Within one hundred years after the death of Mohammed, the Moslem Empire extended from northern Spain to India.

The Moslem Empire faced the same problem as all previous empires. How to govern? The Caliphs, emperors, set up a series of 5 viceregencies. The viceroys were in charge of governance in their region appointing judges and collecting taxes. Over time the viceroys started keeping the taxes for themselves and declared themselves independent.

At first, the Moslem Empire simply absorbed all the learning of the Ancient Civilizations they conquered. They translated the Greek texts of Plato, Euclid and Archimedes, etc. and studied them. Soon they were expanding upon this early learning. They calculated the orbits of the moon and planets. They refined the length of a year to 365 ¼ days. In addition the Moslems made significant advances in science and medicine. They introduced the scientific method, which allowed them to make objective conclusions about an experiment's results. In medicine they made significant advances in anatomy and also in the study of diseases. Their greatest accomplishments however, were in the areas of mathematics. They borrowed the Arabic number system from India and instituted the use of the number 0. With this new number system they were able to found the field of modern algebra.

Ironically, the growth of the Moslem Empire eventually led to a reawakening in Western Europe. Mankind began to play one of his more deadly games: "My religion is better than yours." A series of holy wars, the **Crusades**, from 1096 AD to 1270 AD, were fought to liberate the Holy Land from Moslem occupation. Although the Europeans failed in this objective, the Crusades stimulated trade and commerce, leading to a money economy. Merchants and craftsmen prospered, and European cities began to thrive. Most important of all, the knowledge of geography and navigation gained during the Crusades led to explorations and therefore the beginning of the Modern World.

Many of the Crusaders were were most interested in conquering lands and bringing back riches. Many of the knights were younger sons who had no hope of holding land at home.

As the population moved from the farms to the cities, the feudal lands were combined to form large political states (Spain, England, France, and Portugal). Also, the modern European languages came into popular use, although Latin remained the language of the church and the scholars. The stage was now set for the Modern World.

Before going on with the review, try these sample CLEP questions:

ANSWERS:

9. **The Middle Ages date from:**

    (A) the rise of Greece until the fall of Rome
    (B) the fall of Rome until the European discovery of America
    (C) the fall of Rome until the Crusades
    (D) the beginnings of Christianity until the Dark Ages
    (E) the Crusades until the Renaissance

9. (B) The exact dates usually given for the Middle Ages are 476 AD to 1492 AD. With this type of question, if you know one-half of the answer, you can usually determine the correct choice. Before the fall of Rome are considered the ancient empires. The crusades are considered part of the middle ages.

10. **Throughout the Middle Ages the populations of Europe tended to be fragmented and provincial mainly because:**

(A) the lack of a common language hindered communication

(B) the Europeans lost the Crusades

(C) transportation was primitive, therefore trade routes were not explored

(D) the feudal system tended to isolate the people, as each estate was self-sufficient

(E) the lack of a unifying factor, such as religion

11. **Which of the following statements best summarizes the role of the church during the Middle Ages?**

(A) After attaining a position of pre-eminence at the beginning of the era, the church's influence gradually declined.

(B) The church was the leading cause of feudalism.

(C) The church remained the most important cultural and social influence throughout the Middle Ages.

(D) After a long period of corruption, the church divided and its influence became fragmented.

(E) The church was concerned only with spiritual matters, not political or economic ones.

10. (D) There was little need for trade or commerce under the feudal system. While it is true that there were language and transportation barriers, this was not the reason Europe was fragmented. Each lord was able to do just about whatever he wanted on his estate. There was little movement of trade between the different estates and consequently very little diffusion of ideas.

11. (C) The influence of the church overshadowed every aspect of medieval life. Not only were they one of the largest land owners during the Middle Ages, but they were often challenging the secular governments authority. This rules out choice E as an answer. The churches authority did not wane toward the end of the Middle ages. This eliminates choices A and D. While the church may have been used to keep the serfs in line, it was not the reason for the overall feudal structure.

12. Which of the following is a contribution made by the Byzantine Empire?

(A) preserving the law, culture, and philosophy of the Greco-Roman civilization

(B) expanding Christianity in the form of Eastern Orthodoxy

(C) development of a unique artistic style, using mosaics, gold and marble

(D) preventing the Moslems from entering Europe from the east

(E) All of the above were contributions of the Byzantine civilization.

12. (E) All of the choices are correct. Be sure to consider all of the answers before you make your choice.

Questions 13-15 refer to this list:

I. Allah
II. Koran
III. Mohammed
IV. Islam
V. Moslem

13. Which is the holy book of this religion?

(A) I
(B) II
(C) III
(D) IV
(E) V

13. (B)

14. Which is the name used for a follower of this religion?

(A) I
(B) II
(C) III
(D) IV
(E) V

14. (E)

15. Which term is used for the name of the religion?

(A) I
(B) II
(C) III
(D) IV
(E) V

15. (D) Islam is the religion; Mohammed was the founder; Moslems are the followers; the Koran is the holy book; and God is called Allah.

16. Of the following statements, which best summarizes the effects of the Crusades on Western Europe?

(A) The Crusades had a disastrous effect on all countries involved.

(B) The church became even more powerful after the Crusades.

(C) The Crusades eventually united all the governments of Europe.

(D) The Crusades greatly expanded the Europeans' outlook and their knowledge of the world.

(E) The Crusades had little or no effect on the development of European civilization.

16. (D) The Crusades marked the beginning of a reawakening in Western Europe. While the Crusades cannot be considered a military victory for the Europeans they were also not a disaster. This eliminates choice A. The church did not become more powerful because of the crusades, and they certainly did not unite all the governments of Europe. This eliminate choices B and C. The culture brought back by the crusaders greatly changed the outlook of Europe and caused the countries of Europe to start looking beyond their own borders.

THE MODERN WORLD

Two things have marked the entire Modern Age:

1. **Scientific Achievements**

2. **Revolutions**—political, intellectual, and industrial

The age can be divided into three distinct time periods: 1300 to 1600, 1600 to 1900, and the 20th century.

The early period of modern history is noted for the Renaissance, the Reformation, and the historic voyages, which led to exploration of the entire globe. This was the beginning of European, or Western, primacy in the world.

Perhaps the dividing line between the middle ages and the modern age should be drawn at the time of the great plague that swept through Europe from 1347 to 1350. Nearly a third of the population was wiped out. The plague was hardest on the peasants and the poor in the cities. After the plague had passed, the workers who were left were able to demand better wages from the lords of the estates.

The **Renaissance**, or cultural awakening, began in Italy and later spread to other areas. The Medici family in Florence had made a great fortune in banking and trading. They built many palaces and churches; consequently, they became great patrons of the arts. The Popes of that time were also commissioning great works. Pope Julius II was one of the greatest patrons of the arts; he commissioned both Michelangelo and Raphael.

Although the Renaissance drew inspiration from the ancient Greeks (most notably texts and paintings brought from the Byzantine empire when it fell to the Ottoman Turks), the key ingredient of the Renaissance was **humanism**—the glorification of man, the belief in man's perfectibility, and the emphasis on individual freedom. Leonardo da Vinci is not only famous for his paintings (most notably the Mona Lisa), but also contributed greatly in the area of science. He made very detailed sketches of the human body, designed canals, and even drew up plans for a flying machine similar to a helicopter.

Perhaps the greatest invention of the early modern age was the invention of the printing press. In the middle of the 15th century Johann Gutenberg invented a printing press that allowed the letters to be changed, moveable type. Until the time of the printing press, all books were written by hand. The printing press allowed books to be mass produced, and allowed the great works of the age to be widely disseminated. Cervantes in Spain and Shakespeare in England were just two of the most notable writers of this age.

Galileo made notable advances in astronomy. He even proposed that the Sun, not the Earth, was the center of the Solar System. This ran contrary to the teachings of the church during the Middle Ages and caused him to be jailed as a heretic.

The same humanistic outlook that helped bring about the Renaissance also brought the **Reformation** of the Roman Catholic Church. Most reformers looked at the church and saw a corrupt organization that was more interested in money and power, than it was in doing God's work and spreading his word. Some of the manuscripts that were brought out of the Byzantine Empire were original Greek texts of the Bible. Reformers no longer had to rely on translations that were done during the Middle Ages. They wanted to reform the church back to what it looked like in its very beginning.

The first of the great reformers was Martin Luther, a monk in Germany. He believed that people had a direct relationship with God, and that they did not need to go through priests or the church in order to reach salvation. He also believed that salvation was not reached by doing good, but rather that people were saved by their faith alone. Finally, in 1517 he publicly nailed his list of 95 protests to the door of a church.

Much of the nobility in Germany and Scandinavia converted to Lutheranism. Whether this was done for truly religious reasons, or for more practical political reasons varied. Much of the nobility did not like the fact that the Pope was in charge of appointing bishops. Bishops controlled vast tracts of land and great wealth. When princes went to war, they could not always count on the local bishop to send troops, like they could count on their vassals the barons etc. In Germany this created a conflict with the Emperor, who remained Catholic, and his vassals. The first of many wars between the Catholics and the Protestants was fought, but neither side won. Peace was finally signed in 1555 and the Emperor declared that a prince had the right to choose the religion for himself and all his people.

John Calvin preached a stricter version of reform. He preached that people were predestined to either heaven or hell. Calvinism spread quickly through the merchant class because wealth accumulated through hard work was viewed as a sign that you were in God's favor and were destined for heaven.

England ended up with two types of Protestant faiths. Calvinism gained a fair sized following. Then in 1534 King Henry VIII split the Church of England from the Roman Catholic Church. This was done purely for political reasons. He did not like the secular power of the church. The Anglican/Episcopal Church kept many of the teachings and creeds of the Catholic Church, but no longer looked to Rome for authority.

The Roman Catholic Church finally recognized that some reform had to occur, and in 1563 the Council of Trent finally changed the process of appointments, but kept much of the doctrine the same. This united the Roman Catholic Church and silenced the current dissenters. It was, however, not able to fix the breach with the Protestant churches that had already broken away. They were to remain separate.

This led to many wars over religion throughout Europe. In France the Catholic monarchs slaughtered the Protestant Huguenots. The Spanish had their famous Inquisition, fought a war in the Netherlands and sent their armada against England. England itself was not free of trouble. Both the Protestant and the Catholic monarchs when they came to power were known to commit atrocities against the other.

Overshadowing both the Renaissance and the Reformation were the explorations and discoveries in every part of the world. This eventually led to the establishment of colonies, to the spread of the economic system called **mercantilism,** and to a rapid rise in the standard of living for the population of Europe. Mercantilism was based on trade, and wealth was measured in gold or silver.

The next three centuries, from 1600 to 1900, saw intellectual, political and economic revolutions sweep across Europe which, to an extent, have continued to the present day. The **Age of Reason**, the intellectual revolution in the seventeenth and eighteenth centuries with its introduction of scientific method and new instruments, brought rapid advancement in astronomy, electricity, chemistry and analytical geometry. After much success in finding the laws of nature, the intellectuals of the age tried to apply the scientific method to such "human" areas as economics, government and religion. While failing to find "laws" which govern human behavior, they did maintain their faith in man's ability to solve his problems.

This aspect of the Age of Reason helped bring about a series of **political revolutions** in England, America and France. The most important result of these revolutions was the dominant political aspect of Western civilization—democracy and constitutional government.

The 17th century in England was the scene of turmoil. The **English Bill of Rights** was the culmination of a long period of civil war. The **Cromwell Years** that followed could not provide any stability. This resulted in the restoration of the monarchy. While a democracy was not created, absolution was defeated and Parliament was to remain supreme.

THE COLONIAL YEARS

The great explorations led by Columbus (North and South America), Bartholomue Diaz (west coast of Africa and the Cape of Good Hope), Vasco da Gama (East coast of Africa and India), and finally Ferdinand Magellan (circumnavigation of the world) led to the founding of colonies around the globe.

The Spanish set up colonies in South America, Central America, as well as Florida and Western North America. They sent out Conquistadors and though they were small in number they were able to conquer civilizations that were much larger. Hernando

Cortez was able to conquer the mighty Aztec Empire which was centered in Central America. Francisco Pizzaro headed farther south and defeated the Incas who were based in Peru. Both of these conquests sent huge amounts of gold back to Spain.

The English, French and Dutch colonies in North America will be covered in detail in the U. S. History section. These countries also set up colonies throughout Africa and Asia. The main focus of founding the colonies was to get raw materials and send them back to the mother country and to develop markets for finished goods.

In the English colonies in America, however, strong feelings about democracy developed early and became the rallying point for American nationalism. The intellectual basis of the American Revolution became the political theory that governments exist to serve the citizens; and when a government no longer serves the citizens, they then have the right to rebel and to create another form of government.

While both the English and the American revolutions changed the form of government in each country, the social and economic factors remained relatively unchanged. But in France, every aspect of society was turned upside down and inside out after the revolution that began in 1789. Although there was much more social disorder and violence than in the other revolutions, the **French Revolution** did far more to advance the cause of democracy and nationalism in the rest of Europe. As Napoleon's armies marched across Europe, they spread their slogan of liberty, fraternity and equality to the oppressed people of the continent. Although Europe returned to "normal" after 1815 and the exile of Napoleon, the ideals and goals of the French Revolution continued to ferment as "there is no stopping an idea whose time has come."

The conditions which caused the French Revolution were complex and complicated, but they were by no means unique to France. The ideologies of the Age of Reason, with the emphasis on equality and freedom, influenced the intellectuals, and even some nobles, of the age. The rigid class distinctions favored the first two estates (the clergy and the nobility) at the expense of the third (the middle class and the peasantry), which accounted for four-fifths of the population. The weak, indecisive king, Louis XVI, and the extravagant, unpopular queen, Marie Antoinette, added fuel to the revolutionary fervor. But perhaps the most important factors were the economic conditions. The public treasury had been depleted, the parliament refused to tax the privileged groups, and the country faced bankruptcy. The French Revolution established a pattern that many later revolutions (the Spanish, the Russian) were to follow: reform, tranquillity, more reform, violence, terror and finally dictatorship.

As much as the Age of Reason and political revolutions changed the direction of Western civilization, they were not nearly as extensive or profound as the change known as the **Industrial Revolution**, which began in the eighteenth century. Perhaps as important to mankind's history as the cultivation of crops, the Industrial Revolution has affected every aspect of modern society, for better or for worse. The industrial revolution greatly increased the productivity of the average worker. This means that there were more goods for everyone to buy. Consequently, when the supply increased the prices decreased. This allowed many people to buy products that they previously could not afford.

The Industrial Revolution began in England in the textile industry, but it soon spread to other industries and to other areas in Europe and the United States. Today, one would be hard pressed to find any area or society that has not been affected by the Industrial Revolution.

The importance of the Industrial Revolution or series of events, to Western Civilization lies in many areas:

1. The vast quantities of **manufactured goods** increased the standard of living for almost everyone, not just the wealthy.

2. A **financial revolution** created banks, investors and corporations.

3. The **middle class**, which had been nonexistent in earlier civilizations, became the largest class in industrial societies.

4. The Industrial Revolution brought many **problems**—slums, pollution, overcrowding—which are still unsolved today.

5. The Industrial Revolution led to **imperialism** as the industrialized countries needed more and more raw materials and larger markets for their manufactured goods. The competition for colonies, especially in Africa and Asia, became very intense.

6. But perhaps most importantly, the Industrial Revolution changed the Western World from a basically agricultural society to a basically **urban society**. It is easy to get an idea of how the industrial revolution changed the world. The population of England during the American Revolution (before the industrial revolution) was less than the population of modern day New York City.

By 1900, the close of the second era of the Modern World, the Western countries had complete faith in science. Democracy and nationalism were the wave of the future governments. Capitalism (with reforms) and imperialism ("the white man's burden") were the economic future. All of this was soon to change in the 20th century, as the very foundations of Western civilization were shaken.

By far, the most striking feature of the **20th century** is that of change. A person who was born in 1900 would have seen almost incomprehensible changes in every area, but especially in scientific technology. While not always beneficial to the condition of mankind, the scientific and technological discoveries have brought vastly improved transportation and communication systems; medical advances which have almost eliminated some diseases or conditions; the exploration of outer space; the beginnings of the nuclear age; and perhaps most of all, the material goods—everything from computers to compact disc players—which have contributed to "the good life."

In addition to these changes brought by science and technology, the 20th century has been marked by wars. This has led to the rise of new nations, and also to the rise, and subsequent fall of communism.

World War I, 1914 to 1918, was probably one of the most injudicious and foolish wars since the Children's Crusades of the Middle Ages. The nations of Europe had everything to lose and little to gain by fighting each other. By the end of the war, very few of the problems of Europe had been settled. In fact, the situation was actually worse. World War I helped create the problems that led to World War II.

An extremely tense situation had existed in Europe for many decades, waiting for a spark to set off an explosion. While there were a number of causes, most historians agree that the major factor was excessive **nationalism**. All countries try to foster patriotic feelings in order to bring unity, but excessive nationalism can lead to "my country is better than yours, and I can prove it on the battlefield."

France had long wanted revenge for the humiliations suffered during the Franco-Prussian War. The Balkans had become a "powder keg" of nationalism, with both Austria and Russia trying to control events there. Germany, under policies started by Bismarck, sought the dominant position in Europe. This, plus the competition for colonies, brought Germany into conflict with England.

Secret diplomacy, in which the cabinets and parliaments were not told of treaties and agreements, led to military alliances that divided Europe into two armed camps. When Archduke Ferdinand of Austria was assassinated, these two camps lined up as the **Central Powers** and the **Allies**, and the war began.

Almost everyone expected a short war, but instead it bogged down into trench warfare at great cost to all nations involved. The United States entered the war in response to a combination of German submarine actions and American idealism. Many weapons were first used during this war. The airplane was used to drop bombs as well as locate enemy troops. Also, many chemical weapons were used. Treaties later banned chemical weapons. Finally the submarine, which first was used during the American Civil War, was used to block shipping between the United States and Europe.

The airplane was first used as an offensive weapon during WWI when it was used to drop bombs on enemy troops.

The war ended with an armistice, not a surrender, in November of 1918. The **Treaty of Versailles**, in 1919, guided by the spirits of nationalism and revenge, imposed an extremely harsh settlement on Germany.

Many of the results of World War I are still felt today, but the main effects are:

1. The map of Europe was changed, as many new countries (Hungary, Czechoslovakia, Yugoslavia and others) were created.

2. World War I led to the conditions that allowed the communists to seize power in Russia.

3. The war deepened the feelings of isolationism in the United States.

4. The League of Nations, while a failure, marked the beginning of international cooperation.

5. But perhaps the most important outcome of World War I was World War II. By reducing Germany to a third-rate power, and by creating the conditions that allowed dictators to come to power, World War I, along with the peace treaty, contributed directly to the causes of World War II.

Compared to World War I, the causes of **World War II** are much less complex:

1. the problems created by World War I
2. the rise of dictatorships
3. the desire of Germany, Italy, and Japan for more territory

In terms of lives lost, money spent, and destruction incurred, World War II has been by far the most costly struggle in history. World War II resulted in vast population shifts as the European colonial empires collapsed and new nations were created. The end of World War II marked the beginning of the **Nuclear Age** as well as the beginning of the **United Nations**. World War II also led to the conditions that allowed the spread of communism.

But perhaps the most significant result of World War II was the shift of world leadership from the European nations to the United States and the Soviet Union. For the first time since the rise of the Ancient Greeks, the Europeans did not direct the course of Western civilization.

The political dominance of Europe may have declined, but the European ideologies (democracy or communism), technology, life styles and even nationalism have spread to every corner of the world. In the decades since World War II, although a revolt against the West has occurred in areas of Asia and Africa, a new civilization appears to be emerging which is not Western or Eastern, but rather a World civilization. The world has remained politically divided into "two worlds," with the "third world" left out of the post-war prosperity. However, the nations of the world have tended to move toward an interrelated, interdependent civilization.

Before going on with the review, try these sample CLEP questions:

ANSWERS:

17. **The philosophical movement which emphasized the human condition, rather than religious matters, and led to both the Renaissance and the Reformation, is known as:**

    (A) enlightenment
    (B) the Age of Reason
    (C) humanism
    (D) Counter Reformation
    (E) mercantilism

17. (C) Any word which has the suffix "ism" means belief in whatever the first part of the word is. In this case, the word "human" is used in the question, therefore "humanism" is the logical choice. Enlightenment is another term for the Age of Reason, which came after the Renaissance and the Reformation. The Counter Reformation was the Roman Catholic Church's response to the Reformation. Mercantilism was a set of economic beliefs.

18. **The 17th and 18th centuries, because of the philosophical and intellectual movement which stressed the importance of nationalism, individualism, and human reason, became know as:**

(A) the Renaissance
(B) the Age of Reason
(C) the Napoleonic Age
(D) Edwardism Age
(E) laissez faire

18. (B) Once again, a clue to the correct answer, the word "reason" is used in the question.

19. **The most significant end-result of the English Civil War was:**

(A) the restoration of the monarchy
(B) a written constitution
(C) affirmation of the primacy of parliament
(D) rejection of democracy
(E) election of Cromwell and the Puritans

19. (C) The question asks for the most significant result, not the only one.

20. **Which of the following statements is the best summary of the attitude of other European governments toward the French Revolution?**

(A) They feared the new government and waged war against France.
(B) They tended to ignore the events in France.
(C) They welcomed the liberating aspects of the French Revolution.
(D) While shocked by the revolution, they did not intervene in the internal affairs of France.
(E) After helping the French royal family to safety, the other nations prepared for war.

20. (A) The other monarchs feared the spirit of revolution would spread, so they felt their only recourse was to suppress the French revolutionists by force.

21. Which industry in which country led the way in the Industrial Revolution?

(A) steelworks in England
(B) mining in France
(C) railroads in the United States
(D) textiles in England
(E) textiles in the United States

21.(D) Many questions ask for more than one piece of information, so if you know the answer to only one part, you can eliminate some of the possible answers. In this case, if you know England is correct, you can eliminate (B), (C) and (E). If you know textiles is correct, you can eliminate (A), (B) and (C). You should always make a choice if you can eliminate three of the five possible answers.

22. At the beginning of the 20th century, the nations of Africa and Asia were for the most part:

(A) free and independent nations
(B) unexplored lands
(C) colonies of the European powers
(D) in mass revolt against the West
(E) becoming industrialized and urban

22. (C) Many of the questions on the CLEP examination will ask for trends during a time period, rather than specific dates. In this case, most of the colonial empires collapsed after World War II, so (C) is the correct answer.

23. The Central Powers in World War I were:

(A) Great Britain, Germany, Turkey
(B) Turkey, Russia, Germany
(C) Germany, Austria-Hungary, Turkey
(D) Germany, Great Britain, France
(E) France, Great Britain, Russia

23. (C) The key to answering this question correctly is knowing whom Germany was fighting against, then eliminating the incorrect combinations. The Allies were (E)—France, Great Britain, Russia.

24. Which of the following was the most significant result of World War II?

(A) Russia was seized by the communists.

(B) The United Nations was created.

(C) Many new nations were created in Europe.

(D) Isolationism gained wide support in the United States.

(E) World leadership shifted from Europe to the United States.

24. (E) Answers (A), (B) and (D) happened after World War I. While it is correct that the United Nations was created after World War II, the question asks for the MOST significant result of the war.

25. Which of the following statements is the most accurate regarding the postwar years?

(A) For the most part, the nations of the world have become peaceful and interrelated.

(B) Western civilization has gradually declined in influence.

(C) Europe is no longer the dominant political force in the world.

(D) The third world has rejected the influences of Western civilization.

(E) Western civilization has been spread so far and so wide, it can now be called a World civilization.

25. (C) This question calls for your evaluation of trends and events during the time period in question. (A) is not the correct choice, because there have been many wars and revolutions, in addition to economic tensions. (B) is too general an answer—it may have lost in some areas (politics), but gained in others (technology). (D) is also incorrect—they may have rejected some ideas, but they may have adopted others. (E) is not the best answer because the world may be moving in that direction, but it has not been achieved yet. Therefore, (C) is the best choice.

GLOSSARY OF WESTERN CIVILIZATION TERMS

Age of Reason: the 17th and 18th centuries in Western Civilization.

Allies: the nations that fought against the Central Powers in WWI. They included Great Britain, France, Russia and the nations later allied with them, Japan, Italy and eventually the U.S. They also were the nations that fought the Axis powers in WWII. They were Great Britain, the U.S., the Soviet Union, and others.

Ancient World: the world before the end of the Western Roman Empire AD 476.

Byzantine Empire: the Eastern Roman Empire after the fall of the Western Roman Empire in AD 476. It ended with the fall of Constantinople, its capital, in 1453.

Central Powers: the collective countries who opposed the Allies during WWI consisting of Austria-Hungary, Germany, Bulgaria, and the Ottoman Empire.

Christianity: the Christian religion, including the Catholic, Protestant, and Eastern Orthodox churches.

Communism: the theory or system of social organization based on holding all property in common. Ownership is by the community or the state.

Constantinople: Capital of the Byzantine Empire. Present name is Istanbul Turkey.

Crusades: expeditions undertaken by the Christians of Europe in the 11th ,12th, and 13th centuries to recover the Holy Land from the Muslims.

Cultural Diffusion: the spreading of traditions, ideas, and culture through trade and commerce.

Dark Ages: the period in European history from about AD 476 to about 1000.

Feudalism: the political, military, and social system in the middle ages. Duties were set for both lords and their vassals.

French Revolution: the violent changing of government from monarchy to democracy which occurred from 1789-1799.

Humanism: an ethical theory that often rejects the importance of a belief in god in favor of the importance of mankind.

Imperialism: the policy of extending the rule of an empire or nation over foreign countries

Mercantilism: an economic and political policy in which a government regulates the national economy in order to accumulate gold and silver. Exports are favored over imports.

Middle Ages:	the time in European history between the end of the dark ages and the Renaissance, from about 1100 to 1492.
Middle Class:	a class of people between the lords and the serfs.
Modern World:	after the Middle Ages to the present.
Nationalism:	devotion and loyalty to one's own nation.
Nuclear Age:	the period where nuclear weapons were developed and tested.
Peloponnesian War:	war between ancient Athens and Sparta, which left Greece vulnerable to the invasion of the Romans in 146 B.C.
Reformation:	the 16th century movement for reforming the Roman Catholic Church, which resulted in the establishment of the Protestant churches.
Renaissance:	the great revival of art, literature, and learning in Europe beginning in the 14th century in Italy and extending to the rest of Europe. It marked the transition from the medieval to the modern world.
Revolution:	forceful overthrow and replacement of an established government or political system by the people governed.
Roman Empire:	the imperial form of government established in Rome in 27BC.
Treaty of Versailles:	peace treaty signed at the end of WWI negotiated during Paris Peace Conference in Versailles; signed June 28, 1919.
United Nations:	international organization with headquarters in New York City. It was formed in 1945 to promote peace, security, and cooperation amoung nations.
World War I:	war fought between the Central Powers and the Allies, beginning on July 28, 1914, and ending on November 11, 1918.
World War II:	the war between the Axis and the Allies, beginning on September 1, 1939, with the German invasion of Poland and ending with the surrender of Germany on May 8, 1945, and of Japan on August 14, 1945.

American History

INTRODUCTION

All groups and societies in the world, with all their differences, share two traits—a ban on incest and an **ethnocentric view** of their world. This term borrowed from the field of sociology, means that each group (or nation, or neighborhood, or political party, etc.) assumes a cultural superiority. For example, a typical Frenchman when asked which nation would anyone wish to have been born in, would answer, "Why, France, of course!" This man is expressing an ethnocentric view, as is the New Yorker who thinks the world stops at the Hudson River. Ethnocentricity can be used to help explain why the Nazis were capable of murdering so many—if they were "superior," then all others must be "inferior."

This ethnocentric view of the world begins within the family, and later the schools and other institutions help to foster this attitude in order to bring unity to the group. In the United States the schools, and particularly American history courses, have been seen as the primary factors used to encourage an ethnocentric view of America. In many cases this has led to a subjective whitewashing of American history, with the emphasis on Presidents and wars. While the "real" history of America might be depicted as the story of millions of ordinary immigrants who carved a great nation out of a wilderness, this is not the aspect of the American narrative, which is stressed.

In this brief review of American History, we will present a summary of the major events, trends and issues that have brought the United States from an untamed frontier to our present state. As you study this section, try to gain a broad understanding of the subject matter, rather than to memorize specific dates, facts and names. While you may be asked very specific questions on the CLEP examination, a general comprehension of the material is more important than a mind filled with unrelated details.

FINDING A NEW WORLD AND THE FOUNDING OF 13 COLONIES

Long before Columbus, perhaps 25,000 years ago, the American Indians came from Asia across the Bering Strait. They were probably following the buffalo herds that these nomadic tribes were dependent upon.

There is much evidence to support the theory that Europeans long before Columbus discovered America, perhaps as early as 2,000 years ago. This is why Columbus is often called "the last man to discover America." The debate over who was the first does not detract from Columbus' achievement—it was only after his voyages that the Europeans set about to explore, exploit, and finally to settle the New World.

Columbus made his first trip in 1492. While he was not the first European to come to the Americas, his coming greatly changed Europe. Gold and silver brought back to Europe caused rampant inflation. There was also a tremendous amount of transfer of plants, animals and diseases. Small pox was unknown in the Americas before the coming of the Europeans and had a devastating effect. Horses had died out in the Americas and were reintroduced. Likewise there was a transfer back to Europe. Chocolate, corn, potatoes, tobacco and turkeys were all unknown in Europe.

At first the explorations, discoveries, and claiming of land were accomplished by the Spanish and then the French. But this early exploration had little effect on what was to become the United States. The Spanish were primarily interested in gold, the French in furs; and both were discouraged from making permanent settlements in North America by harsh winters, fierce Indians and thick forests.

The English were latecomers to exploration and discovery but the first to settle in large numbers. England required colonies for two reasons—for a supply of raw materials and as a market for her manufactured goods. This desire for colonies would later be called **imperialism**. Other English settlements were not primarily started for economic reasons, they were settled for religious reasons.

English colonies were not able to find large quantities of gold and silver. They needed to find a new cash crop. Their early southern colonies in the Virginia area turned to tobacco once they were able to convince Europeans to use it.

The first permanent English settlement began in **Jamestown, Virginia**, in 1607. Many of the colonists expected instant wealth and did not prepare for the coming winter. Inadequate food and shelter caused nearly two-thirds of the initial 100 settlers to perish in the first winter. However new settlers soon arrived and the colony became prosperous because of tobacco. Tobacco growers needed large plantations and a steady flow of labor, hence the first indentured servants arrived and then the first slaves in 1619. The Virginia colony was originally settled by the Virginia Company, but reverted to a Royal Colony, a direct possession of the King, in 1624.

In 1620 the Mayflower, which had intended to go to Virginia but was blown off course, landed at Plymouth, Massachusetts. Most of those on board were Pilgrims who drew up the **Mayflower Compact**, in which they agreed to self-government and majority rule.

The Pilgrims initially had a friendly relationship with the Native Americans. The Pilgrims were not looking for instant riches like many of the southern colonists. They left England for religious reasons.

In the **New England Colonies** the tradition of self-government through town meetings continued. Most of the farms were too small to need slaves, and they lacked a major cash crop like the south's tobacco. The lack of a cash crop forced New Englanders to diversify with many becoming ship-builders and merchants.

Later, in 1630, a larger group of Puritans came to Salem with a charter as the **Massachusetts Bay Colony**, which included Plymouth and settlements in Maine. The Puritans were a Protestant group who believed that those destined for salvation were already chosen. The chosen ones could be seen to be living a moral life as expressed in the bible. The strict life lead by the Puritans carried over into their government that carried over into their town planning. Their cities were well laid out and growth controlled.

William Penn founded the Pennsylvania Colony. It was settled largely by Quakers who believed in non-violence and tolerance.

The **Middle Colonies**—New York, New Jersey, Pennsylvania and Maryland—started as proprietary colonies. In these colonies the king gave a large tract of land, such as Pennsylvania, to a single individual, in this case William Penn, usually as a reward for some favor. Penn and the Quakers he brought to the New World believed in tolerance, fairness to the Indians, and culture—**Philadelphia** became the most important cultural center in the colonies. Lord Baltimore settled the Maryland colony, across the Chesapeake Bay from the Virginia Colony as a refuge for English Catholics who were suffering persecution in England. Later it became one of the first colonies to practice religious tolerance.

As Royal Colonies, the **Southern Colonies** developed somewhat differently. In North Carolina most of the settlers came from the northern colonies. They had small farms and little slavery. South Carolina, however, attracted wealthy colonists who had large rice plantations, which needed many slaves. This became the aristocratic colony. Georgia began as an idealistic experiment as James Oglethorpe emptied the debtors' prisons in England by furnishing transportation to the proprietary colony. However, many people began committing "crimes" in order to receive a free trip to America.

In the early stages of colonization there were three types of colonies:

1. **Chartered**, in which the king owned the colony but gave the rights to joint-stock corporations.

2. **Proprietary**, in which the land itself was given to a person.

3. **Royal**, in which the king owned the colony, and the king appointed the governor.

By the Revolution, all the colonies had become royal colonies except for two—Rhode Island and Connecticut, which remained self-governing throughout the Colonial Period.

Before you continue our review, try a few sample CLEP questions:

ANSWERS:

1. The New England Colonies and the Southern Colonies differed the most in regard to:

(A) the size of the farms and the need for slaves
(B) religion
(C) the type of settlers
(D) cultural aspects
(E) amount of self-government

1. (A) is the best answer, because this is the only one which implies the economic differences which defined the colonies from the beginning. Many of the cultural differences were a direct result of the fact that there was no major cash crop. The religious differences, while major were not a colony difference but a settler difference. A settler with southern religious views would still have had a small farm in New England.

2. The term imperialism can best be defined as:

(A) self-rule
(B) the conquest of land
(C) the desire for cheap raw materials and a market for manufactured goods
(D) the belief in democracy as the best of governments
(E) the monarchy system of government

2. (C) Choices (A), (D), (E) can easily be eliminated because they mention nothing about the desire for an expanding influence or cheap raw materials. All types of governments can be imperialistic, but none have to be. When choosing between choices (B) and (C) you have to choose (C) because it is a more precise answer. The conquest of land without gaining a new market would be counter-productive.

THE DEVELOPING COLONIES

In the last half of the 17th century most colonies were experiencing rapid growth. New York, because of its economic system was lagging behind some of the others. After taking New York from the Dutch, the King granted the land to his brother the Duke of York. He set up the colony along traditional English lines. There were large landholders and rent paying workers. Land, however, was cheap in the other colonies so there was no incentive for settlers to come and pay rent to others.

The rapid growth of the colonies did have a negative effect. The addition of new settlers caused the colonies to be ever pushing westward. This caused them to clash with the Native American tribes in the area. This is the first area where the interests of the King and the interests of the Colonist started to diverge. Sending troops and protecting the colonists costs money and the King did not necessarily see a similar return to the treasury through expansion. This juxtaposition came to a head in Virginia. The Governor, the King's man, refused to help western settlers in their fight against the Native Americans. The western Virginians found a leader in Nathaniel Bacon. He not only led attacks on the tribes, whether they had attacked settlers or not, but he also rebelled against the Governor. Although the rebellion was unsuccessful its effects were felt for years to come.

In the early 1700's England largely ignored the colonies. England was experiencing revolutions at home and a war with France. While the French war did spill over to the Americas in the French and Indian war, colonists fought only when their self interests were threatened. This would all change with the end of the war in 1763.

CAUSES OF FRICTION

By 1760 the colonists may have thought of themselves as British subjects, but they had become a new breed—Americans. There were few class differences, most were Protestants, and all were self-governing to a large degree. While the colonists had much political freedom, England had tight economic controls and the colonists grew resentful of any controls. While many of these controls had existed for some time, they had been largely ignored. When England chose to enforce the laws friction occurred.

This was brought to a head with the end of the **French and Indian War** in 1763. This war between England and France grew out of conflicts in Europe, but with the victory England now controlled North America east of the Mississippi River. The conclusion of this war had two effects on the future of the colonies:

1. The colonists felt they no longer needed England for protection and grew resentful of England's continued military presence.

2. England was in debt because of the war and felt the colonists should be taxed since the war was fought to protect the colonies.

George III must also be mentioned as a cause of the friction; but in order to understand the significance of his role, we must look at English history. During the 1400's, England was torn between the two houses, York and Lancaster, each claiming the throne. This led to the War of the Roses, which finally ended when Henry VII married the daughter of the York House. Their son, Henry VIII, brought the Reformation to England. Each of his children reigned, Edward for a very short time. His daughter Mary, known as "Good Queen Mary" to the Catholics and as "Bloody Mary" to the Protestants, is remembered for her attempt to bring Catholicism back to England. Elizabeth I (1558-1603) reigned during the age of discovery and exploration. During the time of her heir, James I—and his son, Charles I—most of the colonies were founded. Charles was beheaded; there was a civil war, followed by 20 years of rule under Cromwell and the Puritans. After the restoration of Charles II, his son, James II, had to flee because he was Catholic. William and Mary (James' daughter) ruled, and then William's sister-in-law, Anne. When she died, the closest Protestant relative was a German, George I, who never learned English. His son, George II, also had little interest in being king of England.

During this time period England was involved in several wars with France, while confronting her internal problems—civil war, Protestant vs. Catholic, and German kings. The question can be raised—who was running the show in the colonies?

When George III came to the throne in 1760 (at the age of 22), he surveyed the situation in the colonies and felt they had been neglected for too long. This, plus the desire for revenue to pay for the French and Indian War, led to a series of acts and incidents.

The first act, the Sugar Act, started the protests. The colonists as a necessary evil however, largely accepted it. The Stamp Act of 1765 however went too far. It required that all wills, deeds, marriage certificates, etc. required an official stamp. Protests were the most pronounced in Boston where an angry mob marched on and attacked the home of the stamp official. Protests got so bad that England ended up repealing the Act after four months.

The Townshend Acts soon followed. They were a series of small import duties imposed on many everyday items used in the colonies. The theory was that colonist would not be as upset by many small taxes. Again, England had miscalculated. The colonists felt that it was unfair for England to impose taxes specifically on them when they did not have representation in Parliament where the laws were passed. After a few years most of the Townshend Acts were also repealed.

Next came the Tea Act of 1773. The act was designed to bail out the East Indian Tea Company by giving it a monopoly to sell tea in the American colonies. While most of the colonies simply boycotted the tea, the colonists in Boston went a step further. They disguised themselves as Indians and snuck aboard East Indian Tea Company ships tied up in the harbor. They then threw the tea overboard.

King George was furious. In response, he forced through Parliament the Intolerable Acts. They were very punishing. The colonies responded together. They called the First Continental Congress. While the first Continental Congress did not pass anything major, it was the first time all the colonies met as a group to protest the way they were being treated by England.

The First Continental Congress met in the fall of 1774.

The climate continued to deteriorate in New England. The Boston Massacre, where a group of English soldiers panicked and fired on a crowd of protesters leaving five dead, occurred. In April of 1775, the colonists fought back in the Battles of Lexington and Concord. Britain wanted to seize weapons stored in Concord. People watched the British troops to see how they planned to attack. They could either come by ship or over land. The colonist could not prepare to defend both ways. When the British started to move, the watchers were told to light lanterns in the North Church. One if the British were coming by land and two if they were coming by sea. The signal was seen by riders who then rode through the countryside waking the militia.

The Second Continental Congress led to the appointment of George Washington to lead the troops.

Before you continue our review, try this sample CLEP question:

3. The conclusion of the French and Indian War led to tensions between the colonies and England because:

   (A) the colonists had supported the French

   (B) the colonies were bankrupt because of the war

   (C) England tried to tighten the economic controls

   (D) George III had not supported the war

   (E) the war had not solved the problem of who would control the area east of the Mississippi River

3. (C) England attempted to levy taxes on the colonies. In addition, England also restricted the colonists to the narrow strip of land along the Atlantic coast. The other choices are all the opposite of what really happened.

WINNING THE WAR AND FOUNDING A NEW NATION

The former colonies faced almost insurmountable difficulties in their fight against England. The new nation had no navy versus the strongest navy in the world. Many citizens called the **Tories**, supported England. Few men had any military experience, and there was little money to pay and train soldiers.

How then was the small band of rag-tag soldiers able to defeat the most powerful nation of the age? England had many logistical problems—it was 3,000 miles away and had primitive means of transportation and communication. In addition, England had great difficulty recruiting her own citizens to fight for so vague a cause. But perhaps England's greatest problem had to do with the type of warfare—she was fighting in the traditional manner versus guerrilla warfare. The Americans simply did not know and did not follow the "rules" of war. While the British would march in perfect formation, the Americans would hide in trees with their Kentucky long rifles.

Initially the war went poorly. Washington was soundly defeated in New York and almost destroyed. In the winter of 1776, many of his troops started deserting. He came up with a bold plan to attack the Hessians, German mercenaries, at Trenton on Christmas Eve. He loaded his troops into boats and crossed the Delaware River from his winter headquarters in Pennsylvania to complete the surprise attack. The victory had very little military significance, but in terms of morale to the Continental Army, it was significant.

The English planned a bold stroke to swiftly defeat the Continentals. In 1777, they planned an attack to capture the entire colony of New York. This would effectively cut the colonies in two. Since the British also controlled the sea, if their plan worked, they would be able to deal with the New England colonies and then the southern colonies separately. Unfortunately for the English their plan failed. The part of the attack coming down from Canada was defeated at Saratoga. General Howe recalled the contingent sent from New York City before they could push north to meet the Canadian contingent. The last British Army in the attack never made it out of western New York.

This was the sign that France needed. They were still angry about their defeat in the French and Indian war and wanted to get back at their long rival the British. They did not want to get involved in a hopeless cause. After the British defeat at Saratoga, they decided to give the colonies some aid.

The war then shifted to the South, and here the colonists did poorly. Every General Washington sent south was soundly defeated by the British commander, Lord Cornwallis. Only a few pockets of fighters who used hit and run tactics remained. In 1781, Cornwallis made a blunder. He retreated his troops to Yorktown Virginia. The only escape was by sea. When the French Navy blocked his escape, Washington surrounded and defeated Cornwallis' forces. The upheaval in England, when the news that the British troops had been defeated, caused Lord North's (the leader in parliament) government to collapse. Effectively this was the end of major battles during the Revolutionary War although minor skirmishes did continue. The **Treaty of Paris** was signed in 1783 ending hostilities completely.

The war had become too costly and too unpopular for England to continue. The English decided they could accomplish their goals economically rather than militarily. England began a policy of deliberately attempting to strangle trade, hoping the new nation would ask to become colonies again—they almost succeeded.

The political leaders of the time may not have known what type of government they wanted, but they surely knew what type of government they did not want—the strong, central government of England. The **Articles of Confederation** was deliberately designed to provide for a very weak central government with most of the power residing in the individual states. Under the Articles of Confederation the United States almost fell apart and became 13 separate states. Each state could print money, and some of it became worthless. By 1787, the new nation was on the verge of chaos: the war debts were unpaid; there were tariff wars between the states; there was a decline in trade, the nation suffered an economic depression, as well as inflation.

Finally a convention was called to revise the Articles, but instead a whole new **Constitution** was written. Some of the men involved with the convention were Washington, Franklin, Hamilton, and Madison, but not Jefferson, who was serving as Ambassador to France. The new constitution required the vote of at least nine of the existing states at special constitutional conventions. Passage of the document was by no means a sure thing. There was a strong feeling that too much power was being given to the federal government and there were too few provisions for the rights of the citizens. Therefore a large number of people opposed the ratification of the constitution. They were called the Anti-federalists. The Federalists supported passage of the Constitution. A group of them wrote a series of articles in newspapers, The Federalist Papers, which explained why the Constitution was a good thing. One of the key factors that helped swing the votes to the Federalist's side was the **Bill of Rights**. The Bill of Rights are the first ten amendments to the Constitution and they state rights citizens have under the Constitution. One of the first acts of the new government was the passage of the Bill of Rights and the creation of the Federal Court System. **George Washington** was inaugurated as the first President.

Before you continue our review, try a few sample CLEP questions:

4. The Americans were able to win the Revolution because:

(A) England was so far away
(B) the French gave aid to the Americans
(C) the war was unpopular in England
(D) the English did not know how to successfully fight against the guerrilla type of warfare
(E) all of the above contributed to the British defeat

ANSWERS:

4. (E)   All of these factors contributed to the American victory. When answering questions, be sure to read all of the answers. If you do not, you may mark the first correct answer and overlook the "all of these" type of answers.

5. Which of the following statements is the best summarization of the nation under the Articles of Confederation?

(A) The Articles of Confederation established such a weak form of government that the new nation was almost overwhelmed with difficulties.

(B) The new government was very successful, and the country prospered under the Articles of Confederation.

(C) Although there were some minor problems, the Articles of Confederation served the country quite well at the time.

(D) The Articles of Confederation was such an ineffective form of government that it brought ruin and destruction to the country.

(E) The Articles of Confederation had little effect one way or the other on the United States.

5. (A) This type of question requires that you make a judgment about degree, based upon your understanding of the material. In general, when answering this type of question, avoid the answers at the extremes (B and D) and the noncommittal type (E).

THE U.S. UNDER WASHINGTON, ADAMS, AND JEFFERSON

Under the new Constitution many hoped that there would be no political parties, but two took shape almost immediately. The **Federalists**, led by **Alexander Hamilton**, the first Secretary of Treasury, favored a strong central government at the expense of the states. They saw the necessity of Congress assuming the national debt, a strong national bank, and a levying of import taxes to provide a cash flow. Hamilton was an admirer of the British and favored the upper class, merchants and businessmen.

Alexander Hamilton favored a strong federal government giving advantages to the rich.

The **Democratic-Republican Party** rallied around **Thomas Jefferson**, the first Secretary of State. They preferred a weak central government, with the emphasis on states' rights. Jefferson admired the French system, with its emphasis on democracy and equality. The followers of the Democratic-Republican Party were mostly small farmers and planters.

The two parties probably differed the most regarding the Constitution: the Federalists believed in a very broad interpretation, while the Democratic-Republicans insisted upon a strict interpretation of the founding fathers' words and intentions. Washington tried to remain above the political process, but he nevertheless tended to favor the Federalists, who gained the upper hand in the early years.

Under Federalist **John Adams**, the Napoleonic Wars between France and England led to problems in the United States. Both nations interfered with American shipping, so **John Jay** was sent to England to work out a treaty. Adams also sent envoys to the French government, who offered the Americans bribes. This incident became known as the **XYZ Affair**, and war with France seemed inevitable. The **Alien and Sedition Acts**, which suppressed liberties, were passed, causing revulsion among the citizens. This series of events killed the Federalist Party and led to the election of Jefferson and the Democratic-Republicans in 1800.

Jefferson stood for peace, democracy, states' rights and promotion of agriculture. His most notable accomplishments were:

1. The **Louisiana Purchase**, which Napoleon sold for $15 million because he needed the money and because he knew he could not defend it if either the United States or England decided to claim it.

2. Keeping the United States out of the growing conflict between England and France.

Before you continue our review, try this sample CLEP question:

6. **The major difference between the Federalist Party and the Democratic-Republican Party revolved around the issue of:**

   (A) the national bank
   (B) farmers' interests versus merchants' interests
   (C) import taxes
   (D) states' rights
   (E) how to interpret the constitution

ANSWER:

6. (E) While all five of the answers are correct, the question asks for the MAJOR difference. The issue of states' rights is just one issue debated when discussing how to interpret the Constitution.

WAR, PEACE, EXPANSION AND SLAVERY

The **War of 1812**, under Madison's administration, was caused largely by England's impressment of U.S. sailors. Under English law, English ships of war could impress, take on to their ship and make them work, any English citizens on merchant ships. Unfortunately they started impressing U.S. sailors too. The War resulted in a stalemate in which neither side won nor lost much. The Americans tried to invade Canada and were defeated. The English did attack and burn Washington DC The most famous conflict, the **Battle of New Orleans**, made a national hero of **Andrew Jackson**. It occurred after peace had already been agreed upon in Europe but news of the peace had not reached the United States yet. The most lasting effect of the war however, was the unifying influence on the country.

Under Monroe, Florida and Oregon were purchased from Spain. The Americans gave up their claims to Texas, and assumed $5 million in American citizens' claims against Spain. The claim to the Oregon territory was not completely clear either; England also had claims, which would be negotiated in future, treaties. The **Monroe Doctrine**, in 1823, told Europeans to keep out of the Western Hemisphere. Before purchasing Florida, Spain had moved the Florida border northwards pinching the United States between Florida and Canada. The Seminole Indians had also been a problem in the early 1800's. Andrew Jackson defeated the Indians and captured all the Spanish forts except St. Augustine.

Monroe's term, often referred to as the **Era of Good Feeling** because political parties almost ceased to exist, brought peace and prosperity to the nation. Most citizens were more interested in growth and expansion into the Western territories than in political entanglements, except over the issue of slavery.

Even in colonial times many people were opposed to slavery, but in the early 1800's the issue began to divide the nation. The South's major crops—cotton, sugar, rice and tobacco—wore out the land, so the Southern states demanded that at least some of the new territories be allowed to enter the Union as slave states. Many Northern states were equally insistent that not one more slave state should be admitted. A careful balance of the number of slave states versus the number of free states was maintained. **The Missouri Compromise** in 1820 prevented a civil war at the time but only postponed the matter until a later date. Under the terms of this compromise,

Missouri entered as a slave state and Maine entered as a free state. Also all new states north of the southern border of Missouri would be free. For a few years the nation could turn to the business at hand—growth and expansion.

Perhaps more than any other leader, Andrew Jackson represented a symbol of the age. He received much support from the old Democratic-Republican Party, renamed the **Democrat Party**, and with his **"let the people rule"** attitude and his distrust of the wealthy, a new political era commenced. Powerful political machines began, as did the **spoils system**, in which the politicians appointed their friends and supporters to office. When Jackson entered office, he removed a large number of people from the previous administration and hired his friends and supporters. Social reforms and public schools were also encouraged under Jackson.

Serious problems over the slavery issue flared again when Texas, a free republic, was admitted to the Union. From the beginning of Texas' independence from Mexico, the republic had applied for statehood but had met resistance from the Northerners who balked at admitting a slave state.

Under **James K. Polk**, Texas finally entered the Union. Polk then tried to buy the land west of Texas all the way to the Pacific Ocean, but Mexico would not sell. General Zachary Taylor moved troops into Texas. The southern border of Texas was disputed. The U.S. said it went all the way to the Rio Grande, but Mexico said it was just south of San Antonio. Taylor moved his army into the disputed area and the Mexican Army led by Santa Anna attacked. The U.S. won easily and gained California and the Southwest Territory in the process. Also under Polk, disagreements with England over the Northwest were settled peacefully, and the U.S. gained the Oregon Territory (Oregon, Washington, and Idaho).

Many Europeans were aghast at how easily and quickly the United States had gained so much new territory, but this was the era of **Manifest Destiny**; that is, most Americans felt it was God's wish that America should rule from coast to coast.

The current inhabitants of the newly acquired lands were treated poorly. The Mexican Settlers were repeatedly swindled and the Native Americans were moved to reservations.

The addition of this new territory was a mixed blessing for the nation. While there was much new land available for farming and settlement, the question of slave state versus free state once more seriously divided the nation. The Missouri Compromise was no longer valid, since California, which had no slaves, would have been cut in two. **The Compromise of 1850** settled the issue for the moment, but it did little to prevent the Civil War. California was to be admitted as a free state; the Southwest was to be organized into two territories with no mention of slavery. In 1854, the Kansas-Nebraska Act was passed. It repealed the Missouri Compromise and allowed Kansas to vote on if it wanted to be admitted as a free or a slave state.

Instead of abating, the tensions increased during the 1850's. If ever a strong voice was needed in the White House, it was during this time—but three weak Presidents (**Millard Filmore**, **Franklin Pierce**, and **James Buchanan**) were elected. The **Abolitionists**, a small but increasingly loud group, continued their vociferous attacks. Kansas, called **Bleeding Kansas** at the time, became a battlefield as settlers from each side moved into the territory in anticipation of the election.

A new political party, the **Republican**, was formed with opposition to the further extension of slavery as the basic platform. In the election of 1860 the Democratic Party split three ways allowing the first Republican President, **Abraham Lincoln**, to be elected with only 40% of the vote. South Carolina seceded the next month, and the fighting began in April, 1861, at **Fort Sumter, South Carolina**.

Before going on with the review, try these sample CLEP questions:

7. **Which of the following statements most accurately describes the Missouri Compromise?**

   (A) There would be no more slave states admitted to the Union.
   (B) Missouri was admitted as a free state, but the other territories west of Missouri could become slave states.
   (C) California was admitted as a free state, with Missouri as a slave state.
   (D) Missouri was admitted as a slave state, but no new state above the southern border of Missouri could become a slave state.
   (E) All of the territories would hold elections prior to statehood in order to determine free versus slave status.

ANSWERS:

7. (D) This type of question is a variation of the true-false type. When answering this kind of question, it is best to eliminate the false answers, rather than to look for the true statement. (A) is false because other slave states could be admitted. (B) is false because the compromise talked about territories north of Missouri's southern border. It said nothing about the west. (C) California was admitted with the compromise of 1850. (E) Kansas was the state that took a vote to see if it would be slave or free.

8. Which of the following Presidents is most associated with the term Manifest Destiny?

(A) Jefferson
(B) Madison
(C) Polk
(D) Lincoln
(E) Jackson

8. (C) This question tests your knowledge of two facts: the meaning of a term, plus a name to go with it. It is sometimes possible to "stretch" a little knowledge into the correct answer. For example, if you know which time period the Manifest Destiny is associated with, you might realize that Jefferson and Madison are too early and Lincoln too late. When left with two possibilities, in this case Polk and Jackson, you should make a choice between the two. Polk is the best choice because he acquired large amounts of land in the Southwest and settled claims in the Northwest.

THE CIVIL WAR AND RECONSTRUCTION

In a discussion of the causes of the Civil War, the slavery issue is usually emphasized, although the subject is much more complicated. Many of the causes of the conflict go back to the founding of the colonies when the economic rivalry began between the North and the South. Most of the people thought of themselves as citizens of a particular state, rather than as American citizens. Therefore, when conflicts arose, the population tended to view the issues as a state rather than as a nation.

By the time of the Civil War, the North had all of the economic advantages: a larger population (22 million versus 9 million); 7/8 of the industry; most of the railroads; and the North even produced more food. In fact, the South had only two advantages: it was fighting to preserve what it had on its own land and therefore knew the territory better (except for the disaster at Gettysburg); and it had better military leaders.

Civil wars are the most costly and the most vicious of wars, and the American Civil War is no exception. The only hope the South had was for a quick victory, but the killing and destruction dragged on for four years. Eventually the North found some good generals and was able to overpower the South.

The first turning point in the war occurred in the battle at Antietam, Maryland. The North had been bungling the war badly, but finally it was able to capitalize on its major advantages. After the battle Lincoln made his Emancipation Proclamation. It stated that all slaves in states that were still in rebellion after January 1st, 1863 would be set free. It said nothing about slaves in states that were fighting for the Union. Lincoln feared that this would cause states like Maryland to switch sides.

The Union then devised a strategy to cut the South in two along the Mississippi River. After Vicksburg fell, they soon achieved that goal. A second strategy of the North was to cut off the Confederacy's trade routes. Their huge advantage of industrial capacity helped them achieve this goal. They built many ships and soon blockaded all southern ports.

The Civil War saw the first use of Ironclad vessels. Putting iron plating on the sides of ships made them almost invulnerable to the opposing wooden ships. The first two, the Monitor for the North, and the Merrimac for the South fought to a draw.

General William T. Sherman captured Atlanta in 1864, after burning a wide path across Georgia. The South was nearly out of resources and men. The Confederate President urge the army to melt into the hills and continue a guerrilla war, but General Robert E. Lee surrendered the Army of Northern Virginia at Appomattox Courthouse effectively ending the war in 1865.

After the war, the North was heavily in debt and had inflated currency. The South, however, was in complete ruin. The old economic way of life was simply gone.

John Wilkes Booth assassinated Abraham Lincoln at Ford's Theater. Without Lincoln to temper the extremists, the Northern leaders were determined to have revenge. **Andrew Johnson,** Lincoln's Vice President, had been a compromise. He was a Southern Democrat-Unionist. He proposed a moderate plan for bringing the confederated states back into the Union much as Lincoln had proposed. The radicals in the Senate wanted a severe program with military rule, and this clash led to the impeachment of Johnson, who was acquitted by one vote.

Johnson's effectiveness as a President ended, and the South entered the period known as **Reconstruction**. **Carpetbaggers**, opportunists from the North, and freed Blacks took over the Southern governments, while many Whites joined the **Ku Klux Klan**. Even after reconstruction ended, the South lagged far behind the rest of the country in economic development.

Before going on with the review, try these sample CLEP questions:

9. **Which of the following statements about the Confederacy and the Union is not true?**

(A) Generally, the South had better generals than the North.

(B) Because the South had large plantations, it was able to produce more food than the North.

(C) The South was fighting to preserve an economic way of life; the North was fighting to preserve the Union.

(D) The North had more of the industry and railroads than the South.

(E) The North had a far larger population than the South.

10. **Which of the following statements regarding Andrew Johnson's administration is the most accurate?**

(A) Johnson was impeached because of his crimes and misconduct.

(B) Compared to Lincoln, Johnson was an ineffectual President.

(C) The Congress was dominated by the moderate groups.

(D) For the most part, the South was treated fairly after the Civil War, with revenge not a motivation for the actions of Congress.

(E) Johnson was able to carry out all of Lincoln's plans for Reconstruction.

ANSWERS:

9. (B) This is another variation of the true-false type of question. In this case you are asked for the false statement, so you should eliminate the true answers. (A) is true because the South had much better Generals at the beginning of the war than the North. (C) is true because the South knew that if it lost, it would not be allowed to keep its old way of life. (D) and (E) are both also true, the North had huge advantages in both population and industry.

10. (B) In this type of question, you must make a judgment about statements which may be partially true. Try to select the best answer, rather than the only correct answer. (A) is false, he was impeached because many Northerners were unhappy with his policies toward the South. (B) is true because after he was impeached Johnson lost all his effectiveness. (C) is false because Congress was mostly made up or radicals. (D) is false because the radicals wanted revenge. (E) because of his ineffectiveness Johnson was unable to carry out Lincoln's plans.

THE GILDED AGE

The 35 years between the end of the Civil War and the end of the century are often referred to as the **Gilded Age.** This era was marked by two notable developments and changes in the country—rapid industrial development in the North; and the taming of the Western Frontier.

The Civil War had quickened the pace of the **Industrial Revolution** in the North as more and more people moved to the cities. The Great Plains, an area thought to be uninhabitable by earlier settlers, was conquered in less than thirty years. Also, the period after the Civil War could be called the **Age of the Immigrants**. Lured by free land in the West and jobs in the factories or on the railroads, immigrants from every part of the world streamed into the United States.

Politics took a back seat during this era. **Ulysses S. Grant**, who served two terms, is remembered for being the second worst President in our history. An alcoholic, he was surrounded by inept, dishonest, unqualified administrators. Although corruption and scandals marked this time period, the attention of the country was focused elsewhere.

Perhaps the most striking characteristic of this era was the astounding rapidity of industrialization. This was the season for the Mellons, Rockefellers, Carnegies, when fortunes were made and dynasties were created—the age of unregulated big business.

This era has been termed "Gilded" rather than "Golden" because there were many economic conflicts beneath the showy veneer of wealth. The almost total lack of regulation of commerce led to monopolies, cartels and other unethical or corrupt business practices. Without unions or government intervention, the workers' conditions grew worse and worse as the century drew to a close. The conflict between farmers who wanted cheap money (silver) and businessmen, who wanted gold to be standard, grew into a bitter debate, which threatened to divide the barely reconciled nation.

The boom or bust type of business cycle also marked this era. **Grover Cleveland**, the only Democrat elected between the Civil War and 1912, was thwarted in his goals by a great panic caused by financial disturbances abroad and over-expansion at home.

Prosperity quickly returned after the election of **William McKinley** in 1896. He defeated William Jennings Bryan in a bitter campaign over gold (McKinley) vs. silver (Bryan) issue.

Under McKinley, the United States had a brief fling with imperialism as a result of the **Spanish-American War**. The Cubans revolted against Spain. Because of the strategic location and the sugar investments, the United States had always been vitally interested in the affairs of Cuba. Sensational newspaper reports, called **yellow journalism,** inflamed the American temper against Spain. When the battleship *Maine* was blown up in Havana harbor, war was declared.

The United States won very quickly and gained the former Spanish colonies of Guam, Puerto Rico and the Philippine Islands. Cuba became an independent nation but remained under American protectorship for many years.

Because of the long anti-colonial tradition in America, a wave of revulsion swept the nation after the war was over. After all, the United States did not really need raw materials and markets abroad (imperialism) as perhaps England did.

By the end of the century, the country was ready for major social reforms and for regulation of some aspects of labor and industry. While America was not quite ready to assume a leadership role in world events, American influence and presence were being felt worldwide.

Before going on with the review, try these sample CLEP questions:

11. **The 35 years after the Civil War can best be termed as an era when:**

(A) there was much progress and wealth on the surface, but many economic disturbances underneath

(B) the government began large-scale regulation of business and industry

(C) little attention was focused on the political happenings in Washington

(D) the workers and the immigrants greatly improved their conditions

(E) there was little economic progress because of the destruction the Civil War had caused

11. (A) This is the best answer because it presents a summary of the era. While (C) may be a true statement, it is too specific and narrow an answer to be the best selection. The other choices are all incorrect.

12. **Which of the following was not a cause of the Spanish-American War?**

(A) The Americans sided with the Cuban protesters, thus angering the Spanish.

(B) The yellow journalists presented a biased view of the Cuban-Spanish conflict.

(C) The United States desperately needed new markets and more raw materials.

(D) The American people thought the Spanish had attacked and sunk the *Maine*.

(E) Many Americans were extremely concerned about the sugar investments in Cuba and therefore wanted Cuba to be an independent nation.

12. (C) You should eliminate the correct causes to find the incorrect cause. Many people did not believe that the United States needed to be an imperialistic nation. It had huge amounts of natural resources. The high standard of living allowed most Americans to purchase goods, so there was no need for companies to look overseas to sell their products.

THE PROGRESSIVE ERA

Teddy Roosevelt, the former governor of New York, became President when McKinley was assassinated. His administration, known as the **Square Deal,** provided the first strong leadership since Lincoln. Domestically his policies included "trust busting" (the breaking up of monopolistic corporations), regulation of the railroad industry, the Pure Food and Drug Act, and perhaps most importantly, the conservation of natural resources. In foreign policy, Roosevelt's motto was **"walk softly and carry a big stick."** His most notable achievements in foreign affairs were the building of the Panama Canal and the Open-Door policy in China.

The first two decades of the 20th century were an era of social reforms. The **muckrakers**, writing about the evils of the Industrial Revolution, helped to bring about a public outcry over such conditions as child labor, poverty in the tenements, and abuses in the business world. **William Howard Taft** tried to continue Roosevelt's reforms, but he was neither as skillful nor as successful.

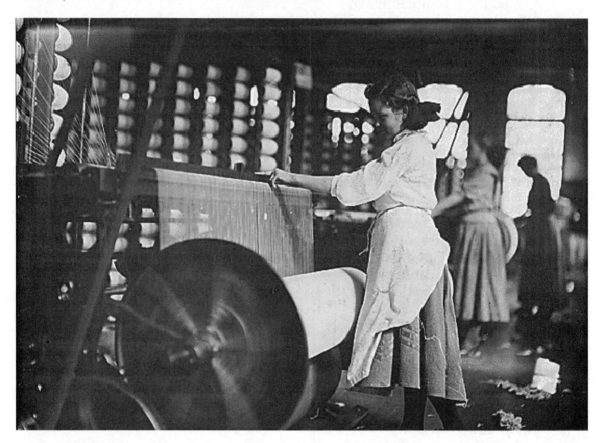

The Muckrackers complained about child labor and other abuses by industry.

In 1912, the Republican Party split over the issue of social reforms. The conservative wing renominated Taft, while the liberal wing nominated Roosevelt as the "Bull Moose" candidate. This division allowed **Woodrow Wilson** and the Democrats to win the election.

Wilson, like Franklin Roosevelt and Lyndon Johnson, began his presidency attempting to reform society, but he then became almost totally involved with war and foreign events. Domestically, Wilson is noted for the income tax; the Clayton Anti-Trust Act, which helped the infant labor unions; and the low-cost loans to farmers.

World War I began in Europe during the later years of Wilson's first term and he won re-election in 1916 largely on the slogan of "he kept us out of war". However, largely because of German interference with American shipping as well as the decidedly pro-British attitude of most citizens, America entered the war in 1917. The infusion of fresh troops helped speed the conclusion of the war in 1918.

The **Armistice** was based upon Wilson's 14 Points, point 14 being the **League of Nations** (similar to the present day United Nations). Although the idealistic Wilson was treated as a hero in Europe, he was a babe in the woods compared to the skilled diplomats who drew up the Treaty of Versailles. In order to convince the others of the dire necessity for the League, Wilson compromised on all the other issues involved with the treaty. Although Wilson knew the treaty was greatly unfair to Germany, he was convinced that all the problems could be ironed out later when the League was in operation.

Although the League of Nations was popular with the American people, it was defeated in the Senate largely because of party politics, a hatred of Wilson, and a fear of European entanglements. The **Progressive Era** came to a close.

Before going on with the review, try these sample CLEP questions:

ANSWERS:

13. **The Progressive Era differed from the Gilded Age in regard to:**

(A) regulation of business and industry
(B) leadership in foreign affairs
(C) social reforms
(D) the leadership of the Presidents
(E) all of the above

13. (E) In all of these respects the two eras differed greatly. The Gilded Age was pro-business and favored monopolies, while the Progressive Era was known for trust busting. The Presidents during the Progressive Era were strong and pushed through many social reforms and took a leadership in foreign affairs, while the Gilded Age Presidents lived by the philosophy of "Lassiez Faire."

14. **In the election of 1912, the Bull Moose candidate for President was:**

(A) William Jennings Bryan
(B) William McKinley
(C) Teddy Roosevelt
(D) William Howard Taft
(E) Woodrow Wilson

15. **During the last two years of his term, Wilson was mainly interested in:**

(A) helping labor unions
(B) punishing Germany
(C) securing approval of the income tax
(D) starting the League of Nations
(E) negotiating the Treaty of Versailles

14. (C) With this type of question, testing specific factual knowledge, you will usually either know the answer immediately or not at all. However, do try to "stretch" the information. For example, if you know that Wilson ran as a Democrat and that Bryan and McKinley ran in much earlier elections, your choices are between only Taft and Roosevelt. Since you have a 50 percent chance of being right, you should always make a choice between the two.

15. (D) The question asks for the main or primary interest Wilson had during the latter years of his terms in office. The early years of his Presidency he was concerned with helping the labor unions and passing the income tax. He was against punishing Germany for WWI and while he did negotiate the Treaty of Versailles, his main point in the treaty was the League of Nations and he tried to get the Senate to pass it for the rest of his Presidency.

THE ROARING '20'S

The mood of the country in 1920 turned conservative, and Republican **Warren Harding**, running on the platform of **"Back to Normalcy,"** was elected. Harding's administration, probably the worst in U.S. history, was characterized by political corruption on a large scale. Among other virulent acts, the Secretary of Interior took bribes for the leasing of federal oil reserves at **Teapot Dome**, and the head of the Veterans Bureau embezzled large sums allocated for hospitals.

Harding died in office and **Calvin Coolidge** became President. Most remembered for his statement, **"The business of America is business,"** Coolidge brought little in the way of leadership to the White House. The country, especially the business world, continued on its way to disaster with little governmental regulation or interference.

After the disillusionment, which followed World War I, the United States entered a long period of isolation. The highest import tariffs in history were passed during the

1920's; this had the effect of shutting out most foreign goods from the U.S. But perhaps the most significant development in foreign affairs in this era was the **Kellogg-Briand Pact**, a disarmament agreement which was widely defied, except by the United States.

Generally, the country prospered throughout the 1920's. It was an age of real estate booms, wild stock speculation, and riotous spending. However, two groups were in trouble: the farmers, who had expanded production during the war years and continued to expand even as demand declined; and the workers, who lost their earlier gains.

But this troublesome aspect of society was hidden behind the symbols of the '20's: Model T's clogging the highways; jazz-bands and flappers; Lindbergh and flagpole sitters; the speakeasy and gangsters; and the **Golden Age of Literature**—Faulkner, Fitzgerald, Hemingway, Lewis and Sandburg.

This was also the era of Prohibition, a brief period in American history where the government tried to make the consumption of alcoholic beverages illegal. While the idea may have been noble, it allowed organized crime to make huge profits bootlegging. A whole underground economy flourished, and instead of strengthening society, Prohibition was tearing it apart.

A Chicken for Every Pot

This ad was from Hoover's 1928 election campaign.

When **Hoover** was elected in 1928 most Americans were convinced their "bubble" would last for at least a lifetime. What, then, caused the greatest economic depression in the history of the nation? The "man-in-the-street" would probably answer, "The stock market crashed." But the crash was only a symptom of the disease, not the cause.

Two groups, the farmers and workers, had been in a depression throughout the decade, with severe limitations on their buying power. Business was already in a decline before the crash, with dangerously high inventories by 1928. By this date, almost everyone who could afford the cars, appliances and other material goods had already purchased them; there were no new markets, yet the factories were kept at high production levels. The rampant speculation in stocks, with no governmental regulations, was really paper **prosperity** with no relation to the actual worth of the stocks. Many people were buying stocks on margin, borrowed money. Therefore, the stock market "crashed"; this brought the value of the stocks in line with their real worth—which in many cases was nothing.

After this happened, the economic well-being of the nation steadily declined: banks failed; factories and stores closed; there were millions of bankruptcies; farm prices fell even lower; and foreign trade ceased altogether. By the end of 1930 there were 6 million unemployed; by the end of 1931, 12 million were unemployed. This was the era of soup kitchens and Hoovervilles.

These men were wondering if they would be able to get their money back out of the bank. Many banks failed.

The Hoover administration took some measures to ease the situation, but they were not enough. Radical governmental intervention was needed.

Before going on with the review, try these sample CLEP questions:

16. **The Harding administration was noted mainly for:**

(A) wide-scale corruption
(B) bringing the country back to normalcy
(C) bringing Prohibition to the country
(D) helping the farmers and the workers make economic gains
(E) extending the vote to women

16. (A) While Prohibition and the women's vote correspond to the beginning of Harding's term, they are separate events; since "normalcy" was never clearly defined, it would be incorrect to say that Harding achieved this. (D) is the opposite of what happened.

17. **"The business of America is business," is a quote by:**

(A) Woodrow Wilson
(B) Warren Harding
(C) John D. Rockefeller
(D) Calvin Coolidge
(E) Herbert Hoover

17. (D) Although Coolidge was known as "Silent Cal" as President, this one quote was widespread and adopted by many.

18. **In the 1920's, the United States' position regarding world affairs was one of:**

(A) active involvement as the world leader
(B) attempted isolation from world events for the most part
(C) involvement with European affairs, but not with Asia
(D) attempting to increase the number of treaties and commitments to the Allies
(E) using the League of Nations to solve international problems

18. (B) This is the best answer. After World War I many Americans simply wanted to be left alone. They feared that any involvement with Europe (through the League of Nations, or in other ways) could only lead to America being dragged into future wars.

19. **Which of the following statements is the most accurate regarding Hoover's part in the Depression?**

(A) All of the blame for the Depression can be laid at his feet.

(B) Hoover did not even take office until after the stock market crash.

(C) Since most of the conditions of the Depression existed before Hoover took office, he should not be faulted for the causes of it.

(D) Hoover can be faulted for not doing enough to halt the further decline in the economy.

(E) C and D

19. **(E)** Both of these statements are true. This type of question often appears to be more difficult than it really is. For example, if you know that Hoover was elected in 1928 and the stock market crash occurred in 1929, then (B) cannot be the answer. Since you should avoid answers with qualifying words such as "all," "none" and "always," (A) cannot be the answer. If you conclude that (A) is incorrect, then you can go on to conclude that (C) is probably correct. Then your decision will be based on whether only (C) is correct, or if (C) and (D) are both correct, which means answer (E) is correct.

ROOSEVELT: THE NEW DEAL AND WORLD WAR II

When **Franklin D. Roosevelt** was elected in 1932 the nation was on the verge of a revolution. Roosevelt realized drastic measures were needed to prevent this upheaval, so the **New Deal**, with relief, recovery and reform as the key elements, was implemented. Relief from the immediate effects of the Depression was provided by such programs as the **WPA** (Works Project Administration), which put people back to work again; huge amounts of money were pumped into the economy (deficit spending) to stimulate recovery. The WPA was responsible for building much of the nation's infrastructure: roads, bridges, dams, and water systems. The reform aspects include the strengthening of labor's right to organize and the initiation of social security, which were undertaken to insure that this type of depression would never happen again.

When Roosevelt came to office he did not have a specific program to implement but rather a basic set of beliefs:

- The government has the prime responsibility for the public welfare.

- Bold experimentation is the way to find solutions to social problems.

- Active leadership of a strong President is needed in times of crisis.

Although the Depression continued throughout the 1930's, these basic beliefs about the government's role have continued to be the foundation of government policy to the present day. Roosevelt's response to the Depression marks a profound shift in who is responsible for the welfare of all and changed, perhaps forever, a small central government into a large federal bureaucracy.

Full economic recovery came with America's entry into World War II in 1941. When the war began in Europe in 1939, Roosevelt and others in his administration knew that the United States could not remain safe in a world dominated by Hitler, Mussolini and the military dictators of Japan. In spite of the strong isolationist feelings at home, which initially kept the U.S. from entering the war, Roosevelt was able to prepare the nation for the eventual conflict. Through such measures as the **Lend-Lease Program**, which sent arms and supplies to the Allies; and the **Good Neighbor Policy** toward Latin America, which solidified the Western Hemisphere against possible attack the U.S. tried to influence the outcome of the war without getting directly involved.

The surprise attack by the Japanese on Pearl Harbor on December 7th, 1941, resulted in the U. S. declaring war on Germany, Italy and Japan. While the U.S. sent many troops to the war, the most important impact the U.S. had was in the huge amounts of material that it could commit to the war once all its industries switched to a war footing.

The first major action US troops saw was in Northern Africa. Germany had been having major success led by Erwin Rommel. Initially the U.S. troops did not fare well going against the veteran German troops. However, the allied troops were better able to maintain their supply lines and were able to use this to their advantage. From Africa, they Allies crossed the Mediterranean and captured Sicily and the rest of Italy. Then the Allies launched the largest amphibious invasion in history to establish a beachhead at Normandy, France. The British and American troops then pushed east to join up with the Russian troops in Germany.

The Japanese enjoyed significant success early in the war. Capturing the Philippines and a large area of Southeast Asia and China. Their fortunes turned at the battle for Midway Island. The Americans island-hopped their way back toward Japan. Truman was faced with a hard decision. Either he could commit troops to a bloody invasion of the main islands of Japan, or he could use the newly developed atomic bombs. He chose the latter, and they were dropped on Hiroshima and Nagasaki. The Japanese finally accepted unconditional surrender.

The atomic bombs were developed with great secrecy and at huge expense. The project was called the Manhattan Project. The U.S. gathered all their greatest minds together under the leadership of Robert Oppenheimer. The first atomic explosion occurred on July 15th, 1945 in Alamagordo, New Mexico.

Roosevelt planned for peace from the beginning of the war, as he sought to avoid Wilson's mistakes. At the **conference at Casablanca**, Roosevelt, Winston Churchill and Joseph Stalin agreed to accept nothing less than unconditional surrender. Another **conference at Yalta** led to a more definite outline for the coming peace. The **Big 3** agreed to divide Germany, and also Berlin, into four military zones. Agreements were reached regarding the elections and boundaries in Eastern Europe. The conference also settled the details for the forthcoming **United Nations**. In addition, commitments were made to the Soviet Union regarding the Far East in exchange for the Soviet promise to enter the war against Japan after the conclusion of the European theater. Roosevelt was widely criticized after the war for his part in this conference, mainly because the Soviet Union failed to honor the agreements.

Roosevelt died shortly before the end of the war, and the little-known **Harry S. Truman** led the nation during the difficult postwar era.

Before going on with the review, try these sample CLEP questions:

20. The most lasting effect of the New Deal was that of:

(A) ending the depression
(B) changing the scope and the emphasis of government
(C) banking regulations
(D) regulation of the stock market
(E) bringing full-scale socialism to the United States

20. (B) Answers (A) and (E) are exaggerations and therefore incorrect; (C) and (D) are true but too specific to be "the most lasting effect."

21. Before the bombing of Pearl Harbor in 1941, the United States was clearly:

(A) unprepared for war
(B) isolated from world events
(C) supportive of the allies
(D) determined to have peace at any price
(E) none of the above

21. (C) The key word in the question is "clearly." The Lend-Lease Program is a clear indication of support for the Allies. The temptation to mark (E) may be strong, but do not choose this as an answer unless you are sure the other answers are incorrect.

THE POST-WAR ERA TO THE PRESENT

Truman came to the presidency totally unprepared for the role of world leader. He had not even been told of the Atom-bomb research. Truman had been selected to be Vice President mainly because he came from the border state of Missouri and would therefore balance the ticket. But Truman, a very intelligent and capable man, quickly overcame these limitations and went on to make lasting contributions in foreign affairs. He ordered the dropping of the A-bomb, thereby eliminating the necessity of invading Japan. The **Truman Doctrine** prevented the expansion of the U.S.S.R., particularly into Greece and Turkey. The **Marshall Plan** rebuilt much of Europe. **NATO** and the **Berlin Airlift** reinforced America's commitment to the nations of Europe, and finally, the **Korean War** was a show of American determination to prevent the further spread of communism.

Domestically, Truman's program, the **Fair Deal,** a continuation and expansion of the policies of FDR, was for the most part rejected by Congress, as the mood of the country became more and more conservative.

Even though Truman was re-elected in 1948, despite all predictions to the contrary, he became an increasingly unpopular president. He was the common man, without the urbane appeal of Roosevelt. He fired the incredibly popular MacArthur during the Korean War; the Korean War itself was unpopular; and Senator Joe McCarthy and others created a public outcry about who "lost" China.

The growing discontent set the stage for a sweeping victory for the Republicans and **Dwight D. Eisenhower** in 1952. During his two terms, "Ike" was one of the most popular Presidents in history, however, later his administration was judged to be only mediocre.

He appointed conservative businessmen to government positions; and while they did not try to turn back the clock, they did little to advance the New Deal policies. Domestically, the most important issue was desegregation of the schools and the budding civil rights movement.

In foreign affairs, Eisenhower continued the Roosevelt-Truman policies as a confirmed foe of communism. Yet he also arranged the truce in Korea and was an avid seeker of peace. The Cold War continued throughout the 1950's.

While Ike was extremely popular, he could not transfer his popularity to other members of his party. His Vice President, Richard Nixon, lost a very close election to the young Senator, **John F. Kennedy.**

Perhaps **Kennedy** is most remembered for the type of man he represented—young, wealthy, sophisticated and intellectual. Domestically, he made many proposals—civil rights, Medicare and housing—but Congress was slow to react. In foreign affairs, Kennedy is remembered most for the **Cuban Missile Crisis**, the **Bay of Pigs** fiasco, and the **Peace Corps**.

After Kennedy was assassinated in 1963, **Lyndon Johnson** was able to push through Congress the social reforms Kennedy had started. But the **Vietnam War** greatly overshadowed Johnson's domestic accomplishments. History will probably place most of the blame for the war on him, mainly because of a series of bad judgments on his part. In addition, violence at home marked the Johnson years. Riots in the cities, peace demonstrations and the assassinations of **Martin Luther King** and **Robert Kennedy** left a lasting scar on the nation.

Under **Richard Nixon**, elected in 1968, the Vietnam War ended, as did the draft. The country was plagued with inflation and recession, and the dollar was devalued. Nixon reopened relations with China and started détente with the Soviet Union. But the growing cancer, known as the **Watergate cover-up**, finally brought about Nixon's resignation in 1974.

Vice President **Gerald Ford** assumed the Presidency upon Nixon's resignation. Amid much public controversy Ford granted Nixon a pardon for any criminal offenses committed while in office. Ford also granted a limited amnesty to Vietnam War draft evaders and military deserters. The rate of inflation increased and continued to do so throughout the 1970's as the price of oil increased dramatically.

In 1977 **Jimmy Carter** took the Presidential oath of office; early in his term of office he granted pardon to almost all of the Vietnam era draft evaders. After years of separation, the United States and the People's Republic of China exchanged full diplomatic relations. Carter also arranged the **Camp David summit** talk during which Premier Manahemi Begin of Israel and President Anwar Sadat of Egypt agreed on a framework for Mid-East peace.

The United States continued to be drawn into world controversies. The rebel Sandinistas opposed the government of President Anastasio Somoza in Nicaragua; in 1979, Somoza resigned amid increased pressure from the rebels. The year before in Iran, Shah Mohammed Riza Pahlavi established martial rule to end anti-government rule. His rule slipped and his health faltered, and the exiled Ayatollah Ruboola Khomeini came to power in Iran.

The United States opened its doors to the ailing shah; in November of 1979, followers of the Ayatollah seized the United States Embassy in Teheran. Carter attempted to achieve release of the hostages and even ordered a rescue attempt, which failed; nonetheless, the hostages' release took place after **Ronald Reagan** came to office. The Carter Administration did participate, however, in the Second Strategic Arms Limitation Treaty—**SALT II**.

As mentioned, the 1970's saw a high rate of inflation as well as high interest rates. Reagan took measures that resulted in far less inflation and much lower interest rates. The national deficit, however, remained astronomically high. Early in his term Reagan made several cuts in social programs, a move which was unpopular with many. His administration also made a larger commitment to arms.

The United States continues to play a strong role in international affairs. The invasion of **Grenada** while unpopular with many Americans at the time, has been accepted as a successful mission. Peacekeeping American troops were sent to **Lebanon** to assist Mid-East peace, but terrorist attacks on the American embassy and the United States troops barracks have been grim reminders of the instability of the region.

The 1984 Presidential election saw the first female candidate, Walter Mondale's running mate for the Vice-Presidency, **Geraldine Ferraro**. A promising economic future at home nonetheless helped re-elect Reagan in a landslide victory.

On the heels of Reagan's popularity, **Vice President George Bush** was elected in 1988. A head-on confrontation in the **Middle East** saw the victory of **Desert Storm** as the United States once again participated as a world leader. The collapse of the Berlin Wall symbolized the undermining of Communism and the dissolution of the Soviet Union. Economic woes at home, including the Savings and Loan scandal and high unemployment, affected the mood of the country. The 1992 Presidential campaign saw the rise of three candidates, **President Bush, Bill Clinton** and the independent, **Ross Perot**. The country looked inward to its own economic worries while trying to reconfigure its role in international affairs.

With the vote split Bill Clinton was able to capture the Presidency. His administration was plagued by many scandals, but he was able to have the first balanced budget in many years. The Presidential election in November 2000 was one of the closest on record. The outcome hinged on the results in a single state, Florida, where the two main candidates **Al Gore** and **George W. Bush** were separated by only a few thousand votes. After numerous court challenges, all the way up to the Supreme Court, George W. Bush was declared the winner. His administration has faced many challenges from a slowing economy to terrorist attacks.

Before you continue our review, try a few sample CLEP questions:

22. Truman was nominated for the Vice-Presidency primarily because:

(A) he was extremely popular with the population

(B) he was a very capable and well-known Senator

(C) he was an intellectual, with a very good education

(D) he was a war hero

(E) he was from Missouri and would balance the ticket

22. (E) With this type of question, if you know one fact for certain but are unsure if the other answers might be correct, mark the one you are sure of.

23. Of the following, which is the best conclusion regarding the popularity of Presidents?

(A) There is a high correlation between a President's popularity and his effectiveness as a President.

(B) In general, the more unpopular a President is the more likely he is to be judged "great" in the future.

(C) Popular Presidents are able to transfer this popularity to other members of their party.

(D) There is little relationship between a President's popularity and how history will finally judge him.

(E) Popularity and public opinion are usually of little concern to the man who is President.

23. (D) This type of question asks you to make a broad generalization based upon your understanding of the relationships of Presidents and their popularity. The best way to answer this type is to think of examples which do or do not fit each answer. (D) is the best answer because some presidents were very unpopular but were later judged to be great or near-great (Lincoln, Truman), while some Presidents were very popular but were later judged to be mediocre or poor (Harding, Eisenhower).

Questions 24 and 25 refer to the following list:

    I.   Truman
    II.   Eisenhower
    III.   Kennedy
    IV.   Johnson
    V.   Nixon

24. **Which President is noted for the Peace Corps?**

(A) I
(B) II
(C) III
(D) IV
(E) V

24. (C)

25. **Which Presidents were Democrats?**

(A) I, II, III, IV, V
(B) I, III, IV, V
(C) II, IV
(D) III, IV
(E) I, III, IV

25. (E) This type of double question can be very confusing at first but really offers the opportunity to expand a little knowledge. Question 24 is a straightforward question, simply asking who started the Peace Corps. In question 25 however, all you need to know is that Nixon and Eisenhower were Republicans. Then all the answers containing either a II or a V can be eliminated. This leaves you with choices (D) and (E). Was Truman a Democrat? If you know that he was the Vice President for one of the most popular Democratic Presidents (Franklin Roosevel) you could safely conclude that he was a democrat.

GLOSSARY OF AMERICAN HISTORY TERMS

Abolition: the movement to terminate slavery in the United States.

Armistice: a suspension of hostilities by agreement of the warring parties.

Articles of the Confederation: the first document establishing the government of the 13 American states in 1781 and replaced in 1789 by the Constitution of the United States.

Battle of New Orleans: fought January 8, 1815 during the War of 1812 between 6500 American troops under Andrew Jackson and 8700 British troops under Sir Edward Pakenham; U.S. defeated the British but peace agreement had already been signed.

Bay of Pigs: site of the attempted invasion of Cuba by anti-Castro forces April 1961.

Bill Of Rights: the formal statement of the rights of the people of the U.S., incorporated in the Constitution as Amendments 1-10.

Bleeding Kansas: violence in Kansas as a result of anti-slavery movement during the territorial legislative elections.

Carpetbaggers: a Northerner who went to the South after the Civil War for profit.

Charter Colony: a colony governed under a charter from the British Crown which allowed much autonomy.

Compromise of 1850: compromise that was intended to bring together the anti- and pro- slavery factions of Congress and the nation.

Constitution: the governing document of the United States.

Cuban Missile Crisis: a military standoff between the U.S. and U.S.S.R. in 1962 that brought the two super powers to the brink of nuclear war.

Democratic Party: one of the two major political parties in the U.S.

Democratic-Republican Party: the U.S. political party opposed to the Federalist Party, founded by Thomas Jefferson in 1792. They favored state's rights over a strong federal government.

Desert Storm: also known as the Persian Gulf War.

Era of Good Feeling: the peaceful period during Monroe's term where political parties were insignificant and the U.S. prospered.

Ethnocentrism: the belief in the inherent superiority of one's own ethnic group or culture.

Fair Deal: the domestic programs of President Harry Truman.

Federalist:	the political party that favored the adoption of the Constitution.
French & Indian War:	the war in America in which France and its Indian allies fought England and the colonies 1754-60.
Gilded Age:	time after Civil War when businesses expanded rapidly.
Good Neighbor Policy:	a U.S. policy of non-intervention among the nations of the Western Hemisphere.
Industrial Revolution:	the mechanization of industry that began in England.
Kellogg-Briand Pact:	U.S. and France cosponsered a pact to renounce aggression and call for the end of all wars.
Korean War:	the war (1950-55) between N. Korea, aided by Communist China, and S. Korea, aided by the U.S. and other United Nations members.
Ku Klux Klan:	a secret organization that aims to suppress rights of African-Americans.
League Of Nations:	an international organization created in 1919 to promote world peace and cooperation.
Lend-Lease Program:	the U.S. supplied material to those opposing the Axis powers prior to entering WWII
Louisiana Purchase:	the territory that the U.S. purchased from France in 1803 for $15,000,000
Manifest Destiny:	the 19th century belief that it was inevitable for the U.S. to expand from the Atlantic to the Pacific Oceans.
Marshall Plan:	U.S. postwar aid program to help Western European nations rebuild after WWII.
Mayflower Compact:	the first colonial agreement signed 1620 aboard the *Mayflower*.
Mexican War:	the war between the U.S. and Mexico that started over the Texas border.
Missouri Compromise:	the political compromise in 1820. Missouri became a slave state, but new states above the southern border of Missouri would be free.
Monroe Doctrine:	President Monroe in 1823, stated that the U.S. opposed further European colonization in the Western Hemisphere.
Muckraker:	someone who searches for corruption and scandal in government.
NATO:	a military alliance of western nations for the purpose of a collective defense.
New Deal:	the economic and social policies and programs introduced by President Franklin D. Roosevelt aimed at ending the depression.

Peace Corps:	a program of the U.S. government that sends volunteers to help developing countries.
Progressive Era:	the period around the 1890's when great changes were made on the local, state, and national levels.
Proprietary Colonization:	colonization where the land is given to an individual.
Reconstruction:	the reintegration of the South back into the Union after the Civil war.
Republican Party:	one of the two major political parties in the U.S.
Royal Colonization:	colonization where the land is owned by a king, and the governor is appointed by the king.
Spanish-American War:	the war between the U.S. and Spain in 1898.
Spoils System:	public offices are filled with supporters of the victorious political party.
Square Deal:	Theodore Roosevelt's plan to try and balance the wealth of Americans.
Teapot Dome:	political scandal during Harding's term where federal oil reserves were illegally sold to private oil companies for the personal financial gain of the Secretary of the Interior and Secretary of the Navy.
Tories:	colonists who remained loyal to England during the Revolutionary War.
Treaty of Paris:	treaty to end the French and Indian War and the war in Europe.
Truman Doctrine:	policy set by Harry Truman in 1947 to send U.S. aid to anti-Communist forces in Greece and Turkey.
United Nations:	an international organization with headquarters in New York City, formed in after WWII to promote peace, security, and cooperation.
Vietnam War:	military struggle fought in Vietnam 1959-1975 in which the U.S. helped South Vietnam fight North Vietnam.
War of 1812:	conflict between the U.S. and Britain that began in 1812 and lasted until early 1815.
Watergate:	a political scandal during the 1972 presidential campaign, arising from a break-in at Democratic Party headquarters at the Watergate building complex in Washington D.C.
WPA:	Works Project Administration
XYZ Affair:	the French government offered the U.S. bribes to regulate U.S. trade with England.
Yellow Journalism:	the use of scandalous or sensationalized stories to attract readers.

Native American, African and Asian History

INTRODUCTION

Until very recently, Native American, African and Asian histories were ignored or neglected as academic courses of study. Courses labeled World History were actually the history of Western civilization; in the study of American history, the role of the Black-American was almost totally ignored (except for the slavery issue). But the civil rights movement, the rise of pride in ethnic heritage and interest in non-western cultures have sparked interest, and therefore college courses, in all of these areas. While only about eight percent of the questions on the CLEP Examination will cover these areas of study, this review will present the highlights of each.

AFRICA

The lack of written records has long hidden the rich and colorful past of the African empires. Except for ancient Egypt and its successor, the Kingdom of **Kush**, little research and few discoveries were made until very recently.

At one time the powerful Kush ruled the entire Nile Valley. Until about the fourth century A.D., it ruled the middle Nile when the King of Axum and his army destroyed the Kush culture.

According to Arab records, great nations of West Africa arose about the eighth century. The three largest, **Ghana**, **Mali** and **Songhai**, all followed a pattern of war and conquest, corruption and inefficiency, and then invasion by a stronger group. Under these empires, trade and commerce flourished, and Timbuktu became a center of Moslem learning.

One of the first times Ghana is mentioned in the Arab records the writer referred to it as the land of gold. Much of the gold in Europe before the Spanish conquests in the Americas came from the trade routes from West Africa to the Arabs to the Europeans. The trade routes had to cross the **Saharan** Desert. They ended in cities along the Niger River (**Timbuktu**, **Gao** etc.) and then the goods travel on from there by boat.

After the West African bulge, East Africa came under the influence of the Arabs. The **Swahili** culture, a mixture of **Zanj** and **Islam**, produced language, poetry and architecture; and its people traded extensively with India and even China.

There is much physical evidence throughout Africa that advanced civilizations existed—**Zimbabwe**, **Monomotapa**, **Mapungubwe**—but without written records, these cultures remain a mystery.

In the fifteenth century, the first Europeans, the Portuguese, began to explore the west coast of Africa. They were lured by the prospect of trade and gold, and they were able to establish friendly relations with the Africans.

In the sixteenth century, first the Dutch and then the English and the French colonized many areas of Africa, as the Portuguese became more interested in Asia.

The Dutch turned the existing slave trade into an efficient and ever-expanding operation. As the Dutch dominance declined, the French and the English competed with each other until the English won control of the slave trade toward the end of the eighteenth century. Between the years 1530 and 1900, about 24 million Africans were removed from the continent, but only 15 to 20 million survived the crossing to America. In addition, many millions were killed or died during the raiding attacks or during the march to the coast. Although Parliament in 1807 abolished slavery in the British Empire, not until the European nations actually settled in the African colonies did the slave trade halt.

In 1850, Africa was still called the **Dark Continent**, as the interior was unknown to the world. But by 1890 the major geographical features were discovered and mapped, and the scramble for colonies became intense. By 1900 the partition of Africa by the European countries left only two independent countries, **Liberia** and **Ethiopia**.

King Leophold II of Belgium established a very profitable colony in central Africa, the Congo. The Germans colonized Southwest Africa, as well as **East Africa** (Tanganyika) and the **Cameroons**. Meanwhile, Great Britain, after gaining control of Egypt in 1881, began building a colonial empire from **Cairo** to **Capetown** in South Africa. This attempt to expand South African territory led to a war between the British and the Boers (former Dutch colonists who had developed their own culture in the **Transvaal** and the **Orange Free State**). After three years of fierce fighting, the **Boer** states were incorporated in the Union (Republic) of South Africa.

The Italians laid claim to **Somaliland** in East Africa, but they were defeated in their attempts to conquer Ethiopia (until 1936 when Mussolini's troops occupied the country for five years). The French were also actively creating colonies at this time. Not content with Algeria, Tunisia, and Morocco along the Mediterranean, the French advanced into North and West Africa. Portugal and Spain also had a few smaller colonies in Africa.

Each European nation differed greatly in its approach to governing the colonies. The British, for example, encouraged indirect rule and self-government, which eventually led to independence. On the other hand, the French tried to integrate their colonies into the mother country; the Portuguese made Angola and Mozambique provinces of Portugal; while Belgium encouraged economic, but not political, integration.

Economic development of the African colonies slowed after World War I and the worldwide depression which followed, as the impoverished ruling nations did little more than preserve law and order. However, during and after World War II the economic importance of Africa's vast resources (gold, chromium, copper, uranium and petroleum) was clearly demonstrated. The economic development of the colonies also brought social and political awareness as African nationalism and self-government grew into full-fledged movements.

Led by Western-educated urban Africans, one by one the colonies demanded and received independent status during the 1950's and '60's. Underdeveloped and poverty-stricken, the new nations have been subject to political upheavals and armed conflicts. African leaders, while determined to raise the standard of living for their citizens, have remained distrustful of both the East and the West. Africa, like other third world areas, remains a potential "powder keg" as developed nations compete for influence and resources.

Before going on with the review, try these sample CLEP questions:

1. **Which of the following established a great kingdom along the middle Nile?**

   (A) Rome
   (B) Kush
   (C) Ghana
   (D) Moslems
   (E)   Portugal

2. **Why is so little known about many of the early civilizations of Africa?**

   (A) The Europeans were not interested in Africa.
   (B) They were primitive, food-gathering tribes who left little evidence of civilization.
   (C) Few written records were found.
   (D) Africa remained unexplored for so long.
   (E) None of the above.

3. **Who were the first Europeans to explore the west coast of Africa?**

   (A) Italians
   (B) British
   (C) French
   (D) Dutch
   (E) Portuguese

ANSWERS:

1. (B) The Kingdom of Kush controlled all the Nile at one time. Rome and Portugal are in Europe. The Moslem Empire was centered in the middle east and the Ghana empire was in West Africa.

2. (C) With this type of question you must decide what was the cause (no written records) for the effect (little is known). While other answers may be true statements, they are not the cause of the effect. Most test-takers dread the possible choice, "none of the above," as this choice tends to make even the most knowledgeable person feel insecure. Do not mark this as the answer unless you are almost certain that all the other choices are incorrect.

3. (E) The Portuguese, attempting to find a sea route to the Far East, were the first Europeans to explore the west coast of Africa. By contrast, the north coast had been explored, conquered, and settled by Europeans since ancient times.

4. **Which of the following statements is the most accurate regarding the slave trade?**

   (A) The Europeans introduced slavery to the African cultures.
   (B) By the end of the eighteenth century, the slave trade had ended.
   (C) Slavery was outlawed in the British Empire before the American Civil War began.
   (D) Most of the slaves died during the crossing to America.
   (E) The Dutch were never involved in the slave trade.

5. **The Boer War was fought between:**

   (A) the British and the Dutch
   (B) the British and the French
   (C) the British and the Swahili
   (D) the British and the East Africans
   (E) the British and the former Dutch colonists

6. **Which of the following statements is the most accurate regarding the British and their colonies?**

   (A) The British encouraged self-government as soon as the colonies were ready.
   (B) The British exploited the colonies economically, but they did not establish political units.
   (C) The British dominated every aspect of colonial life, and the natives were completely excluded.
   (D) The British were eager to grant independence to the colonies as soon as possible.
   (E) The British confined their colonial interest to South Africa.

4. (C) Slavery in the United States did not end until 1865; the British government ended slavery in its empire in 1833. For the CLEP Examination, while it is not necessary to memorize a large number of dates, it is desirable to develop a grasp of time sequence and to know which events occurred before the others.

5. (E) The Boers were descendants of the original Dutch settlers. One of the amazing facts of the colonization of Africa by Europeans is that while the colonists fought each other, their battles did not draw the mother countries into direct conflict with each other.

6. (A) Because the British policy encouraged self-government, most of the British colonies made the transition to independence with less internal conflict than the other colonies in Africa.

7. **What effect did World War II have on colonial Africa?**

    (A) The colonial empires collapsed.
    (B) The economic importance of Africa was widely recognized.
    (C) The demand for independence began in earnest.
    (D) Many armed conflicts took place on the continent.
    (E) All of the above.

7. (E) All of the choices are direct results of World War II.

ASIA (FAR EAST)

Because the Far Eastern civilizations and cultures are so vastly different from Western civilization, Asia has remained an enigma to the Western world. Seen first as a source of raw materials and later as a battleground, only recently have the Far Eastern cultures, religions and philosophies been studied by Westerners. British rule in India, broken after World War II, created means whereby the culture of India became known to the West. Desire for trade on the part of Westerners broke the isolationist stance of Far Eastern countries. Even today the Peoples' Republic of China remains somewhat a mystery despite the establishment of more open communications.

The nations and the people of Asia are as varied as everything else on the continent. The religions, customs, life-styles, political systems and economic conditions are as diverse as the geography. Asian countries today, notably India, Japan and the Peoples' Republic of China, share a common problem—overpopulation. India and China have not experienced the economic growth enjoyed by Japan since World War II and, therefore, have not the same means to provide for their people.

RELIGION

Religion has always been important in Asia and in some areas remains the dominant influence. **Lao-tse**, in China about 500 B.C., was the first to formulate a golden rule. His followers, known as **Taoists**, have changed his simple teachings into many complex rites and ceremonies. Shortly after Lao-tse, **Confucius** set forth his beliefs, which are more philosophy than religion. Confucianism, more concerned with the present than the hereafter, stresses the five characteristics of a superior person—dignity, sincerity, earnestness, benevolence and kindness. The Chinese retain the deep reverence for their ancestors and deep respect for tradition. **Shintoism** is a nationalistic elaboration of this attitude in Japan.

Hinduism, the faith of the majority in India, is composed of a trinity—**Brahma**, the creator; **Vishnu**, the sustainer; and **Shiva**, the destroyer—plus a host of lesser divinities. The doctrine of transmigration of souls forbids the taking of animal life and consigns the population to a rigid caste system. **Gautama Buddha** broke with traditional Hinduism and taught that the only permanent good in the world is the dreamless state of **Nirvana**. His moral teachings are still followed by many millions of Asians.

Islam, a faith based on strict moral codes, is practiced by the people in western Asia, the Middle East and Pakistan. Christianity has more followers than any other religion in the world, but it has never been a major faith in Asia, except for the Philippines and a few spots in the Middle East.

HISTORY

Civilization began in Asia long before Western civilization developed. The Asians were the first farmers and merchants and founded the first cities. Asia moved far ahead of the West in cultural and scientific development. Paper, gunpowder, movable type and navigation instruments were developed in Asia long before they were in the West. Dragonbones, bone fragments dug up while Chinese peasants plow their fields, are really oracle bones foretelling the future. They were buried carefully, and the inscriptions they bear indicate much about ancient Chinese life.

Little is known about the early Indian civilization, mainly because many of its written records have not been translated. Long before the birth of Christ, **Aryan** (Indo-European) invaders overran the northern areas of India, pushing the **Dravidian**, or original, population to the south of the peninsula. Alexander's armies brought the Greek influence to the area. **Asoka**, a native ruler, established a peaceful, Buddhist nation (**Mauran** Empire) in the second century B.C. Under his rule, travel and trade were safer, and the merchant class increased its wealth. Buddhism is opposed to the **caste system** of Hinduism and so the merchants abandoned their lower status as decreed in the Hindu religion. People from on caste were forbidden from marrying people from a different caste, and there was no way to change from one cast to another. Soon after Asoka's reign, peace dissolved. In the fourth century A.D., India was to some extent at peace under the **Gupta Empire**, during which the arts and sciences flourished. It was during the Gupta Empire that "Arabic Numerals" were invented and replace Roman Numerals. Indians also made great stides in astronomy which aided their navigation of the sea.

During the Medieval period, 500-1500 A.D., internal strife and foreign invaders increased, and Hinduism took the place of Buddhism. It was during this time that Islam was introduced to India.

**Tourists from all over the world visit the Taj Mahal.
It is a moseleum for an ex-emperor's wife.**

In China the first civilization appeared along the Hwang Ho River. The ruthless **Shih Huang Ti** (246-210 B.C.) was the first emperor and built the first part of the **Great Wall**. The **Ch'in Dynasty** ended shortly after his death, but the **Han Dynasty** which followed maintained the unity he established and accepted Confucianism as the official set of beliefs. The most powerful of the Han Emperors was **Wu-ti**. His armies pushed west conquering the Huns. Traders soon established trade with the Persians setting up the **Silk Road**. Some notable achievement of these two dynasties were paper making, sun dials and porcelain.

The Great wall of China streaches for hundreds of miles.

The Han Dynasty lasted for four centuries after which there was disorder and confusion until the **Sui Dynasty** (589-618 A.D.). The Sui were a powerful family that came about from the union of an old influential Chinese family and one of the Hun invaders. Among other achievements, the Sui created a system of canals in central China (to bring rice from the south to the armies that guarded the north) and to some extent unified the country. During the **Tang** and **Sung Dynasties** (618-1279 A.D.), Chinese civilization flourished. Poetry, arts and science, and government expanded, making this time a classical period. Trade and the resulting transfer of culture flourished at this time. Chinese Junks, ocean-going vessels, traveled from Japan to the Persian Gulf. All types of religion spread to China at this time, but Buddism took the firmest hold.

Chinese Emperors were able to maintain a stable government without having to fight off the other nobles by the use of civil servants. Civil servants advanced by how well they did on test and if they supported the Emperor, and not by which of the noble families they belonged.

About 1200 A.D. **Genghis Khan**, from the wilderness of central Asia, and later his grandson **Kublai Khan** conquered much of Asia and even the European areas of Russia. The **Monguls** had two great tactical advantages. Their bows were much more powerful and their horses allowed them great mobility. Another descendant, **Baber**, invaded India and founded the Mogul Empire which reached its peak under **Akbar the Great** during the **Yuan Dynasty** (1279-1368 A.D.), but the cultures were so different that there was unrest.

The **Ming Dynasty** (1368-1644 A.D.) extended the Chinese influence to most of Asia. The last dynasty was the Ch'ing (1644-1912); the rulers were **Manchus**, not Chinese, yet they adopted much of Chinese culture which no doubt aided the rule's stability. However, this dynasty (often referred to as the **Manchu Dynasty**) was replaced in 1910 by a weak republic, which became corrupt and unable to stop the Japanese invaders of the 1930's.

Around the second century B.C. Japan slowly formed itself into a single nation. The Emperor was said to be descended from the sun goddess and the Shinto religion was closely tied to the politics of Japan. The Japanese copied China's strong central government. In the middle of the 9th century the powerful Fujiwara clan challenged the Emperors for power. This power struggle lasted until the 12th century when the Shoguns, military dictators, took over.

Japan was ruled by powerful shoguns, military dictators.

Japan, after an unsuccessful attempt to conquer Korea in the sixteenth century, had become withdrawn and isolated until the mid-nineteenth century. But Japan was the first Far East nation to adopt Western technology.

About 1500, Asia entered a cultural and scientific decline at about the same time that the West began to make rapid progress. By 1800, many areas in Asia had become European colonies.

The Portuguese were the first to establish colonies, but they soon lost their colonial empire as the Dutch, French and British gained strongholds. For nearly two hundred years, India was the crown jewel of the British Empire. Holland controlled the East Indies, while France dominated Indo-China.

Japan, competing with Russia for more territory in the early twentieth century, emerged triumphant after a war in 1905. Until World War II Japan was the dominant military power in the Far East.

The end of World War II brought even more turmoil to Asia. India broke away from British control but split into the Hindu republic of India and the Moslem Dominion of Pakistan. China, Manchuria, Tibet, and later what had been French Indo-China became communist nations. The Dutch East Indies became the Indonesian Republic.

The economic gap between the East and the West has become even wider as Asia has experienced a population explosion. The political disputes and many on-going wars have disrupted attempts to increase industrial production and agricultural output. The economic and education progress has been uneven in Asia. Japan, one of the richest nations in the world, experienced an economic boom that now shows some signs of slowing down. On the other hand, some nations such as Cambodia and Laos show little progress. India, China and Pakistan have seen some progress, but they have also seen it wiped out by the population explosion. At the present, Asia consists of a few wealthy nations existing beside many poverty-stricken ones.

Before going on with the review, try these sample CLEP questions:

ANSWERS:

8. **Shintoism is associated with which nation?**

    (A) China
    (B) India
    (C) Japan
    (D) Pakistan
    (E) Indonesia

8. (C) Japan

9. **Which religious leader taught that Nirvana is the ideal state?**

    (A) Buddha
    (B) Hindu
    (C) Confucius
    (D) Lao-tse
    (E) Mohammed

9. (A) Buddha

10. **The Han, Tang and Ming were ruling families in which country?**

    (A) Japan
    (B) China
    (C) Indonesia
    (D) Indo-China
    (E) India

10. (B) China

11. **Which of the following statements is the most accurate regarding Japan?**

(A) Japan remained untouched by Western influence until the twentieth century.
(B) The Japanese were unaffected by the developments in China.
(C) Japan extended its territory until its defeat by the Russians in the early part of the twentieth century.
(D) The Japanese were the first Far Eastern culture to adopt Western technology.
(E) After the invasion by the Chinese, Japan lost its earlier economic gains.

11. (D) Japan became the most advanced nation in the Far East. Answer (A) is incorrect because while Japan did not have a colonial period like the other countries in Asia, it was greatly affected by their culture and by trade.

12. **Which of the following was a result of the conditions in Asia after World War II?**

(A) The colonial empires collapsed as most nations won independence.
(B) Asia became a battleground between communist and non-communist forces.
(C) Some areas of Asia (Japan, Singapore, Hong Kong, Taiwan) experienced an economic boom.
(D) New nations were created.
(E) All of the above.

12. (E) All of the above.

North and South American History

At least by about 20,000 years ago during the last great ice age groups of people crossed the Bering Strait which connected Siberia to Alaska. They then moved south to populate both North and South America. Many of these people were hunters and gatherers. Some however developed farming and were able to build great civilizations. One of their main crops was maize or corn.

In North America one of the earliest civilizations was the **Mound Builders** of the Mississippi Valley, however their civilization had collapsed around 1000 b.c. and we know little of them. In the Southwest the Native Americans learned how to work in clay. The built cities up the sides of cliffs for protection. When they were threatened, they could simply pull their ladders up and they were safe from harm. When Spanish explorers came upon these towns they called them **pueblos**.

The rest of the North American Indians were not able to build great civilizations, there were not enough farmers to allow them to concentrate into large cities. In Central and South America this was not the case.

Central American civilization history starts with the **Olmecs**. They were found in the area around the **Yucatan Peninsula**. Their civilization arose around 900 B.C. They were the first to use written language in the Western Hemisphere. The Olmecs gave way to the **Mayans**. The Mayans were very good astronomers. They were able to accurately predict ecliplses of both the sun and the moon. They built observatories where their priests, the only ones who could be astronomers, plotted the movements of the heavenly bodies. The Mayan civilization died out around 1000 A.D.

Ancient ruins in Central America.

The last great civilization in Central America was the Aztecs. Their capital city was **Tenocititlan** (modern day Mexico City). They ruled the area of Mexico down to Guatemala. Their priests believed in human sacrifice and they had a very warlike culture. They were defeated in 1519 by a small Spanish Army led by **Hernando Cortez**. When the Spanish first landed the Aztecs believed them to be Gods. The Spanish also brought many new diseases with them which ravaged the native population.

The Great civilization in South America was the **Incas**. They controlled a region of the Andes moutains that measured approximately 2000 miles. They were the first farmers to grow potatos and were excellent metal workers in bronze, silver, and gold. Their civilization too was destroyed by the Spanish. In the 1530's they were conquered by a Spanish are lead by **Francisco Pizarro**. In November 1532 Pizarro invited **Atahulpa**, the Emperor of the Inca to a feast. Atahulpa came with many of his nobles. Pizarro's men suddenly attacked and captured Atahulpa killing many of the nobles in the process. The Emperor then bargained for his release agreeing to fill one room with gold and two more with silver. After the ransom was paid Pizarro went back on his word and had the Emperor excuted. The empire was left leaderless and put up little resistance after that.

NATIVE AMERICAN RELATIONS TO THE UNITED STATES

There were no provisions for relations with the Native Americans in the treaty to end the American Revolution. Soon settlers were pushing westward from the original 13 colonies over the Appalachian Mountains and into new territory. This brought them into direct confrontation with the Native Americans who lived there.

The first formal treaty between Native Americans and the U.S. Government occurred in 1795 after **General Anthony Wayne** had been victorious in 1794. This treaty specified "Indian Territory". In 1830 Congress passed the **Indian Removal Act** which allowed the removal of all Native American east of the Mississippi to Indian Territory west of the Mississippi.

When settlers from the United States continued their western movement and started crossing the Mississippi, people in Washington, D.C. felt that the boundries in the Indian Territory needed to be more sharply defined and evolved it into the reservation concept. The Native Americans resisted and the U.S. government sent the calvary in to force them onto the reservations. This resulted in the Plains Indian War in the last half of the 19th century.

AFRICAN AMERICAN HISTORY IN THE UNITED STATES

The slave trade in colonial times is usually called the **triangular trade** because of the ships' routes. Products from New England were taken to the West Indies and exchanged for molasses and sugar, which were shipped back to New England to be turned into rum. The rum, in turn, was shipped to West Africa and exchanged for slaves who were shipped to the West Indies and the southern colonies. This triangular trade made many New Englanders wealthy—as ship builders, rum distillers and slave traders.

Although the first **Black Africans** arrived in the colonies as free workers (in 1619, in Virginia), the demands of the large plantation owners for a cheap labor supply brought slavery on a large scale to the colonies. At one time there were slaves in every colony, but the different farming and economic conditions in the North made slavery unprofitable. The peak years of the slave trade were between 1700 and 1750. Officially, an act of Congress in 1808 ended the slave importation, but it continued illegally for many years.

After the Revolution and independence, there was a move toward abolition of slavery in the North. Even in the South, slavery might have died had it not been for the invention of the **cotton gin** in 1793, which made cotton a profitable crop but required a large labor force.

Fear of slave revolts led to severe laws regarding education, property ownership and movement of African Americans. Even in the North, every state had restrictions on the freedom of the African Americans. This helped lead to a **Back to Africa** movement. In 1817, the American Colonization Society founded the African country of **Liberia**, which in 1847 became the first Black self-governing country in Africa. But only about 12,000 Americans settled there as the primary goal shifted to abolition of slavery in America, not resettlement in Africa.

As far back as 1688, the **Quakers** in Pennsylvania had called for abolition. In the early 1800's, the Quakers helped start the **Underground Railroad** which brought slaves to the North and freedom. Also at this time, **David Walker** urged the slaves to fight for their freedom. His main was of disseminating his information was through pamphlets.

But it was not until the 1830's that abolition became a crusade: **William Lloyd Garrison** was the chief spokesman; **Frederick Douglas**, a fugitive slave, wrote for newspapers and gave lectures; and **Harriet Tubman**, also a fugitive slave, led the Underground Railroad.

Frederick Douglas was very influential in spreading the word about the evils of slavery

Nat Turner led a slave revolt in 1831. He was a slave in Virgina. First, he killed his owner and his family. He ended up with about 50 followers. The militia soon put down the revolt, but it had a lasting effect because it had scared the Southern slave owners. They passed many new laws, and the Southern abolitionist movement died out. Abolition became a more important goal of people residing in the North.

Freedom for the slaves finally came in 1865, with the passage of the **13th Amendment**. The **Emancipation Proclamation**, in 1863, applied only to the states in rebellion against the federal government, not to the four slave states still in the Union. The federal government did little to help the freed slaves, except for **the Freedman's Bureau** which provided education.

After **Reconstruction**, which ended in 1877, most ex-slaves still worked in cotton. One by one the states withdrew the African Americans' right to vote, and a gradual pattern of the separation of the races took hold in schools, railroads, hotels, churches, barbershops, etc. The famous court case, **Plessy versus Ferguson** in 1896, upheld this separate but equal doctrine. The African Americans had little opportunity to develop leadership abilities, except in their local churches.

The outstanding leader and educator in the late 1800's and early 1900's, **Booker T. Washington**, founded **Tuskegee Institute** which stressed vocational training, especially for African American farmers and mechanics. He urged that the African Americans respect the laws and develop friendly relations with the Whites. **George Washington Carver**, working at Tuskegee Institute, helped to diversify agriculture in the South.

Booker T. Washingron was responsible for educating many African Americans

Washington's main opponent, **W.E.B. DuBois**, became the first African American to receive a Ph.D. from Harvard in 1895. He felt that the African Americans should actively seek equal rights, voting rights, justice in the courts, an end to lynching and violence, and an end to other forms of discrimination. DuBois was one of the founders and leaders of **the National Association for the Advancement of Colored People (NAACP)**.

After the end of World War I, many African Americans began the migration northward. While escaping the rural poverty of the South, the newly urbanized African Americans faced many problems—slums, unemployment, riots and a different form of discrimination. **Marcus Garvey**, who had a large following at the time, opposed integration and urged racial pride and a return to Africa. But also in the 1920's, African Americans began to win distinction in various fields such as jazz and boxing.

During World War II, as an experiment, the Army was partially desegregated. In 1947, President Truman issued orders for equal treatment in the Armed Forces, the first institution to be desegregated.

After the war, the northward migration became a tidal wave, and African Americans entered many fields. In 1947, **Jackie Robinson** became the first African American in major league baseball. In 1950, **Gwendolyn Brooks** won the Pulitzer Prize, and **Ralph Bunche** won the Nobel Peace Prize for his work in the United Nations.

Also after the end of World War II, the civil rights movement picked up momentum as the need to end racial discrimination and to guarantee civil rights became more and more urgent. Some of the highlights of the civil rights movement include:

1. The Supreme Court, in **Brown versus the Board of Education** in 1954, ruled that states could not have separate schools for African American and White children.

2. In 1955, in Montgomery, Alabama, **Mrs. Rosa Parks** was arrested for sitting in the front on a bus. **Martin Luther King, Jr**. led a successful boycott of the local bus company. This event helped convince African Americans that they could win their goals by direct actions, such as freedom marches and sit-ins.

3. The **Civil Rights Act** of 1964 outlawed segregation in public places, voter registration tests, and discrimination by employers and unions. In addition to court actions against those who did not comply, federal funds were withheld.

4. The **Voting Rights Act** was passed after the march on Selma, Alabama, in 1965.

5. In the North, the fight was against de facto segregation, which led to such emotionally charged issues as court-ordered busing of school children.

African American nationalist groups, such as the **Black Muslims** led by **Malcolm X**, opposed this civil rights activity and demanded separation of the races. The call for **Black Power** split the civil rights movement and spawned more radical groups, such as the **Black Panthers (Huey Newton, Bobby Seale, Angela Davis)**.

After 1965, there was a movement away from the fight for legal equality to demands for social and economic equality. The nonviolent groups gave way to the violent ones; and riots, caused mainly by poverty and frustration, occurred in Watts, Newark, Detroit and other cities. The worst race riot of the twentieth century occurred in Los Angeles following the not-guilty verdict reached by the jurors of the **Rodney King** trial.

Today, while African Americans have made many political and legal gains, economic and social equality has not been fully realized.

Before going on with the review, try these sample CLEP questions:

Questions 13-15 refer to this list:

I. Marcus Garvey
II. Booker T. Washington
III. Nat Turner
IV. Ralph Bunche
V. W.E.B. DuBois

ANSWERS:

13. **Which two of the above people were contemporaries and had opposing views about the direction African Americans should take to achieve their goals?**

    (A) I and IV
    (B) II and III
    (C) II and V
    (D) III and V
    (E) IV and V

13. (C)

14. **Who of the above led a slave revolt?**

    (A) I
    (B) II
    (C) III
    (D) IV
    (E) V

14. (C)

15. **Who of the above won a Nobel Peace Prize?**

    (A) I
    (B) II
    (C) III
    (D) IV
    (E) V

15. (D) Garvey urged a return to Africa; Washington advocated a more passive role than did DuBois; Turner led a slave revolt; and Bunche won the Nobel Peace Prize.

16. **The process by which fugitive slaves were brought to freedom in the North was called:**

    (A) triangular trade
    (B) freedom march
    (C) civil rights
    (D) Underground Railroad
    (E) Reconstruction

16. (D) The Underground Railroad became a symbol of hope for the slaves and a rallying point for the Northern abolitionists.

17. **Which American institution was the first to fully desegregate?**

    (A) the churches
    (B) the public schools
    (C) the Armed Forces
    (D) the universities
    (E) the labor unions

17. (C)   The Armed Forces, after a presidential order.

18. **Which of the following is the most accurate statement regarding the civil rights movement?**

    (A) It was short-lived and did little to achieve equality.
    (B) After achieving its goals of equality, the civil rights movement was disbanded.
    (C) Although helping to bring about equality under the laws, the civil rights movement has not brought full economic and social equality.
    (D) The civil rights movement became fragmented after desegregation of the schools was achieved.
    (E) The civil rights movement was supported by all African Americans in its demand for desegregation.

18. (C)   Economic and social conditions are more difficult to change than laws are.

19. Which group of natives was conquered by Cortez?

    (A) The Incas
    (B) The Spanish
    (C) The Pueblos
    (D) The Aztecs
    (E) The Mayans

19. (D)   Cortez conquered the Aztecs.

20. **Which Native Americans built mud homes up the sides of cliffs?**

    (A) The Incas
    (B) The Spanish
    (C) The Pueblos
    (D) The Aztecs
    (E) The Mayans

20. (C)

GLOSSARY OF NATIVE-AMERICAN, AFRICAN, & ASIAN HISTORY TERMS

American Colonization Society: a group who tried to send freed slaves back to Africa during Abolution.

Aryan: (in Nazi doctrine) a non-Jewish Caucasian, esp. of Nordic stock.

Black Muslims: a member of the Nation of Islam.

Black Panther: a member of a militant black American organization active in the 1960s and 1970s.

Brown V. Board of Education: landmark court case of 1954 in which the Supreme Court unanimously decided that it was unconstitutional to create separate schools on the basis of race.

Ch'in Dynasty: the dynasty of ancient China, 221-206 B.C., marked by the emergence of a unified empire and the construction of much of the Great Wall of China.

Ch'ing Dynasty: see Manchu Dynasty.

Civil Rights Movement: in the U.S., the political, legal, and social struggle to gain full citizenship rights for black Americans and to achieve racial equality.

Confucius: 551? - 478? B.C. Chinese philosopher and teacher.

Dark Continent: term formerly used to refer to Africa before large areas of the continent had been explored.

De Facto: actually existing, esp. without lawful authority.

Emancipation Proclamation: proclamation issued by Abraham Lincoln on January 1, 1863 during the Civil War, declaring all slaves free.

Freedman's Bureau: March 1865; the U.S. War Department established the Bureau of Refugees, Freemen, and Abandoned Lands to furnish food and medical supplies, establish schools, and negotiate fair wages and working conditions for freed slaves.

Gupta Empire: a dynasty of N. India (A.D. 329-540) whose court was the center of classical Indian art and literature.

Han Dynasty: a dynasty in China, 206 B.C.-A.D. 220, characterized by consolidation of the central state, territorial expansion, and cultural and scientific achievements.

Hinduism: the common religion of India, based upon the religion of the original Aryan settlers as expounded and evolved in the Vedas, Upanishads, Bhagavad-Gita, etc.

Islam:	the religion of the Muslims, as set forth in the Koran, that teaches that there is only one God, Allah, and that Muhammad is His prophet.
Kush:	an area mentioned in the Bible, sometimes identified with Upper Egypt; an ancient kingdom in North Africa, in the region of Nubia.
Manchu Dynasty:	also known as Qing or Ch'ien dynasty; last of the Chinese dynasties in which Imperial China reached its zenith of power and influence.
Ming Dynasty:	a dynasty in China, 1368-1644, marked by the restoration of traditional institutions and the development of the arts, esp. porcelain, textiles, and painting.
Mogul:	a member of the dynasty of Muslim rulers that dominated N. India and parts of the Deccan from the 16th to early 18th centuries.
NAACP:	National Association for the Advancement of Colored People.
Nation of Islam:	an organization composed chiefly of American blacks and advocating the teachings of Elijah Muhammad: members are known as Black Muslims.
Plessy v. Ferguson:	the landmark court case where segregation in railroad cars was upheld.
Shintoism:	the native religion of Japan, primarily a system of nature and ancestor worship.
Sui Dynasty:	581-618; brief Chinese dynasty where China was reunified, its economy was revitalized, and its rulers began to support Buddhism.
Taoism:	a Chinese philosophic tradition founded by Lao-tzu, advocating a life of simplicity and naturalness and of noninterference with the course of natural events, in order to attain a happy existence in harmony with the Tao.
Triangular Trade:	trade of slaves and commodities among Europe, the Caribbean Islands, and North America.
Underground Railroad:	(before the abolition of slavery in the U.S.) a system for helping fugitive slaves escape into Canada and other places of safety.
Yuan Dynasty:	1279-1368; Chinese dynasty established by Mongol Kublai Khan.

Sociology

Sociology is the study of human interaction, the way that individuals and/or groups influence the behavior of others. The study of human social behavior goes back to the ancient Greeks; Plato and Aristotle considered the importance of organized social life. It was not until the nineteenth century, that sociology was considered a separate discipline. Like psychology, sociology for centuries had been included as an aspect of philosophy. The Frenchman **Auguste Comte** designated sociology as a distinct study. He stated that just as the natural scientists had uncovered laws, so too could the social scientist discover social laws. For this effort, Comte is called the Father of Sociology. In England, **Herbert Spencer** developed a theory of society in his Principles of Society (1876). **Emile Durkheim** of France utilized Comte's ideas in a scientific study of suicide, gathering facts, observing rates and drawing conclusions about suicide based upon his observations and data. In the United States, **Lester F. Ward** initiated inquiries in sociology.

The work of these people was prompted in part by the social ills resulting from the Industrial Revolution. However, sociology today is a science which concentrates on acquiring knowledge about human interactions, not on applying this knowledge to actual situations. The generalizations arrived at through this study are often used, nonetheless, by social workers, correctional officers and others who work with individuals and groups in society. The methods of this science can be broken down into three parts: concepts, theories and research. A **concept** is a generalization concerning behavior which applies to a group of people. **Theories** are generalizations founded on observation and based upon relevant facts. A hypothesis is a hunch which at the present lacks enough evidence. When enough evidence is obtained, a hypothesis can become a theory. **Research** is conducted to test hypotheses and to improve the reliability of theories; five steps are followed. The first is to define the topic to be studied, followed by planning the research design to outline type of data and procedures for collecting it. The third step is to collect the data, followed by statistical and other analysis of the data. Drawing conclusions is the fifth and final step.

There are two basic types of research designs: experimental and observational. The **experimental design** is used less frequently because it is costly and may be hazardous. In this type of design, two groups are formed either by matching the groups for specific factors such as age or sex, or by random selection. One group is the control group, the other experimental. If a stimulus which is introduced to the experimental group (but not to the control group) causes a change, it can be concluded that the stimulus had an independent effect on the experimental group. Testing for stress, for example, could be harmful to the experimental group. In observational studies, on the other hand, the events being studied occur incidentally.

There are four types of **observational studies**, one of which is the **impressionistic** in which the observer makes an informal report from his observations, which may in turn provide hypotheses for other, more detailed studies. Another approach is the **comparative** study, which isolates distinct features among groups, uses questionnaires and interviews, and relies on statistical analysis. **Participant observation** studies take place when the observer himself joins the group he is observing; one problem, however, is that emotional involvement may create bias in the report. The **case-study** method collects accurate and complete details about a group using questionnaires and interviews. It differs from the comparative study in that it focuses on one particular group and examines as many features as possible. One disadvantage of the case-study method is that conclusions drawn about one group may not apply to all similar groups.

Other criticisms have been made about sociology in addition to the disadvantages of the various methods. Some claim that social behavior is obvious and reflects common sense, and therefore, the science of sociology is not necessary. However, when tested, many such notions do not always prove to be true. The fact that individuals are unique and complex does not refute the usefulness of sociology. This science frequently describes patterns of behavior common to many. Many books have been written in recent years to communicate the findings of sociologists to the laymen. In conducting these studies, sociologists must strive not to influence their subjects and not to allow their own values to color their objectivity.

Before going on with the review, try these sample CLEP questions:

1. Who of the following is the Father of Sociology?

(A) Plato
(B) Aristotle
(C) Auguste Comte
(D) Herbert Spencer
(E) Emile Durkheim

ANSWERS:

1.(C) August Comte is called the Father of Sociology. Aristotle and Plato considered social behavior in their philosophical studies. Herbert Spencer was an English sociologist known for his theory of social evolution which states that with time society becomes more heterogeneous. Emile Durkheim is known for his belief that sociology should concentrate on social facts, beliefs and behaviors common to people.

2. In which of the following did sociology have its roots?

(A) psychology
(B) economics
(C) history
(D) philosophy
(E) statistical analysis

2. (D) Sociology and psychology have their roots in philosophy; sociology concentrates on group behavior, while psychology emphasizes individual behavior. History studies unique human events; economics studies a particular aspect of human interaction. Statistical analysis is used frequently in all the social sciences to understand data.

3. **Which of the following best describes a hypothesis?**

   (A) an unproved concept
   (B) a proven theory
   (C) a proven concept
   (D) a law
   (E) an axiom

4. **One of the disadvantages of experimental research designs is which of the following?**

   (A) cost
   (B) objectivity
   (C) hazard
   (D) A and B
   (E) A and C

5. **The proper order of steps for research is which of the following?**

   (A) define topic, plan research design, analyze data, collect data, draw conclusions
   (B) plan research design, define topic, collect data, draw conclusions, analyze data
   (C) define topic, collect data, plan research design, analyze data, draw conclusions
   (D) plan research design, define topic, collect data, analyze data, draw conclusions
   (E) none of the above

3. (A) A hypothesis is an unproved concept; once enough evidence is gathered to support a hypothesis, it is called a theory. Events that occur uniformly time and again are considered laws. An axiom is a truth that is self-evident.

4. (E) Experimental research designs in sociology are both costly and may present hazards to the people being studied.

5. (E) The proper sequence of steps to be taken in a research design is as follows: define the topic, plan research design, collect data, analyze data, draw conclusions.

6. A complete, detailed report of the New City High School teachers would most likely be which type of the following studies?

(A) participant observation
(B) comparative
(C) experimental
(D) case
(E) impressionistic

6. (D) The researcher would most likely use a case-study method to study a group of high school teachers. Since his purpose would be to learn about this group at work in detail, he would not use an experimental, impressionistic or comparative approach. Chances are slim that such a researcher would actually be a staff member (participant observer); most researchers work for colleges and universities.

SOCIETY AND CULTURE

Society can be viewed in a number of ways. First, it can be seen as a group of persons who share a culture and are relatively organized. Society can also be the largest group to which an individual can belong; this also includes all the groups which make up society. Finally, society can be viewed as the network of social relationships whose system is largely determined by culture. No matter how society is viewed, however, it tends to persist because it does not readily change, and through its customs and laws it meets the needs of its members. Society both influences and is influenced by its members.

Status is the position held by a member of a society, and **role** is the expected, appropriate behavior of his status. **Ascribed status** is determined at birth; **achieved status** is acquired though individual effort. When a society is undergoing rapid social change, more and more emphasis is placed on achieved status. Sex, age and sometimes race are used to determine ascribed status. **Social rank** is the hierarchy of status with those at the top of the system receiving a greater degree of prestige. An individual usually possesses several statuses and therefore, roles. Roles differ from society to society; roles may also change over time. Some are voluntary, others are involuntary. Difficulty in performing a role is called **role conflict**, and it may arise because an individual is inadequately prepared for a role, must perform incompatible roles, or is facing a role incompatible with his own characteristics. Sometimes society itself is not clear about expected roles, e.g., the young woman and the marriage-children-career decisions. Mental and physical illness, crime and unhappiness can result from unresolved role conflicts.

Sociologists have presented society as divisible into two parts. **Herbert Spencer** broke society into industrial and militant segments. **Ferdinand Tonnies** presented the concepts of *gemeinschaft*, the community (family, etc.) and *gesellschaft*, the society (government, etc.). **Howard Becker** presented sacred and secular societies, and **Robert Redfield** presented folk and urban societies. The last three concepts are similar in that folk and sacred societies tend to be small, revolve around family ties, are based on agriculture and rely on customs and traditions. Urban, secular societies tend to be modern and diffuse and experience rapid change. Industrialization brings about modern, secular societies. However, large, modern societies are not necessarily cold and their members isolated; new associations such as clubs, professional groups and recreational organizations provide a network for communication and sharing in a way similar to the old kinship ties. Folk societies, furthermore, do experience tensions despite the fact that many yearn for the "good old days."

Culture is the whole of learned behavior in a society shared by its members and passed on to future generations. Culture depends upon man's interaction with man and language, symbolic communication. While many cultures coincide with national boundaries, this is not always the case; furthermore, groups that have some elements in common with the culture yet are in some ways distinct are called **subcultures**. Many cultures are comprised of various subcultures. While cultures vary from one to another, they all have developed customs and laws regarding marriage, leadership, religion and other factors of society. Some sociologists state that culture exists in the minds of the people and that inventions are the result of these ideas, while others say the inventions are actually part of culture itself; this second approach is called **material culture**. Just as society persists, so does culture; like society, culture does not determine absolutely the behavior of an individual.

The **trait** is the smallest unit of culture; a group of related traits forms a **cultural complex**; a combination of several complexes makes up a **cultural pattern**. A wedding ring is a trait; the wedding ceremony is a complex; the customs and rules regarding marriage make up a pattern. Since man does not have instincts to guide patterns of behavior, as do many animals and insects, he uses symbols, or language, to transmit learned behavior, or culture. **Symbols** are either referential (denotative) or expressive (connotative). Culture determines what man thinks. **Language** is used to focus on certain aspects of experience and therefore determines reality. This focusing is called **selective attention** and reflects the reality that each culture creates. It is for this reason that some structures and vocabulary can not be translated exactly from one language to another.

A **value** is a judgment as to the worth of an object or idea. An **attitude** is a manner of thinking which influences the way an individual will react to a situation. Some values and attitudes are covert, or concealed, and not reviewed or discussed in public, while others are openly displayed in public. There is never complete adherence to values and attitudes in any society. Values and attitudes based on incomplete information or ignorance are called **stereotypes**. These notions are always false to some degree, but nonetheless may influence the behavior of those stereotyping and those stereotyped.

A **norm** is a rule stating how the individual should behave in a certain circumstance and therefore reflects the values and attitudes of a culture. Norms vary from culture to culture but help to standardize behavior within each culture. Not all norms are obeyed; individuals may behave otherwise because of ignorance, defiance or conformity to a special subgroup. Conformity to norms generally exits, however, because of habit, teaching, usefulness, desire for acceptance or fear of punishment. **William Graham Sumner** pointed to three norms in his work *Folkways*. **Folkways** are customs of behavior, actions that are desired or permitted, but do not result in punishment if disregarded. **Mores** are required ways of behaving which can result in punishment if violated. **Laws** are norms put into force by some central authority. A combination of these norms usually are organized within one or more institutions.

The most prevalent institutions are the family, religion, government, education and the economic system.

Among cultures and societies, there is much variation concerning the norms of each group. While all groups set norms concerning marriage, some permit only **monogamous** unions (one husband, one wife) while others allow **polygamous** marriages (one man, several spouses, or one woman, several spouses). Just because norms differ, however, does not indicate a lack of morality. Every society has a sense of good and evil. Different conceptions emerge because of the needs and circumstances of each group. **Ethnocentrism** is the belief that one's own society or culture is superior to others. While such beliefs make the society stronger and more unified, they also hinder the understanding and good will among differing groups.

Before going on with the review, try these sample CLEP questions:

ANSWERS:

7. **Which of the following statements is not true about society?**

   (A) It can be a network of social relationships.
   (B) It can include a series of subgroups.
   (C) It changes readily with any stimulus.
   (D) Its members can share a culture.
   (E) It influences its members.

7. (C) Societies tend to resist change and provide stability to the group. They can be viewed as a network of social relationships and as a series of subgroups. Members frequently share a culture, and they are influenced by the society.

8. **Which of the following is an achieved status?**

   (A) the Prince of Wales
   (B) the eldest brother
   (C) a Brahman
   (D) a working mother
   (E) none of the above

8. (D) A working mother is an achieved status because it is acquired through the effort of the individual. The Prince of Wales, the eldest brother and the rank of Brahman are all determined at birth, ascribed status.

9. **In which of the following societies is a role conflict most likely to occur?**

   (A) tribal
   (B) urban
   (C) rural
   (D) sacred
   (E) folk

9. (B) Role conflict is most likely to occur in an urban society because more options are open to its members. Tribal, rural, sacred and folk societies are smaller and less complex; roles are more likely to be clearly defined.

10. How does the sociologist define culture?

(A) the whole learned behavior of a group
(B) the learned behavior of civilized groups
(C) the expected behavior of a status
(D) the appreciation of the arts by a group
(E) the acquisition of language

11. The smallest unit of a culture is which of the following?

(A) role
(B) trait
(C) norm
(D) pattern
(E) comple

12. As a symbol, the word "lamp" is which of the following?

(A) denotative
(B) connotative
(C) expressive
(D) B and C
(E) none of the above

10. (A) The sociologist defines culture as the whole learned behavior of any group. While civilized groups are studied by the sociologist, he does not exclude others. A role is an expected behavior of a status. Culture can also be used to describe an appreciation of the arts; this is a more general use. Acquisition of language is a universal feature of humans.

11. (B) A trait is the smallest unit of culture. Complexes are groups of related traits; patterns are combinations of complexes. Role is expected behavior of a status. Norm is a standard of behavior.

12. (A) As a symbol, the word "lamp" is denotative, or referential. It is a physical object which is manmade and gives light. The Iron Curtain is a term suggesting the secrecy of the former Soviet Union; it expresses the barrier that existed between the Soviet Union and other countries. This is a connotative, or expressive, term.

13. According to William Graham Sumner actions that are desired but do not result in punishment if omitted are called which of the following?

(A) folkways
(B) mores
(C) values
(D) laws
(E) attitudes

13. (A) Folkways are desired or permitted behaviors for which there is no punishment if omitted. According to Sumner, mores are required ways of behaving; violation of these beliefs is punishable. Laws are norms enforced by a government and punishable if violated. Values are judgments, and attitudes are predispositions to situations.

SOCIALIZATION

Socialization is the transmission of culture to an individual which in turn helps develop his personality. The development of **personality** gives rise to knowledge of the self, or identity. Socialization is a continuing process which spans the individual's entire life. Though different groups will emphasize various values and information, certain behaviors are taught by all and include: basic skills such as eating manners, goals, learned skills such as a profession, and roles. Other factors that vary the socialization process for individuals include biological differences among individuals, different experiences, changes in the culture itself and differing values among the socializing institutions themselves. Socialization can occur in both formal and informal situations.

Some sociologists state that culture produces a **modal personality**, one that reflects the values of the culture. However, there is little evidence that this influence is pervasive in forming basic personality. Other sociologists claim that complex, modern society produces individuals that are alienated and lonely, or anomic. This suggestion does not have ample evidence to be considered a fact. What is known is that there are several **institutions** which contribute to the socialization process, the most crucial of which is the family. It is within the family that the individual first interacts and learns values and information. The school is another institution fostering socialization; it provides both training and knowledge as well as basic values. The peer group as an institution provides the individual with modern values, equalitarian relationships and an identity apart from the family.

Television, radio, magazines and other media also have a socializing effect. Since the adult may encounter changes in status and roles in a modern society, he is often called upon to make adjustments. Marriage, divorce or a new career are examples of situations requiring **adjustment**, and the individual can make such adjustments more smoothly if he can anticipate the new role, a process called **anticipatory socialization**. **Resocialization** is the process of learning values and norms different from those previously learned; an example is the training of an army recruit.

The **self** is the way a person feels about his personality. **Charles Horton Cooley** stated that the individual views himself as he believes others see him, a notion called

The Looking-Glass Self. In this concept, a person first imagines how he appears to others, imagines their judgment of his appearance, and then reacts to these imagined judgments. The process is particularly important in early life. How the individual sees himself is not always accurate, however. **George Herbert Mead** built on Cooley's ideas, emphasizing the importance of language in interactions. Mead stated that the self is composed of two parts, the "I" which is subjective and unknowable, and the "Me" which is objective and knowable through the personality. The interaction of the "I" and "Me" lead to self-awareness. According to Mead, socialization takes place in three distinct steps: the **Stage of Imitation** occurs first when the child imitates parents, brothers and sisters; the **Play Stage** occurs at age two when the child recognizes his "Me" aspect and role-plays; the **Game Stage** occurs when the child recognizes his "I" aspect, plays games with several roles and anticipates the actions of others. In this final stage the individual learns proper behavior in society by learning his roles.

Before going on with the review, try these sample CLEP questions:

ANSWERS:

14. **Which of the following statements concerning socialization are true?**

    (A) It is an on-going process.
    (B) Some basic behaviors are taught by all societies.
    (C) It occurs only in formal settings.
    (D) A and B only
    (E) B and C only

14. (D) Socialization is an ongoing process with some basic behaviors common to all societies such as the establishment of guidelines for marriage and child-rearing. Socialization can occur in formal and informal settings.

15. **The institution that most clearly provides equalitarian relationships is which of the following?**

    (A) the family
    (B) religion
    (C) the school
    (D) the peer group
    (E) the government

15. (D) Peer groups are the individual's contemporaries. Friends provide equalitarian relationships and help the individual develop apart from the family.

16. **Which of the following is an example of anticipatory socialization?**

    (A) a period of engagement before marriage
    (B) boot camp
    (C) recovering from the loss of a friend
    (D) brainwashing
    (E) none of the above

16. (A) A period of engagement before marriage helps to prepare for marriage and is an example of anticipatory socialization. Boot camp and brainwashing are examples of resocialization. Recovering from the loss of a friend is adjustment.

17. **During which of the following stages does the child recognize his "I" aspect of self, according to George Herbert Mead?**

    (A) Game
    (B) Imitation
    (C) Play
    (D) A and B
    (E) B and C

17. (A) A child recognizes his "I" aspect of self in the Game Stage. In the Stage of Imitation, he has no awareness of self and copies the behavior of those around him. In the Play Stage, he is aware of the "Me" aspect of self and plays roles.

DEVIANCE

Role is the expected behavior of an individual in his status. As such, roles allow people to be aware of patterns of behavior which add order to social life. **Social order** is the interaction of people made smooth because of role expectations. Methods used to guarantee adherence to roles and norms are called **social controls. Conformity** is adherence to roles and norms; there is never, however, absolute conformity, only degrees of conformity. Socialization fosters conformity, as does identification with a group. The fact that division of labor in society creates interdependence among individuals also results in conformity. Rewards for good behavior and punishment for bad behavior, further increase conformity to society's norms.

Rapid social change can bring about **social disorganization**, whereby individuals feel they are no longer part of a group. Sometimes suicide, mental illness or drug abuse will result. Alienation may also result. Some sociologists, however, point out that such social disorganization may lead to the rise of a new social order. All societies, nevertheless, do have accepted ways to let off frustrations and tensions, e.g., games, sports, jokes.

Deviance is behavior that varies from the norm. **Variation** is measured both by degree (how much) and direction (approved-disapproved by society). Frequently there is debate as to where to set the norm, so deviance is difficult to measure. There also exists a range of **tolerance**, where a certain amount of variation from the norm is accepted. Groups, as well as individuals, can behave in deviant ways. There are also distinctions between cultural and psychological deviance. In trying to learn the causes of social deviance, sociologists have examined both biological deficiencies and environmental factors affecting the individual; however, no clear case has been made for either hypothesis. Sociologists now look at the socialization process itself by studying the behavior of the deviant, not the individual himself. It has been realized that criminal behavior is learned behavior, and that deviant subcultures form their own sets of norms and values and pass these on to new members. If the society itself is experiencing conflicting roles, some members will reject both and adopt a deviant role. If the society cannot provide the lifestyle that its expectations suggest, some members will opt for deviant behavior. Four responses to such frustrations include **ritualism, retreat, innovation** and **rebellion**. In ritualism the individual continues to work hard for goals he can not attain, while others may retreat from the scene altogether through, for example, drug abuse. Some will create deviant approaches to goals, such as cheating or stealing, while others will rebel, seeking a new social order.

Punishment is the consequence of criminally deviant behavior. Not all deviant behavior is bad, however; the American Revolutionaries displayed deviant behavior. Because deviant behavior can be positive and/or approved of by society, it can provide fresh approaches to problems and situations. All deviance can also work to further define norms and ranges of tolerance.

Before going on with the review, try these sample CLEP questions:

ANSWERS:

18. **Which of the following best describes social order?**

    (A) adherence to role expectations
    (B) smooth interactions among people
    (C) sanctions
    (D) absolute conformity
    (E) none of the above

18. (B) Social order is the smooth operation of interactions among people in a society. Conformity is adherence to role expectations, which while never absolute, aids the social order. Sanctions are rewards and punishments which aid conformity.

19. **Which factors are modern sociologists inclined to examine when studying deviant behavior?**

    (A) school experiences of the individual
    (B) the behavior itself
    (C) the individual's upbringing
    (D) the biological makeup of the individual
    (E) the genetic makeup of the individual

19. (B) Modern sociologists look more at the deviant behavior itself. Studies of biological and/or genetic causes and of environmental causes have yielded contradictory conclusions. While upbringing and school experiences seem to have some effect, the exact relationship is not known.

20. **Watching a boxing match or playing a hard game of racquetball could be considered which of the following?**

    (A) deviant behavior
    (B) retreat
    (C) tension-reliever
    (D) rebellion
    (E) none of the above

20. (C) Sports, either observed or played, serve not only as recreation but also as socially accepted ways of relieving tension. Since many observe/participate, sports are not considered deviant behavior. Retreat is to give up both means and ends of society's values through escape such as alcoholism. Rebellion is to defy the existing social order to bring about changes.

21. **Protest marches as a means to bring about social changes would be an example of which of the following?**

(A) retreat
(B) ritualism
(C) innovation
(D) rebellion
(E) none of the above

21. (D) Protest marches would be considered rebellion. Retreat is escape. Ritualism is to perform duties without reward. Innovation is to make one's own rules and commit crimes.

SOCIAL ORGANIZATION

Sociologists classify unions of people in three ways. **Groups** are made up of persons who interact, see themselves as distinct from other groups, have a communication pattern and share values and norms. **Categories** are numbers of people who share characteristics but do not communicate, such as all married women with two-year old children. **Aggregates** are numbers of people who are in close proximity with one another but do not have on-going communication, such as riders on a bus. Individuals can be members of these classifications simultaneously, and the classifications themselves may overlap over time. Memberships to these classifications may be voluntary or involuntary. An individual's close attachment to a group makes it an in-group; lesser attachment makes it an out-group. **Social distance** defines the degree of closeness or distance for each group. A group may be primary, with close, personal ties, or secondary, lacking those ties. It may be formal or informal, horizontal (members from the same class or of equal status) or vertical (members from several classes).

There are several forms of interaction between members or groups. **Cooperation** is the joint effort of two or more members of groups in attaining a goal. While it is necessary for survival, the fruits of cooperation are not necessarily shared equally by those who join in the effort. **Competition** is the individual member's or group's effort to obtain items which are scarce and desired by many. Competition is necessary for survival, but competition does not revolve around only survival items. The culture determines what objectives may be competed for in a society as well as the rules of the competition. Competition helps to bring out the best in people, but it also may discourage anxious, fearful people or those who continually fail in competitive situations. Competition fosters hostile feelings and may lead to conflicts. In **conflict**, the members or groups not only compete for scarce goods but also may harm one another to obtain their goal. While conflict can be destructive, it is useful because it makes issues clear, can help to unify the group and identifies the enemy.

When arguing groups cease fighting, **accommodation** occurs. There are several types of accommodations including truce, superordination, compromise, third party assistance, and tolerance. In a **truce**, fighting stops without a final solution to the conflict. When one power is stronger than the other, the **superordination** takes place, the weaker power subordinate to the stronger. **Compromises** are reached by opposing powers of relatively equal strength. **Third parties** can reach agreements through conciliation (encouraging negotiation), mediation (suggestion of solutions), and arbitration (decisions for solution made by third party). **Tolerance** is the putting up with the difference of another. Another way to end conflict is **assimilation**, which is the blending of two groups or cultures into one. This takes time and occurs more readily if the groups share similarities of culture, physical features, or if the incoming group is small.

Primary groups are small, close-knit groups whose members interact in a personal way for reasons of satisfaction and pleasure. Such groups endure, offer relative equality and tend to be stable. Proximity aids the formation of such groups, but modern transportation and communication help to maintain primary group members who are at a distance. The family is an example of a primary group, as is a street gang. Primary groups aid social order, provide intimacy and warmth to its members, but may also be repressive for independent people. Such groups may also approve socially deviant behavior (e.g., a street gang).

Secondary groups have numerous members, formal structure, and offer impersonal relationships. Secondary groups are also called formal organizations and are formed for specific, utilitarian reasons. Members can change without affecting the stability of the group and there tends to be a hierarchy of status. Primary and secondary groups can overlap, however. A **bureaucracy** is a prime example of a secondary group; **Max Weber** studied bureaucracies and noted that sets of rules and a ranking of authority are developed, that there is division of labor and employment based on qualifications, and that such organizations tend to be impersonal. He also stated that authority is the cornerstone of the bureaucracy. Other sociologists have noted other features of the bureaucracy power, the Protestant (Work) Ethic, communication, and the professionalization of managers. Drawbacks of the bureaucracy include "red tape," overemphasis of the rules ("going by the book"), negative effects of seniority systems, and workers' feelings of alienation. Nonetheless, bureaucracies do have the potential for efficient, beneficial improvements for society.

For the sociologist, **community** can mean either a geographic location, a group sharing an identity, or both. Communities tend to be organized, to divide labor and to be relatively self-sufficient. Sociologists have studied what is called the **rural-urban dichotomy**. Rural, or folk, communities tend to be small, stable, independent populations whose members are homogeneous and rely strongly on the family. Urban communities have large populations with high density (number of people per square mile), whose members have varied backgrounds and interests and who tend to exhibit more tolerance and innovation. In the United States the majority of people live in urban areas, but throughout the world more than two-thirds of the population live in rural communities.

Cities have central business districts, slum areas and better residential areas which are affected by land values. Groups of common heritage, race or class tend to live in the same area, a process called **segregation**. New groups of people moving into an area is called **invasion**. **Succession** results when an area has been completely invaded by a new group. Centralized businesses and services are located in one area. Decentralization occurs as, for example when highway shopping malls are constructed.

Before going on with the review, try these sample CLEP questions:

22. **A collection of people who share characteristics but do not communicate are considered which of the following?**

   (A) class
   (B) group
   (C) aggregate
   (D) category
   (E) none of the above

22. (D) A collection of people who share characteristics but do not communicate is called a category. A class is a collection of people who share the same status, level of wealth, etc. A group is a collection of people who interact, see values and communicate. An aggregate is made up of people in close, physical proximity who do not have continuing communication.

23. **An individual's class attachment to a group makes that group which of the following?**

   (A) informal
   (B) horizontal
   (C) secondary
   (D) vertical
   (E) in-group

23. (E) An individual has class ties to an in-group. An informal group is loosely structured. A horizontal group has members of equal status; a vertical group has members of different statuses. A secondary group is large and impersonal.

24. **If two nations jointly develop a public works project that benefits both, they would be employing which of the following processes?**

   (A) conflict
   (B) cooperation
   (C) competition
   (D) assimilation
   (E) accommodation

24. (B) Joining forces to create a public works project is an example of cooperation. Conflict is competition for scarce goods involving harm to other competitors. Competition is vying for scarce goods. Assimilation is the blending of two or more cultures. Accommodation is a process to bring about the end of conflict.

25. **Which of the following is not a feature of primary groups?**

   (A) numerous members
   (B) personal interactions
   (C) relative equality
   (D) enduring relationships
   (E) formed for pleasure and satisfaction

25. (A) Primary groups are small, personal, offering relative equality and enduring relationships. They are formed for mutual pleasure and satisfaction.

26. Which of the following is a benefit of bureaucracy?

(A) "red tape"
(B) efficiency
(C) loss of pride in craftsmanship
(D) overemphasis of regulations
(E) none of the above

27. Which of the following is not a feature of urban communities?

(A) sophistication
(B) greater tolerance for deviant behavior
(C) low density
(D) heterogeneous groups
(E) large populations

28. The process by which new groups of people move into an established area is called which of the following?

(A) rural-urban dichotomy
(B) centralization
(C) succession
(D) invasion
(E) segregation

29. The Bowash is an example of which of the following?

(A) metropolis
(B) megalopolis
(C) centralization
(D) decentralization
(E) none of the above

26. (B) Efficiency is a benefit of bureaucracies. "Red tape," loss of pride in craftsmanship, and overemphasis of regulations are drawbacks which hinder efficiency and affect workers negatively.

27. (C) Urban communities have high density, that is, a high number of people per square mile. Because urban residents are exposed to more ideas and are large, heterogeneous groups, they tend to show more sophistication and tolerance of deviant behavior.

28. (D) Invasion is the moving in of new groups of people to an established area. Segregation is the tendency of members of the same ethnic or racial group to occupy an area. Succession occurs as new groups take over an established area. The rural-urban dichotomy is a term identifying these two types of areas. Centralization is the tendency of businesses and services to locate in one area of a city.

29. (B) The Bowash, running from Boston to Washington, D.C., is an example of a megalopolis, a series of metropolitan areas. A metropolis is made up of a central city (or cities) and surrounding suburbs. Decentralization is the tendency of businesses and services to locate away from the center of the city, e.g., industrial parks and shopping malls.

SOCIAL STRATIFICATION

All modern societies are stratified to some degree. Inequalities, as manifested by differing life-styles and opportunities, exist everywhere. This stems from, among other factors, the unequal distribution of goods. Societies, of course, differ in terms of the degree to which inequality exists. Class, status and power also contribute to stratification.

Several theories and approaches to stratification exist. The **functional theory** states that complex societies have a number of needs to fulfill in order to survive, and so those individuals who meet those needs are rewarded. This theory, however, does not come to terms with the fact that many people have potential talent and yet are discriminated against in their attempts to achieve. On the other hand, the **conflict theory** states that stratification is based on competition for the rewards that society can bestow, whereby the group with the most power lays claim to most of the rewards. What probably exists is a combination of the two.

Approaches to studying stratification include the **subjective**, **objective** and **reputational** methods. In the first, people are asked to rank themselves as members of the upper, middle or lower class. Invariably, most people rate themselves middle class, even though many are in fact much higher or lower. The objective method takes into account factual information such as education, occupation and income. However, this does not give a clear picture either; sanitation engineers may receive greater pay than college professors. The reputational method has community leaders rank others by class. This method also has drawbacks; are these leaders accurate in their assessment? Thus, a combination of these approaches might yield more useful, accurate information.

Stratification can occur in a number of ways. **Caste**, for example, is a rigid system of ranking members of society such as existed in India. Possession of land, or **estate**, is another type which is seen in the feudal system. **Class distinction** is based largely on economics; relying on occupation and income, it is less rigid than caste or estate. Closely related to class are status and party; Max Weber stated that these last three combine to differentiate people. **Status** ranks people by prestige; **party** groups people as they seek power.

The **Industrial Revolution** gave rise to a "working" class with its division of labor; thus, occupation in part determines class, but it is not the only factor. Education, family background and power are also important. Being a member of a higher class has certain rewards; the higher the class, the more likely the individual member is to enjoy good health, live longer, have greater educational opportunities and be less likely to be arrested, tried and convicted for a crime. This does not mean that lower classes commit more crimes.

The **social mobility** is change from one place in the rankings to another; it may be horizontal (a change in position without a change in status or class), or it may be vertical (upward or downward). Occupational and/or geographic mobility are two examples which indicate social mobility; promotions and/or transfers frequently mean enhancement in our society. Such change does have a price, however; role conflict may result and friends may be lost as the individual moves up (or down) the social ladder.

Before going on with the review, try these sample CLEP questions:

30. **In a society, arranging people by rank is which of the following?**

   (A) stratification
   (B) differentiation
   (C) conspicuous consumption
   (D) status
   (E) A and B

30. (A) Stratification is the arranging of people in a society by rank. Differentiation is the recognition of different categories of people such as by age or sex not based on rank. Conspicuous consumption is extravagant spending on luxury items by those of the higher classes; this term was coined by sociologist Thorstein Veblen. Status is the ranking of individuals by honor.

31. **Which of the stratification systems below is most likely to be open?**

   (A) caste
   (B) slavery
   (C) feudal
   (D) class
   (E) estate

31. (D) Of the systems listed, class, based on economic position, is the most likely to be open. Slavery, caste, feudal and estate would tend to be fixed and closed.

32. **Max Weber's term "party" means which of the following?**

   (A) political parties in America
   (B) any political party
   (C) a group working together to consolidate power
   (D) any group
   (E) A and B

32. (D) While political parties may in fact obtain a degree of power, Weber's term does not refer specifically to a political group but rather to any group forming to gain power.

33. A lateral move from Pittsburgh, Pennsylvania, to Chicago, Illinois, is most likely to be an example of which of the following?

(A) intergenerational mobility
(B) intragenerational mobility
(C) occupational mobility
(D) geographic mobility
(E) none of the above

33. (D) A lateral move does not involve a promotion, and so this type of mobility is geographic in nature. Intergenerational mobility is movement to higher (or lower) positions across generations (father to son). Intragenerational mobility is movement to higher (or lower) position within a generation (the occupation you begin with and the one you end with). Neither type of mobility occurs with great frequency for the large majority in the labor force.

SOCIAL CHANGE

Social change is transition within a society. Often it is caused by a change in the behavior of people, but this is not always the case. People who conform as well as those who deviate from society's norms may contribute to social change. Societies change at different rates; forces outside the society may contribute to change; change may or may not be deliberately initiated.

Many factors can contribute to change such as technological developments, environmental conditions, shifts in population size and location, type of social organization and the attitude of society's members toward change. There can be varying degrees of change within a society, a condition known as **cultural lag**. Change is more likely to occur where the society is receptive to the changes presented.

A **social movement** is an organized effort on the part of many people to bring about change in a society. **Reform movements** seek to bring about change by using the current system in a way acceptable to society. **Revolutionary movements,** on the other hand, seek to overthrow the existing order to establish a new one. Social movements provide direction to the change that develops in society.

MAJORITY-MINORITY RELATIONS

Several approaches have been taken in trying to define and classify by race. One divides the people of the world into three general groups, **Caucasoid, Negroid** and **Mongoloid** race. The Caucasoid race is characterized by white skin, wavy hair and brown, blue, green or hazel eyes. There are variations in this group such as type of hair; some have curly hair while others have hair that is straight. So too are there variations among those of the Negroid race although generally the skin is brown/black, the hair is black and curly and the eyes are brown in color. Members of the Mongoloid race usually have yellow/brown skin, straight black hair and dark eyes.

Any group can constitute a **minority**, for it is not numbers alone that constitute a minority in a sociological sense. This term can also refer to people who suffer disadvantages as compared to others in society. Because one's race is usually highly visible, it is frequently used to make distinctions; distinctions, moreover, can also be drawn along ethnic lines. Distinctions giving inferior or superior status to the various minority/majority groups are social in nature, not biological. The behaviors displayed by the various groups as well as the attitudes shown by them and towards them by others are all learned. This learned attitude toward a group of people is called **prejudice**. It can generate both feelings and thoughts about a group which are either positive or negative. **Discrimination** can also be either positive or negative, but it differs from prejudice in that it is actual behavior, not just thought or feelings. Discrimination is the treating of people differently because of classification in a particular ethnic, racial or some other type of group.

Discrimination can be found in many areas such as education, employment, politics and place of residence. Furthermore, it can take many forms, from conflict to segregation, partition and annihilation. Discrimination can bring about a number of results ranging from the minority group becoming subservient to the majority, to adaptation, to aggression. Discrimination can be averted to some degree by legal sanctions; prejudice requires that new values be taught.

Before going on with the review, try these sample CLEP questions:

34. **The rise of the Bolsheviks in early twentieth century Russia is an example of which of the following?**

    (A) reform
    (B) revolution
    (C) cultural lag
    (D) diffusion
    (E) none of the above

ANSWERS:

34. (B)   The Bolshevik uprising was a revolution bringing about the fall of Czarist Russia and the rise of communism. A reform movement seeks changes within the current system.

35. **Which of the following statements is NOT true concerning social change?**

(A) It is more likely to occur where society is receptive to change.

(B) Where a society is located can affect the rate and degree of change it experiences.

(C) Change is progress.

(D) Conservative societies tend to view change cautiously.

(E) A society is more likely to change if the adjustment fits in well with its already existing culture.

35. (C) Change can be progress, but it is not necessarily so. While some changes improve conditions for man, others destroy past gains or are simply "bad" for man.

36. **Which of the following is the most accurate description of "the White Man's Burden"?**

(A) discrimination against racial minorities on the part of the white majority

(B) prejudice against ethnic minorities on the part of the white majority

(C) assumption on the part of white colonists that black native peoples need their guidance and help

(D) assimilation of the white minority into the black majority

(E) annihilation of the black minority by the white majority

36. (C) When European and American colonial powers made inroads in foreign countries, they often assumed the attitude that, since their cultures were "superior" to that of the native population, it was their duty, or burden, to care for and assist them. Discrimination is behavior which treats people differently, while prejudice is an attitude towards people based on stereotypes. Assimilation is the merging of different cultures. Annihilation is the extermination of one racial or ethnic group by another.

37. **Which of the following statements about race is true?**

   (A) There are no biological differences making one race superior to the others based on skin color.

   (B) Prejudice is a learned attitude.

   (C) No significant differences in intelligence exist among races.

   (D) Intermarriage exists in all races.

   (E) All of the above.

38. **In American society, blacks have experienced discrimination and prejudice against them in which of the following areas?**

   (A) education

   (B) housing

   (C) employment

   (D) political activities

   (E) all of the above

39. **The Nazi death camps represent which of the following racial/ethnic processes?**

   (A) segregation

   (B) competition

   (C) conflict

   (D) annihilation

   (E) assimilation

37. (E) All of the statements are true. Research indicates that there are no inherent biological differences among the races based on type of skin or other physical attributes. Prejudice is a learned attitude, and as a result, discrimination has led to different groups being afforded unequal opportunities. Lack of opportunity, in turn, contributes to different life-styles and attitudes among groups.

38. (E) American blacks have experienced discrimination in all the areas listed. Civil rights legislation addresses the need for equal opportunity and treatment by law, and the United States Supreme Court decisions such as Brown versus The Board of Education of Topeka (1954) have declared segregation and unequal treatment illegal.

39. (D) The Nazi death camps were used in an attempt to annihilate Jews and other categories of people such as the deformed, the mentally retarded and Nazi dissenters. Segregation is the separation of racial/ethnic groups. Competition aims at putting minority groups at a disadvantage in the society. Conflict occurs when a minority refuses "second-class citizenship" and combats its subordinate position. Assimilation is the merging of the cultures of two or more racial and/or ethnic groups.

MARRIAGE AND FAMILY PATTERNS

In all societies the **family** is the basic living unit. This is so because the family fulfills certain needs including reproduction, economic needs, child-rearing and a place in society. The family also serves to limit sexual activity of married partners to one another and provides its members with warmth and affection.

The family unit varies in form from society to society. In the Untied States and Europe the family typically consists of a father, mother and children, a unit known as the **nuclear family**. The **extended family** on the other hand, consists of additional members to the nuclear unit, grandparents, aunts, uncles and cousins. Both types can be found in any given society.

Marriage patterns can vary from society to society. **Monogamy** is the pattern consisting of one man and one woman; **polygamy** calls for more than one male or one female. **Polygyny** consists of a man and two or more wives; **polyandry**, one woman and several men. Family trees can be traced through the male line of descent (**patrilineal**) or through the female (**matrilineal**). Dating and courtship generally precedes marriage in Western societies; some societies arrange marriages, sometimes at birth. In choosing a partner the individual will frequently seek out a person with like characteristics, intelligence, education and social class and attitudes.

In the last century, the size of the average American family has decreased. Since that time also, the age at time of marriage has declined although a recent trend indicates that at least in some segments of society marriage is being postponed a few years. Attitudes toward divorce have changed as the divorce rate in Western societies has risen. Romantic love is an ideal, and while divorce is disruptive to the family, many people have observed that it may be a healthy alternative to an unhappy union. The number of married women entering and/or staying in the labor market has increased. Schools, religious, social and government institutions provide education and services previously done by the family unit such as education, career training leading to employment, and welfare and social security assistance.

Research in the area of family and divorce patterns indicates that certain factors contribute to a higher success rate in marriage. They include similarity in religion, happy childhood, comparable education attainment and average financial standing at the time of marriage. A period of engagement and post-teen years marriage contribute to the success rate.

Before going on with the review, try these sample CLEP questions:

40. **The family need least likely to be assumed by an outside agency is which of the following?**

(A) reproduction
(B) child-rearing
(C) economic needs
(D) feeling of belonging
(E) social placement

40. (A) Reproduction is the family function least likely to be assumed by an outside agency. Day care centers and schools assist in child-rearing. Social and government agencies assist in financial matters. Social placement and a feeling of belonging are aided by institutions such as schools, employment and social/recreation groups. The advent of the test-tube baby may, at some future date, impact on reproduction as a function strictly within the family unit.

41. **Descent traced through the family males is called which of the following?**

(A) matrilineal
(B) patrilocal
(C) bilateral
(D) neolocal
(E) none of the above

41. (E) Descent traced through family males is patrilineal; through the females, matrilineal; through both, bilateral. Patrilocal residence occurs when the couple lives in the male's village or family; matrilocal refers to the female's; neolocal indicates that the couple lives in an area away from both families.

42. **Dating is best defined as which of the following?**

(A) activity of intense interaction with one other likely to lead to marriage
(B) activity which always leads to marriage
(C) activity which allows for one to become acquainted with another/others
(D) A and C
(E) none of the above

42. (C) Dating is a preliminary activity allowing a person to become acquainted with potential spouses. Courtship is more intense relationship with one person which often leads to marriage.

43. Which of the following is NOT likely to encourage divorce?

(A) ease with which a divorce can be obtained legally
(B) social acceptance of divorce
(C) high unemployment
(D) A and B
(E) B and C

43. (C) High unemployment is not likely to encourage divorce; couples in financial straits are more likely to remain together to pool resources. Divorce costs are another factor. Changes in state laws regarding divorce have made them easier to obtain, and social stigma attached to those divorced has lessened.

DEMOGRAPHY

Demographics is the study of human population. Factors influencing demographics include fertility, morality, migration and trends. The **crude birth rate** is the fertility measure which indicates the number of births per 1,000 people a year. These measures alone do not give the whole picture; for example, how many women are presently of child-bearing age? Because of such factors, demographics also examines age groups and life expectancy rates.

Other factors increase population size. New medicines and better medial techniques have significantly lowered the **infant mortality rate** (the number of infant deaths per 1,000 births). Better farming techniques have improved the quality and quantity of food, lowering the mortality rate. Cultural attitudes can also affect population size, as can **immigration** (movement to a country) and **emigration** (movement from a country).

Introduction of modern medicine and agricultural techniques has had a dramatic effect on the population growth of underdeveloped nations. Death rates have been lowered as well as the infant mortality rate while birth rates have increased. Food production has not kept pace, however, and so many people face starvation. However, not only has the population increased, but so has the rate of population. In 1650, the Earth's estimated population was 500 million; this figure doubled by 1820. Population doubled again by 1930, and doubled yet again by the 1970's. Obviously, as population increases, strains are placed on the Earth's resources for they are limited. There can be no doubt that we must come to grips with the problem of over-population.

Before going on with the review, try these sample CLEP questions:

44. **Which of the following is the number of births per 1,000 people per year?**

(A) crude birth rate
(B) actual birth rate
(C) rate of population growth
(D) infant mortality rate
(E) none of the above

44. (A) The crude birth rate is the number of births per 1,000 people per year; an actual, or exact birth rate would be virtually impossible to assess. The rate of population growth considers the crude birth rate minus the crude death rate. The infant mortality rate is the number of infant deaths per 1,000 births.

45. **Movement of people from one foreign country to another is an example of which of the following?**

(A) demographic transition
(B) population explosion
(C) immigration
(D) emigration
(E) C and D

45. (E) Immigration is movement to a country; emigration is the movement from a country. Demographic transition is a shift between the birth and death rates, whereby modern technology reduces the death rate while the birth rate remains high (population explosion); eventually the birth rate declines. When birth and death rates are low, there is little population increase.

GLOSSARY OF SOCIOLOGY TERMS

Accommodation: behavior which reduces conflict

Anomie: a person's feeling of alienation and rootlessness

Charisma: magnetic attraction of followers due to one's extraordinary qualities and characteristics

Community: a group of people who possess a sense of belonging

Correlation: the degree to which two variables are related to one another

Culture Complex: a group of traits

Diffusion: the spread of traits from one social group to another

Empirical Information: facts based on concrete evidence

Fad: behavior that is short-lived

Fashion: behavior that is somewhat more lasting than a fad

Identification: an individual's acceptance of the group's norms and values

Innovation: a new approach to an end

Legitimacy: the group's consensus that the individual is conforming to his role

Mobility: physical and/or social movement

Mores: norms essential to the group which must be conformed to by its members

Norm: the expected pattern of behavior

Power: the degree to which one has the ability to control another (or others)

Propaganda: information presented in such a way as to influence and/or manipulate the audience

Sanctions: rewards or punishments for certain behaviors

Sect: a small religious group which requires the complete faith of its members

Social Distance: the degree of separation between two or more groups

Symbol: an object that represents something else

Taboo: a behavior forbidden by the society

Psychology

HISTORICAL BACKGROUND

Psychology is the study of human behavior. A word of Greek origin, psychology literally means the study of the mind. During the Golden Age of Greece, there developed two approaches to the study of the mind. One said that man is a rational creature born with all the ideas needed to guide his behavior; **Plato** developed this rationalistic viewpoint. **Aristotle**, a materialist, said that man is a biological creature influenced by experience and his environment. Modern psychology tends to work from the position held by Aristotle.

Plato was a rationalist. Modern psychology teaches that people are more affected by their environment. This view was developed by Aristotle.

Psychology and philosophy were closely related in Greece, and **Rene Descartes** (1696-1650) used a philosophical approach in explaining human behavior. He believed that man is made up of both body and mind, that they are separate but that they do interact. The body's actions are reflex responses, while ideas are innate, or present at birth. By the early eighteenth century, however, psychology began to be approached more scientifically. Descartes' concept of **dualism** (separation of the mind and body) was kept, but the thinkers of the day believed that the mind is blank at birth (*tabula rasa*, or blank slate) and that a person's experiences and environment as sampled through the senses contribute to ideas and intelligence. In order to explain this complex development of ideas, the concept of association was developed which states that we associate or connect events which occur together. The men of this period relied on direct observation and logical reasoning and were therefore called **empiricists**.

Wilhelm Wundt is called the Father of Psychology by many. He and others such as **Hermann von Helmholtz** combined the observation of the empiricists with precise measurements. Wundt set up the first formal psychological laboratory; Helmholtz measured the speed of the nerve impulse. Their approach is called **structuralism** because they attempted to study the structure of the mind; this approach did not work well, however, because it was based upon introspection, the observer's report of

109

his own feelings. The problem was twofold: no one can verify another's self-analysis, and as Sigmund Freud pointed out, many thoughts lie in the unconscious, beyond awareness.

The philosophy of **William James**, pragmatism, and the theory of evolution proposed by **Charles Darwin** contributed to the development of **functionalism**. **Pragmatism** requires that theories be tested and that the result have some practical use; the **theory of evolution** suggests that man has the capacity for further development. These ideas suggested that not only the functions of the mind be studied, but also that the differences between individuals be observed. To see the differences between man and other forms of life, animals were used in laboratories for the first time. This approach still concentrated on the working of the mind, however, even though it did subdivide the field into such areas as industrial and educational psychology.

Emphasis gradually shifted to human behavior which can be observed. **Ivan Pavlov** of Russia and **John B. Watson** of the United States contributed to this change of emphasis. Pavlov observed that dogs would salivate when hearing the bell usually rung before the presentation of the food; he called his system **reflexology**, which studied behavior without referring to the mental process. Watson, who was studying glandular reflexes, developed the concept of **behaviorism**, stating that behavior which can be observed should be the focus of psychology. The subdivision of functional psychology, such as clinical and educational, were kept, but emphasis was placed on learning and adaptive behavior. The physiological activities of the organism being studied also received more investigation.

In the twentieth century, behaviorism has been the basis for much of the experimental and applied psychology. The **Gestalt school** asserts, however, that behavior must be studied as organized patterns, not as isolated incidents of activity. **Wolfgang Kohlor** is associated with this school.

Before going on with the review try these sample CLEP questions:

1. **Plato developed which of the following viewpoints?**

   (A) Man is composed of the body and mind which interact with one another.
   (B) Man is a rational creature.
   (C) Man is a biological creature.
   (D) The mind at birth is a *tabula rasa.*
   (E) none of the above

ANSWERS:

1. (B) Plato believed that man was essentially a rational creature, that by reason alone could discover the truths about himself and his universe.

2. In psychology as outlined by Descartes, automatism means which of the following?

(A) innate ideas
(B) *tabula rasa*
(C) empiricism
(D) reflex action
(E) none of the above

3. The theory of evolution suggests which of the following concepts?

(A) survival of the fittest
(B) natural selection
(C) continuation of man's development
(D) variation of structure and function
(E) all of the above

4. Ivan Pavlov did which of the following?

(A) studied salivating response of dogs
(B) was the only scientist to use animals in experiments
(C) stated the tenets of pragmatism
(D) stated that behavior should not be studied in isolated instances
(E) none of the above

5. Who of the following would place the most emphasis on human behavior in studying psychology?

(A) Plato
(B) Aristotle
(C) Descartes
(D) James
(E) Watson

---

2. (D) For Descartes, automatism meant reflex action, that is, the body exhibits reflex, or automatic, responses to external stimuli.

3. (E) The theory of evolution as proposed by Darwin features all of the points listed. Variation of structure and function makes some organisms more fit to survive; these variations also cause some organisms to be selected for continued survival. Since man, too, has gone through this process and continues to do so, it is reasonable to project future developments.

4. (A) Ivan Pavlov conducted a classic experiment in which he observed that dogs would begin to salivate upon hearing a signal which preceded the presentation of food, a learned behavior. He is not, however, the only psychologist to use animals in his studies. William James helped to formulate the philosophy of pragmatism. (D) is a tenet of Gestalt Theory.

5. (E) Watson would place the greatest emphasis on human behavior in psychology. The behaviorists shifted the definition of this term from study of the mind to study of human behavior.

EXPERIMENTAL DESIGN AND METHODOLOGY

Since the time of the Greeks, efforts have been made to make the study of psychology a science. As a science, psychological information is gathered through observation and experimentation. The **naturalistic method** involves careful observation of animals in their natural habitat. Investigators are trained to carefully record the behaviors shown by the group or individuals. The **case study method**, developed by Sigmund Freud, involves the collection of information about an individual; this biography includes the individual's childhood and present, his dreams and his fears. The **statistical method** is the observation of people's attitudes and practices through data collected in questionnaires or samples.

The **experimental method** tests a suspected relationship, a **hypothesis**, between two factors by varying one and observing its effect on the other. The factor that is manipulated is the **independent variable** and the factor that is observed, or measured, is the **dependent variable**. All other factors which might affect the outcome other than the independent variable must be held constant. For example, in order to test the effectiveness of a medicine, it must be administered to subjects to test the properties of the medicine completely. Some members of the experiment, called the **control group**, will be given a sugar pill, or a **placebo**, which looks identical to the medicine. The testers can then determine if it is the medicine that brings about a change, not the expectations of the ill persons being treated.

In studying the causes of behavior, a scientist looks at a specific response, identifies it, studies it for consistency and frequency, and tries to determine its relationship to a stimulus. These responses can be either bodily movement that can be observed, verbal behavior, or physiological reactions such as chemical or electrical action within the body. **Consistency** must be considered to see if the behavior is common to all of a species, only to individual members or to all organisms. **Frequency** of a behavior is measured as is **intensity** (the amount of energy released by a physical, chemical or electrical response), and **latency** (the time lapse between the introduction of the stimulus and the response).

The growth and development that must take place before a behavior can occur is called **maturation**. In studying maturation, scientists look at three groups of structures: the **receptors** (sense organs), the **effectors** (muscles and duct glands) and the **adjustors** (nervous system and endocrine glands). The functioning of each of these groups depends upon the structure; if the structure is malformed, the function will not occur as well as if the structure were sound. Maturation has been studied in a number of ways: by direct observation, by comparison of species (human babies and young chimpanzees) and by comparison of twins (one trained, one not trained for specific behaviors).

Psychological tests are used to measure samples of behavior. Most psychological data is scaled by **ordinal numbers**, that is, the number assigned to each subject represents the order in which it belongs. If subject number 1 is the least intelligent and number 10 is the most intelligent, observers would know the rank order of the rest. This system does not tell the observer the degree of difference between the subjects. **Nominal scales** are used to differentiate between categories, but like ordinal numbers, do not indicate the degree of difference. **Interval scales** categorize, order and indicate degree of difference, but do not give ratios. Only **ratio scales** categorize, order and give equal intervals and ratios, and are used primarily in measuring physical properties such as loudness or brightness.

Psychological tests can test directly for achievement or inferentially for aptitude or intelligence. Test items are the independent variables, answers are the dependent variables and other factors affecting the test are controlled. **Raw test scores** (what a person obtains) are compared to **norms** (objective standards derived from administration of the test to a representative sample, or test standardization). To account for errors within the test itself, the **reliability** (consistency) and **validity** (truthfulness of the test) are determined by comparison of test scores.

Descriptive statistics are used to collect, organize and describe data. A frequency distribution indicates frequency of scores; this information can be plotted to give a polygon or histogram.

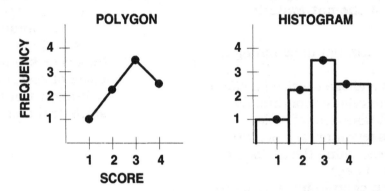

The normal probability curve is a polygon with a theoretical curve representing distribution by chance; it is often called the **bell curve**. If this curve is off-center, it is skewed.

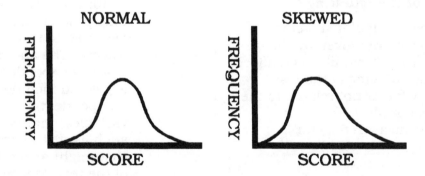

The **mean** is the number representing the common average; the **median** is the number representing the middle score; the **mode** is the number representing the score appearing most frequently. These measures are used to indicate central tendency. Measures of variability indicate the way in which scores vary within a distribution; one of the most useful is the **standard deviation** (SD), which indicates the degree of deviation of each score from the mean. The smaller the SD, the closer the scores are to the mean. Measures of correlations describe the relationship between sets of measures quantitatively.

Inferential statistics allow the scientist to make generalizations from his data and to determine the likelihood that he is correct. A random sampling is used so that the group studied is representative of the whole. Where this is not feasible, a controlled sampling is used. A statistic called the **standard error** of the mean is used to be sure that the characteristics of the sample do not vary from those of the whole. The **critical ratio** indicate the significance of the difference between the sample means.

Two methods of study include the cross-sectional and the longitudinal. The **cross-sectional** method studies people within specific age groups for certain characteristics, attitudes, etc. The **longitudinal** method studies the same individuals over a long period of time.

Before going on with the review, try these sample CLEP questions:

ANSWERS:

6. **Which of the following is an example of the naturalistic method?**

   (A) a psychiatrist questioning a patient
   (B) a psychologist testing a client
   (C) an interviewer conducting a blind taste test of soda
   (D) a conservationist observing and recording the actions of a herd of deer
   (E) a man conducting a door-to-door poll

6. (D) The naturalistic method studies the species in the natural habitat. A psychiatrist questioning a patient would be a case study method. The psychologist, interviewer and poll-taker would all be using statistical methods.

7. **In an experiment, the independent variable would be which of the following?**

   (A) the manipulated factor
   (B) the answer given by the test
   (C) any factor at all which affects the outcome of the test
   (D) any factor not related to the test at all
   (E) the measured factor

7. (A) The independent variable of an experiment is always the factor that can be manipulated, changed or designed to test for a certain feature. The answer given by a test is a dependent variable. (C) would include both independent and situation variables, that is, elements such as distracting noises that might affect the outcome of the test. Measured factors are the dependent variables.

114

8. **The receptors would include which of the following structures?**

   (A) the heart
   (B) the spinal cord
   (C) the pituitary gland
   (D) the muscles
   (E) the nose

9. **The scale most frequently used in psychological tests is which of the following?**

   (A) ordinal
   (B) nominal
   (C) interval
   (D) ratio
   (E) none of the above

10. **An example of a direct test would be which of the following?**

   (A) an intelligence test
   (B) an achievement test
   (C) an aptitude test
   (D) A and B
   (E) B and C

11. **A histogram is which of the following?**

   (A) a frequency polygon
   (B) a visual representation of frequency distribution
   (C) the normal probability curve
   (D) a measure of variability
   (E) a measure of correlations

12. **The standard deviation is which of the following?**

   (A) the mean
   (B) the median
   (C) the mode
   (D) the degree of deviation from the mean
   (E) the degree of deviation from the median

8. (E) The nose is a sensory organ. Muscles and the heart (also a muscle) are effectors. The spinal cord and the pituitary gland (known as the master gland because its hormones regulate both growth and other endocrine glands) are adjustors.

9. (A) The ordinal scale is used most frequently in psychological testing. Nominal scales differentiate between categories. Interval scales give degree of difference. Ratio scales give ratios.

10. (B) Only an achievement test is direct. Intelligence and aptitude tests are inferential. The score on an achievement test tells what has been achieved. Intelligence and aptitude tests tell potential ability.

11. (B) A histogram is a visual representation of frequency distribution; a polygon is another type of representation of frequency distribution. The normal probability curve is theoretical representation of chance distribution. Measures of variability and correlations are descriptive statistics used to summarize data.

12. (D) The standard deviation is a measure indicating the degree of deviation of the scores from the mean.

13. **A cross-sectional survey would study which of the following?**

(A) a student's reading scores through all of elementary school

(B) a worker's income throughout his lifetime

(C) the mating habits of wild ducks

(D) the attitudes of thirteen year old males toward school

(E) the childhood memories of a patient

13. **(D)** A cross-sectional survey would be most likely to be used in studying the attitudes of thirteen year old males toward school. Longitudinal surveys would be useful in studying reading scores through elementary years and lifetime income of individuals. Naturalistic method would be used to study wild ducks. Case study method would be used to record childhood memories.

PSYCHOLOGICAL APPROACHES

There is a variety of approaches that psychologists can take in explaining human behavior. Some schools of thought place different emphasis on mental and physical aspects, while others argue the relative importance of the environment on the individual. Four of the basic views include **behaviorism**, **Freudian psychology**, **structuralism** and **humanism**.

Behaviorism developed because of the difficulty in cataloging and studying introspection, the method used by the early structuralists. Pavlov and his classic experiment with salivating dogs illustrates the process of **classical conditioning**. The dogs were conditioned to respond by the combination of two stimuli, the food and the sounding of the bell. In this case, food is the unconditioned stimulus and salivation the unconditioned response. The bell is the conditioned stimulus because it could cause salivation after combination with the food. The salivation at the sound of the bell is the conditioned response.

Stimulus generalization is the subject's response to a similar stimulus; in this case, a buzzer might provide the same stimulus. **Stimulus discrimination** is the subject's ability to discern similar stimuli. **Extinction** is a process which can eliminate the conditioned response as is **desensitization**; ringing the bell without presenting food will eventually cease to cause salivation, an example of extinction.

Watson was one of the leaders of psychology placing emphasis on such observable behavior. **Operant (or instrumental) conditioning** is a form of behaviorism which states that learning is achieved by reinforcement. **Edward Thorndike**, and more recently, **B. F. Skinner** have contributed to this theory. The **reinforcement principle** states that if a response is followed by a reinforcing stimulus, the likelihood increases that that response will occur. The **operant level** is the normal number of times that a behavior will occur before reinforcement. Skinner designed a container called the **Skinner box** in order to demonstrate operant conditioning. A rat placed in such a box with nothing to do will eventually press the bar in the box; the frequency with which it occurs is the operant level. By a process called **shaping**, the rat learns to press the bar because it yields reinforcement, a pellet of food. Food is given only after the rat has behaved in specific ways, pressing the bar with two paws, for example. Reinforcement must follow the behavior immediately or else extinction will occur.

Primary reinforcers can work in two ways, either to increase pleasure or to decrease pain. **Secondary reinforcers** are used to get to primary reinforcers such as chips received by an animal for pressing a lever used in turn to "buy" pellets of food. **Positive reinforcers** increase the frequency of behavior and give the subject what it wants. **Negative reinforcers** increase the frequency of behavior but allows the subject to avoid a stimulus it does not want. **Punishment** is different from negative reinforcement because it is presented after a response, not before it, and it usually decreases the frequency of a response. In real life situations, continuous reinforcement does not usually exist; **intermittent reinforcement** is much more likely. It can occur at fixed intervals of time or a ratio schedule based on number of responses; the time or number of responses needed for reinforcement can also be made to vary.

Skinner's theories have been proven in the laboratory; he believes that they apply to humans and that people do not truly have free will. His theories do not explain, however, the complexity of human behavior. An approach that does not view man as a machine is **Freudian psychology**, named after **Sigmund Freud**. Freud was a medical doctor who treated patients for hysteria. His knowledge of the autonomic nervous system contributed to his theories. The sympathetic system of the nervous system mobilizes the body while the parasympathetic slows it down. **Libido** is growth energy and is released by behaviors which reduce tension or stress. By using **free association** with his patients he learned that much of the libido's energy is sexual in nature. This talking cure is called **psychoanalysis**, and it revealed to Freud that many conflicts arise because biological urges are frustrated by society's rule.

Freud believed that many problems occurred because society repressed many of our biological urges.

Freud outlined three levels of the mind, the **conscious** which contains thoughts and memories which can now be described, the **preconscious** which is the border line between the conscious and the third level, the **unconscious** which holds thoughts and memories that a person can neither recall nor express. Freud also described the **id, ego** and **superego** as parts of the mind. The id contains all the biological urges of the libido, does not know right from wrong and acts on the principle of seeking pleasure. The ego contains the thought processes used to meet the needs of the id in a rational way; it develops as the child gets older. The superego contains the conscience and a picture of the ideal self; it opposes the id. When the child adopts the values of his parents and society, the superego helps to resolve earlier conflicts. Unnatural attachments, or **fixations**, to ways of seeking pleasure and satisfaction may occur in the oral (sucking), anal (bowel), or phallic (genital) stages if the child is not satisfied.

An **inferiority complex** is a feeling of inadequacy experienced by a child who feels powerless; **Alfred Adler** described this condition. **Erik Erickson** has proposed psychosocial stages of child/adult development which place more emphasis on the environment than on biological urges.

Despite the shift to behaviorism and Freudian psychology, scientists such as **George Kelly** returned to the **structuralist, or cognitive, approach**. This viewpoint sees people as scientists who act according to the way they perceive and interpret a stimulus, not just out of pure reaction to the stimulus. Concepts, or constructs, are thoughts which classify stimuli. Examples of a concept share characteristics known as relative attributes.

There are two ways to learn concepts, one by seeing examples and being told the concept, the other by testing hypotheses about the characteristics of the concept; this second method is more efficient because the person can be selective and can look for other relative attributes. This approach suggests that people are primarily searchers of information seeking to form new concepts. In doing so they develop strategies of either focusing on one or more attributes at a time or scanning one or more hypotheses at a time. With practice and experience, people tend to focus on attributes when solving logic problems. The more attributes there are, the more complex the concept; however, if some attributes are more important, the concept can be identified more readily. Concepts which have conjunctive rules are easier to learn. Learning concepts through language tends to be **deductive** (given the concept, the student is then asked for examples) rather than **inductive** (given examples, the student is then asked for the concept).

Kelly views behavior as the result of learning concepts. New environments and situations present new concepts, and therefore some anxiety, but these become situations for learning new concepts and adapting.

Humanism, unlike the other approaches discussed, focuses on emotional growth and the qualities that make people human. There is no one humanistic approach, but a number of psychologists have made contributions including **Carl Rogers** and **Abraham Maslow**. Because emotions are centered upon, some researchers do not consider the humanistic approach scientific. Carl Rogers developed the notion of unconditional positive self-regard. A baby experiences this when he is loved and nurtured unconditionally. When judgment is made of a child because of his actions, he develops a conditioned worth and learns to act to please others. Since this child needs to please others in order to feel good about himself, his positive self-regard is lowered. As he grows, this child will not take risks for fear of losing the approval of others. A healthy person has positive self-regard.

Maslow developed the concept of the self-actualizing person which is based on a hierarchy of needs ranging from basic biological requirements to those which make life truly worth living when fulfilled. Both Maslow and Rogers studied healthy people (as opposed to Freud) in conducting their studies. Humanists concentrate on understanding the behavior of individuals, not predicting or controlling those behaviors or logical thinking processes.

Before going on with the review, try these sample CLEP questions:

Questions 14 through 18 refer to the following list:

I. Freud
II. Pavlov
III. Skinner
IV. Kelly
V. Rogers

ANSWERS:

14. **Who of the above is associated with the term "positive self-regard"?**

    (A) I
    (B) II
    (C) III
    (D) IV
    (E) V

14. (E) Carl Rogers originated the concept of positive self-regard.

15. **Who of the above would be most likely to describe people as scientists in their thinking processes?**

    (A) I
    (B) II
    (C) III
    (D) IV
    (E) V

15. (D) George Kelly belongs to the structuralism school of psychology which views people as scientists in their thinking processes.

16. **Who of the above is often called the Father of Psychoanalysis?**

    (A) I
    (B) II
    (C) III
    (D) IV
    (E) V

16.(A) Sigmund Freud is often called the Father of Psychoanalysis.

17. **Who of the above studied reflexive responses in explaining behaviorism?**

    (A) I
    (B) II
    (C) III
    (D) IV
    (E) V

17. (B) Ivan Pavlov was the behaviorist who studied reflexive responses.

18. Who helped to develop the concept of reinforcement?

(A) I
(B) II
(C) III
(D) IV
(E) V

18. (C) B. F. Skinner helped to develop the concept of reinforcement.

19. Which of the following is the role of the ego?

(A) to contain the energy of the libido
(B) to act as a buffer zone between the conscious and the unconscious
(C) to seek pleasure
(D) to oppose the id
(E) to meet the needs of the id in a rational way

19. (E) The role of the ego is to meet the needs of the id in a rational way. The id seeks pleasure and contains the energy of the libido; the superego, the seat of conscience, opposes the id. The preconscious acts as a buffer zone between the conscious and unconscious.

20. Which of the following is an example of the cognitive approach?

(A) emphasis on human emotions
(B) action based on perception of stimulus
(C) direct reaction to stimulus
(D) emphasis on the environment
(E) emphasis on reinforcement

20. (B) The cognitive, or structural, approach states that behavior is based on the person's perception of the stimulus. Humanism emphasizes human emotions and the effects of the environment. Classical conditioning studies the direct reaction of an organism to a stimulus; so does operant conditioning, but this approach includes emphasis on reinforcement.

MOTIVATION

In the study of behavior, **motivation** is the reason for an action. Every response is motivated, whether it is a reflex response or the more complex response of solving a problem. All living things exhibit signs of motivation which become more complex the more complex the organism.

Tropism is the simplest form of behavior; it is the movement of an organism away from or toward a stimulus. Usually found in plants and insects, tropism can take several forms, such as phototropism, which is movement away from or toward light, or geotropism, which is movement in relation to the force of gravity.

A **reflex response** is the automatic reaction of a muscle or gland (effectors) to a stimulus. Groups of muscles may also be involved. This response is found in all complex organisms including man. Examples of the reflex response include the knee-jerk reflex, sneezing, yawning and withdrawal from pain. Some reflex responses can be conditioned.

Instinctive behavior is a pattern of action with which the organism is born. Migration, nest-building and mating are examples of instinctive behavior; the information is passed genetically from generation to generation and tends to be specific to species and the same for all members. This behavior is more complex than reflex response, but not as influenced by experience as in more complex forms of behavior. Imprinting is an example of experience affecting instinct and can be seen in young chicks and ducklings. Whatever moving stimulus a newly-hatched chick is presented with, that object will be followed by the chick, be it its mother, a toy truck or a man.

Physiological drives are more complex than instinctive behaviors. A drive is a state of internal arousal caused by a physical need. It is different from instinct because the drive is frequently caused by a learned stimulus and satisfied with a learned pattern of behavior. Sexual drive is an example of this behavior.

Acquired drives are behaviors guided by learned habits and values. They may have their roots in physiological drives but are removed from direct contact with physiological stimuli. For example, the need for food is basically a physiological drive which can be satisfied in a number of learned ways; the need for money to buy food is an acquired drive.

Activation is a general state of arousal that is essential to most motivation. It releases the energy necessary for activity by working through the nervous system, the brain and certain glands.

Before going on with the review, try these sample CLEP questions.

ANSWERS:

21. **Which of the following is movement away from or toward light?**

(A) reflex response
(B) phototropism
(C) geotropism
(D) galvanotropism
(E) none of the above

21. (B) Phototropism is movement away from or toward light. Plants act in this way as do cockroaches. Geotropism is movement in relation to gravity's forces; galvanotropism is movement with regard to electric current. Reflex response is a reaction to a stimulus by a muscle or a gland.

22. **Which of the following is an example of a reflex response?**

(A) moving your hand away from intense heat
(B) migration
(C) mating
(D) hunger
(E) desire for money

22. (A) Moving your hand away from intense heat is a reflex response. Migration and mating are instinctive behaviors. Hunger is generally a physiological drive; desire for money is an acquired drive.

23. **Habits and values are most important in which type of response listed below?**

   (A)   reflex
   (B)   tropism
   (C)   instinctive behavior
   (D)   physiological drive
   (E)   acquired drive

23. (E)   Habits and values are most important in acquired drives because these needs are learned and may be only indirectly related to more basic drives and needs.

PERCEPTION

Sensation is the psychological effect of a stimulus acting upon a sense organ and interpreted by the brain. For example, eyes are the receptors of light; the effects of light are detected by the eye, carried by the optic nerve to the cerebral cortex where light may be interpreted as color. **Perception** is response to a stimulus which uses other information besides the stimulus itself, such as other stimuli present at the moment or stored stimuli. A dress may be red; judging by other red dresses around it which are different shades, the shopper may call it fire-engine red. Judging from past experience, the shopper may think this color does not suit her.

Perception influences human behavior, and there are several types of perception. **Figure-ground perception** is based on changes of stimulation at the edges of figures. The print on this page is an example; the black print stands out from the white paper. Forms and patterns also help perception. Contrast is another aid to perception. Most perceptions occur within a frame of reference, that is, a background or environment that helps to determine the perception. An illusion is a false perception. In order to reconcile the pattern of stimulation at the receptor (**proximal stimulus**) with the actual pattern of stimulation in the real world (**distal stimulus**), complex mechanisms, some in-born and some acquired, go into action. For example, an apple is three dimensional but human retinas are equipped to handle only two. In perception of motion, stability is perceived because of compensation; even though the eye moves, surroundings remain stable. Motion is perceived correctly because of rational analysis; a person in a moving car "sees" the sun follow him, but he knows that this is an illusion.

Perception of constancy is achieved by judging the object in relation to a frame of reference. In a candle-lit room, a fire-engine red dress would be subdued; in sunlight it would be bright. Having binocular vision helps humans with depth perception, but other cues such as **interposition**, (nearer objects have unbroken lines), **linear perspective** (railroad tracks appear to converge), shadows and difference of texture are other aids. Infants have these mechanisms to some degree, but it appears that many develop more fully as they get older. All these perceptions are interrelated and judgments are made so quickly that humans are usually not conscious of all the "decisions" made in perception.

Identification of people and objects is based on experience; man constantly labels and classifies. **Redintegration** is the ability to perceive objects from incomplete information, such as four dots forming a square if placed properly. **Prejudice** is a perception based on irrelevant cues, insufficient or incorrect information; this creates problems in interpersonal relationships. **Perceptual set** is the influence of needs, motives and values on perception which can increase or decrease the likelihood of a behavior. If the shopper thinks the red dress is too bright, or inappropriate for the occasion, or if she already owns a red dress, she probably will not buy it even if it is, objectively speaking, the best dress for her. Perceptual set is learned, for it is based on the past experience of the individual.

Before going on with the review, try these sample CLEP questions:

24. **Which of the following best describes sensation?**

    (A) a physical effect
    (B) a psychological effect
    (C) a frame of reference
    (D) A and B
    (E) B and C

24. (A) Sensation is a physical effect, the result of stimulation upon a receptor of the body. Perception is a psychological effect, a response to a stimulus using additional information.

25. **A silhouette of a child's head is which type of perception?**

    (A) frame of reference
    (B) constancy
    (C) depth
    (D) form-ground
    (E) none of the above

25. (D) A silhouette of a child's head is an example of form-ground perception. Frame of reference is background or context which helps to determine perception. Perception of constancy is the ability to recognize objects even though stimulation may be inconstant. For example, move your finger closer to your eye and the finger appears to grow larger. Perception of depth is the ability to make judgments about a three-dimensional world with eyes that see in two dimension.

26. Perception of constancy is achieved by which of the following?

(A) compensation
(B) proximal stimulus
(C) frame of reference
(D) rational analysis
(E) prejudice

26. (C) Perception of constancy is achieved by a frame of reference. Compensation is the complex, automatic system which gives stability of perception even as the eyes move about. Proximal stimulus is the pattern of stimulation at, for example, the retina of the eye. Frame of reference is context. Rational analysis is the process whereby an object perceived as moving is known to be stable. Prejudice is perception based on incomplete or incorrect information.

27. The ability to perceive objects from incomplete information is which of the following?

(A) perceptual set
(B) redintegration
(C) identification
(D) recognition
(E) prejudice

27. (B) Redintegration is the ability to perceive an object from incomplete information (or insufficient stimuli). Perceptual set is the influence of needs, motives and values on perception. Identification and recognition are responses to a concept. Prejudice is a misconception of reality.

DEVELOPMENT

In order for behavior to occur, the organism must be able to receive stimuli, be able to react to stimuli, and be able to coordinate these processes. The human body is equipped with sense organs, muscles and duct glands, and a nervous system and endocrine glands to carry out behaviors. The structure of the organism will indicate how it will function. Humans behave in more complex ways than do lower animals for this reason. Maturation of the body structure must occur before any behavior can take place; this is an important fact to remember when rearing children. The environment also plays a role in the development of behavior. A child will learn to speak the language of his parents.

Heredity, too, is influential in development. A child of English-speaking parents may have inherited genetically the ability to learn a second language at a young age. If, however, he is not tutored, he will not acquire the language even though he has the ability. These potential abilities depend upon the structure of the organism and the environment. At conception the organism consists of a single cell complete with the genetic information it needs. Even after a few divisions, the cells are still undifferentiated. Normally, however, the cell divides and subdivides until chemical changes, pressures from the cells themselves and electrical changes cause the various cells to differentiate and become specific structures, e.g., bones, organs, glands, muscles. The human organism will react to stimuli in a head-to-tail fashion (**cephalocaudal**) when the embryo becomes a fetus, about eight weeks after conception. Limbs become capable of movement independent of the trunk about fourteen weeks after conception; this movement is called the **proximodistal sequence**.

Both head-to-tail and shoulder-to-finger development sequences continue after birth. A baby will lift his head before it can raise his torso with his arms; he will reach for things before he can grab them well in his hand. Thus development of behavior follows the gradual development of the nervous system and other structures. However, this does not apply to all behaviors. Studies indicate that creeping and walking will occur spontaneously under normal conditions without training, but activities such as bicycle-riding and reading, which are not characteristic of the species, must be learned. Training will not have a positive effect until the child has matured enough to benefit from training. Training before maturation may even have negative effects such as frustrating the child.

With this in mind, educators have developed **maturational norms**; for example, most kindergartens require that the child be five years of age. While norms are useful for most children, each child should be assessed individually because rate of maturation differs from child to child and from structure to structure. Such detailed assessment may not, however, be possible. For some children, the **critical period**, that is, the time when maturation has occurred and the effects of training will be maximized, might be missed. A child not trained at this point might not learn to his potential. Educators have tried to take these points into account with assessment tests for school-readiness and reading-readiness.

Before going on with the review, try these sample CLEP questions:

ANSWERS:

28. **In order for a behavior to occur which of the following must occur?**

    (A) The organism must have the ability to receive stimuli.
    (B) The organism must be able to react to stimuli.
    (C) The organism must be able to coordinate these processes.
    (D) The organism must have reached the necessary point of maturation.
    (E) All of the above.

28. (E) All of the conditions listed must be met before behavior will occur.

29. Which of the following describes a cephalocaudal sequence?

(A) shoulder-to-finger
(B) thigh-to-toe
(C) toe-to-thigh
(D) head-to-tail
(E) tail-to-head

29. (D) A cephalocaudal sequence moves from head-to-tail, a proximodistal sequence begins at the point where the limb meets the trunk and then extends to regions at the end of the limb.

30. A baby learning to pull himself up by raising his head and chest is showing which type of sequence?

(A) proximodistal
(B) prehensive
(C) cephalocaudal
(D) postnatal
(E) Moro

30. (C) A baby raising himself up on his arms is showing a cephalocaudal sequence. The prehensive response is grasping. Postnatal means the time after birth. The Moro reflex is a baby's response when startled; his head falls backward and he throws out his arms and extends his legs.

31. Frustration is most likely to occur in which of the following instances?

(A) teaching a ten-year-old child with linguistic ability a second language
(B) teaching a four-year-old how to ride a tricycle
(C) toilet-training a three-month-old child
(D) helping a fourteen-month-old child to walk
(E) none of the above

31. (C) Most three-month-old babies can not sit up, and so, to try to toilet-train them would be frustrating to them (and the parent). The other behaviors are in keeping with maturational ability factors.

CONFLICT AND ADJUSTMENT

Man is a creature that has needs and drives and sets goals to meet them. When he is prevented from achieving these goals, he experiences **frustration**. This state of being results in **stress**, an organized pattern of response in the body to resist threat or injury. Sometimes this is called the **fight or flight response** because the body gears up to either confront the source of stress or run away from it. Frustration can arise from many sources including the physical environment, society and its rules, or a person's conflict of motives. Man has been somewhat successful in controlling his physical environment, although slums do exist and disasters such as earthquakes and war do occur. He has not been as successful in exerting control over society; instead, society tends to control individuals. Since there are many options and choices that man has to make for himself, often under societal pressure, he frequently experiences conflict and, therefore, frustration. **Culture Shock** and **Future Shock**, for example, are sources of frustration and stress because new situations (e.g., new technology) require new responses (e.g., retraining, new job, new location). Experience and information about a new situation help to reduce stress.

Psychologists have studied and outlined three basic **types of conflict**, approach-approach, avoidance-avoidance, and approach-avoidance. The **approach-approach** conflict occurs when the person is faced with two attractive choices. Since one may be slightly more attractive or better known or understood by the person, the choice is usually not difficult. Frustration, if there is any, is short-lived. In the **avoidance-avoidance** conflict, the person has to choose between two unattractive situations. Usually an outside force is requiring the choice, not personal motives. Sometimes the person will attempt to escape the choices or somehow alter the situation and relieve frustration. Frustration can also be relieved by making a choice (the lesser of two evils). If a choice is not made and the situation not escaped or changed, frustration will continue. An action that will have both positive and negative results is an **approach-avoidance** conflict. In this situation, frustration tends to last because doing the action can be neither postponed nor escaped. Joining a club may be fun, but the person may not be accepted by the members. In order to join, the person must run the risk of not being liked. This type of conflict is the most common, especially for adults, is the most difficult to solve, and tends to be the most frustrating. As models, of course, these three descriptions tend to be simplifications.

The behavior that arises from frustration can be better understood by examining the source of frustration, the drives that are being thwarted, and the responses displayed by the person. If a person is frustrated close to the goal, he is likely to try again. If he has dealt with a similar frustration before, he can handle this situation better. If frustration is severe and prolonged, apathy, or inertia, may set in. The emotional responses to the frustration itself may initiate new drives and sources of frustration (such as being angry with yourself for being angry).

Coping responses, which an individual develops because of reinforcement and other factors, include aggression, withdrawal and defense mechanisms. **Aggression** is physical or verbal attacks on people or things, but it can also be passive, as in ignoring another. Physical aggression is frowned upon by some parts of society and, if produced, can arouse feelings of guilt in the aggressor. Angry aggression can release strong emotions. Sometimes aggression can be displaced, and anger can spread to other frustrations great and small. Chronic emotional aggression is hostility.

Withdrawal is the retreat from a source of frustration. Since no direct satisfaction can be gained from this behavior, the reinforcement is negative; there is escape from threat. Indirectly, there may be some satisfaction because another drive is satisfied, e.g., a child will not fight a bully (withdrawal) which will please his mother, who disapproves of fighting. Withdrawal does reduce fear, a reinforcing aspect. **Anxiety** is generalized fear. **Phobia** is fear of something that is usually not dangerous. Like physical aggression, fear is frowned upon by society, especially in males. Fear and withdrawal are adaptive responses at times, as when threatened by a robber with a gun.

Defense mechanisms are a series of coping behaviors which people employ to avoid anxiety, fear and other emotional responses to frustration. These responses tend to distort reality and are used by normal and abnormal people alike. Sigmund Freud studied these responses because his methods for helping people required that they talk about past experiences. **Repression** is the forgetting of significant events which have been painful. These thoughts are inhibited from passing into consciousness because of the emotions they would awake. **Reaction formation** is the concealing of unacceptable desires by acting in a way that is opposite to the person's true motivations. A mother who has angry feelings toward her child may spoil him with toys. **Fantasy** is daydreaming which is a universal behavior, but which becomes troublesome when used excessively to avoid dealing with a problem. **Displacement** is venting anger upon a substitute person or object. **Projection** is avoiding unacceptable desires in the self by assigning them to others and then condemning them. **Rationalization** is avoiding one's shortcomings and failures by explaining the behavior in logical, acceptable ways. **Regression** is the turning to childhood behavior when faced with frustration, e.g., a temper tantrum.

Before going on with the review, try these sample CLEP questions:

32. Future Shock could best be described by which of the following?

(A) frustration caused by societal traditions

(B) frustration caused by new technologies

(C) frustration caused by travel to a foreign country

(D) frustration caused by parental demands

(E) all of the above

33. Which of the following is an example of approach-approach conflict?

(A) choice between a movie and a play

(B) buying a dress which is too expensive

(C) choice between two equally unattractive job offers

(D) eating ice cream which has excessive calories

(E) choice between finishing a boring job or being reprimanded by the boss

ANSWERS:

32. (B) Future Shock is frustration and stress caused by the new technologies. The changes are happening at a fast rate, and people are having difficulty adapting to some aspects. Culture Shock can be the result of travel to a foreign country or different region of one's own country. Societal traditions and parental demands cause frustrations but have been with us for centuries.

33. (A) An approach-approach conflict represents two attractive goals, in this case, a play or a movie. The dress and the ice cream would present an approach-avoidance conflict. The job offers and the boring task/reprimand are examples of avoidance-avoidance conflicts.

34. **Apathy can best be described by which of the following?**

(A) anxiety
(B) frustration
(C) inertia
(D) stress
(E) conflict

34. **(C)** Apathy is inertia, the inability to act as a result of excessive frustration as seen in wartime bombed-out cities. The other items can contribute to an apathy-producing situation.

35. **Ignoring the request of another to prevent them from doing their job is an example of which of the following?**

(A) withdrawal
(B) repression
(C) reaction formation
(D) aggression
(E) projection

35. **(D)** Ignoring another to hurt him is passive aggression. Withdrawal is escape from coping with a conflict. Repression is the inhibition of recollection of past events. Reaction formation is avoiding fear or guilt by acting the opposite of what one really feels. Projection is pinning the faults one has on others and then condemning them.

36. **A person who takes excessive risks to cover up his fears is displaying which behavior?**

(A) repression
(B) regression
(C) rationalization
(D) reaction formation
(E) displacement

36. **(D)** Taking an excessive risk to disguise fear is reaction formation. Regression is reverting to childhood behavior. Rationalization is making excuses for faults with "logical" arguments. Displacement is kicking the dog when angry with mother.

PERSONALITY

Personality is the organized behavior of an individual, combining his development, motives, intelligence, conflicts and adjustments. In studying personality, psychologists look for themes and recurring patterns of behavior because it would be impossible to catalogue every single aspect of an individual's personality. Through the years, categorizing people by type (**typology**) has been done by many. In ancient Greece, **Hippocrates**, the Father of Modern Medicine, grouped people according to four basic body fluids, called **humors**: blood was associated with cheerful people; phlegm with calm, accepting people; yellow bile with hot-tempered people; and black bile with gloomy people. A person's temperament was governed by balance, or imbalance, of these humors. Excess of any would produce the associated characteristic.

While it is known today that the body is not constructed this way, modern scientists have developed other systems for characterizing personality by studying the body. **W. H. Sheldon** built upon Ernst Kretschmer's earlier theories and developed a system based on body types. **Endomorphs** have round, soft body types, tend to be relaxed, sociable and love to eat. **Mesomorphs** have muscular, strong bodies and tend to be energetic, assertive and courageous. **Ectomorphs** have long fragile bodies and tend to be restrained, fearful and artistic. The approaches of Hippocrates and Sheldon are, however, too simple to explain the complex personalities possessed by man.

A second approach is the **study of traits** in order to analyze personality. In this study the psychologist identifies and measures the components of personality, the important qualities of behavior such as intelligence. He also keeps in mind that individuals display different traits under varying circumstances, and so the psychologist looks at how these traits relate to one another. There is not always agreement concerning what should be called a trait. Studies using a clinical approach have outlined basic needs that man has. Theoretical approaches have outlined values held by man. Statistical analysis of the data yielded by the researchers produce polar traits. These extremes, e.g., cheerful versus depressed, are used in personality questionnaires. The trait approach, like the type approach, does not, however, give much information about how people act in real-life situations.

A third approach is one of **dynamics**, of seeing personality as a process. As such, personality is viewed as always developing, interacting with present situations and past influences. Psychoanalysis as developed by Sigmund Freud is an example of the dynamic approach. Freud believed that a healthy personality resulted from successful passage through the oral, anal, phallic stages, through the latency period and into the genital state. The **oral stage** is the infant's interest in sucking, and later biting (0-18 months); the **anal stage** centers on the young child's interest in his bowel movements (18-36 months); the **phallic stage** is characterized by the child's interest in his genitals (3-6 years). He also develops a strong attachment to the opposite-sex parent, wishing the same-sex parent will leave or die; however, fear that the same-sex parent will punish him by castration causes the child to identify with the same-sex parent. In boys this is the **Oedipus complex**, in girls, the **Electra complex**. A further result is that the child enters a **latency period** of decreased sexuality (6-12 years) until puberty brings about the **genital stage** (12-19 years) and interest in sharing love with a member of the opposite sex.

Through the years there has been criticism of Freudian psychoanalysis, but Freud's work did demonstrate man's irrational behavior and his desire to understand it, the importance of sexuality in development and the need to treat mental illness.

Assessment of personality can be done in a number of ways. One method of diagnosis is the **interview**, the gathering of information in a face-to-face setting. The value of the interview depends in part on the interviewer who tries to create an environment where the person is relaxed. Open-ended questioning, which leads the person to talk more about himself, usually yields useful information. Because of the nature of this technique, however, it lacks standardization.

A **rating scale** is an instrument in which the rater makes a judgment about the degree to which a trait is present in a person. While the information yielded can be analyzed statistically, the data are still judgments by the rater. **Personality inventories** are standardized questionnaires to give information about the subject's personality. The information can be studied statistically, but it is information resulting from self-perception which may not be accurate. **Projective tests** are designed to allow the subject self-expression. Examples are the Rorschach Inkblot Test, free association, storytelling, painting and drawing. Because the tests themselves are the same, there is some control and objectivity; responses are, of course, highly individualistic. In doing a personality profile, a psychologist would be likely to use a number of different approaches.

Before going on with the review, try these sample CLEP questions:

ANSWERS:

37. Typology as an approach can use which of the following guidelines?

(A) the dynamics of the personality
(B) categorization of personality by bodily structure
(C) the search for important qualities of behavior
(D) the listing of man's values
(E) the fundamentals of psychoanalysis

37. (B) Typology would include categorization by bodily structure. Psychoanalysis is a dynamic approach which is interested in the process of personality. Traits include important behaviors, needs and values of man.

38. The most objective approach to personality study is which of the following?

(A) psychoanalysis
(B) theoretical approach based on observation
(C) typology
(D) statistical analysis and polar traits
(E) projective tests

38. (D) Statistical analysis is used to develop polar traits tests. Psychoanalysis, theoretical approaches based on observation, and typology are approaches that tend to be subjective (based on the tester's viewpoint). A projective test has some objective qualities (same test) and some subjective qualities (answers are infinite in variety).

39. Which of the following occurs in the Electra complex?

(A) the girl child favors her mother
(B) the girl child imitates her mother
(C) the boy child favors his mother
(D) the boy child imitates his mother
(E) none of the above

39. (B) In the Electra complex, the girl child favors her father, wishes her mother would leave, but because of fear and guilt, imitates the mother. The Oedipus complex affects boys in a similar fashion.

40. **In the phallic stage, which event occurs?**

(A) the child seeks pleasure in sucking

(B) the child has interest in bowel movement

(C) the child decreases his interest in sexuality

(D) the child seeks a loving relationship with a member of the opposite sex

(E) none of the above

40. (E) In the phallic stage, the child has interest in his genitals and experiences the Oedipus/Electra complex.

41. **The Rorschach Inkblot Test is an example of which of the following?**

(A) polar traits questionnaire

(B) projective test

(C) rating scale test

(D) personality inventory

(E) intelligence test

41. (B) This ink blot test is a projective test.

ABNORMALITY

Abnormal psychology is the branch of this science that studies maladjusted and disorganized behavior. It is difficult, however, to separate clearly normal from abnormal behavior. Many behaviors displayed by disturbed people are exaggerations of actions performed to some degree by healthy people. In trying to define abnormality, psychologists have used three basic approaches. The first is **statistical** in nature; behavior is abnormal if it deviates sufficiently from the norm. While this does standardize the term, it does not take into account the direction of deviation, e.g., a very bright person. This approach suggests that the norm is the best. The **theoretical** approach states that the quality of adjustment sets the standard of normality. In this way behavior is abnormal only if it indicates poor adjustment. However, there still is no definitive answer as to what is normal. The third approach is **clinical** and looks for symptoms of abnormality, behavioral disturbances that suggest maladjustment. In this approach, psychologists can look for signs of disturbance, but these are subjective evaluations.

In assessing abnormal behavior psychologists must look at **symptom syndromes**, the grouping of symptoms, because one symptom can indicate many disorders and other symptoms can appear at a later time. The absence of a symptom can also help the diagnosis. Types of behavior disorders include neuroses, psychoses, character disorders and psychosomatic disorders.

A **neurosis** is an emotional disturbance characterized by extreme defensiveness. While all people have defenses, neurotic people develop symptoms of excessive defensiveness which interfere with normal functioning and cause stress. Anxiety is a frequent symptom, but because the neurotic is still anxious despite his defenses, he becomes involved in a vicious cycle, never learning the source of his anxiety. **Phobias** (unwarranted fears), **obsessions** (persistent undesired thoughts), and **compulsions** (urge to carry out certain acts) are additional symptoms displayed by neurotic people. **Depression**, massive repression (**dissociative reaction**) and **conversion reaction** (symbolic resolution of conflict taking the form of an illness) may also be present.

A **psychosis** is a disorder in which the person afflicted is unable to cope with conflict and stress. **Hallucination** (experiencing sensations that are not real) and **delusion** (false beliefs) are two symptoms of psychosis. One type of psychosis is **psychotic depression** in which the person experiences extreme sadness. **Schizophrenia** is characterized by bizarre behavior, emotional withdrawal and illogical thinking. Types of schizophrenia include simple (apathy), hebephrenic (extreme regression), catatonic (bizarre motor behavior) and paranoid (unsystematized delusions). **Paranoia** is a form of psychosis whereby the person believes he is being persecuted by others.

A **character disorder** is a lack of personality development in the area of values, sexual identification or self-control. Symptoms can include antisocial, irresponsible behavior that is not followed by feelings of remorse or guilt. **Psychopathic**, or **sociopathic**, behavior is characterized by antisocial acts; this person may make promises not to repeat such acts and appear to be sincere, but he is basically unsocialized.

Psychosomatic disorders are physical disorders caused by emotional stress. Internal organs are affected and damage may be severe. The person is usually not aware of the condition until damage to the organs is life-threatening. Back pain and ulcers are often psychosomatic.

The causes of many of these disorders is not known, although there is, for example, evidence that some psychoses may have structural causes such as genetic deformation. There are various techniques for treating the symptoms of abnormal behavior. **Somato-therapies** involve medical procedures or some type of physiological technique. From ancient times through the middle ages, **trepanation** was performed, by which a hole was drilled into the skull to allow evil spirits to escape. **Electroshock therapy** reduces symptoms in some people, but the reason why the therapy is successful is not understood. **Psycho-surgery**, particularly the frontal lobotomy, is used in extreme cases of psychosis. **Drug therapy** includes antianxiety drugs such as Valium and Librium, antipsychotic drugs (Thorazine), antidepressants, and antimanic drugs.

Psychotherapy seeks to change behavior in treating disorders. Freudian analysis encourages **free association**, the free flow of thoughts. **Resistance** occurs when the patient comes to a thought that he tries to repress. Freud also analyzed dreams for latent, or hidden, content. **Transference** occurs when the patient transfers feelings held for people in his past to his therapist. It is the therapist's task to analyze the information revealed in the patient's free association, dreams and transference.

Carl Jung developed **analytical psychology** which has a mystical approach and considers symbols of ancient history and ritual. **Carl Rogers'** approach is **client-centered therapy**. Assertiveness training is based on classical conditioning as are programmed learning, modeling (social learning) and biofeedback (learning to control biological activity through the use of electronic devices).

Gestalt therapy encourages people to choose changes that they desire and emphasizes the here and now. Family therapy and group therapy allow families and groups to explore problems and look for solutions through the help of the therapist. Psychodrama encourages behavior changes because it encourages people to play out roles.

Mental health clinics have been established to provide information and services to encourage mental health and to aid those who need assistance.

Before going on with the review, try these sample CLEP questions:

42. In defining abnormality, which of the following is true?

(A) It is difficult to separate normal from abnormal behavior.
(B) Abnormal behavior is always exhibited by one symptom.
(C) Some abnormal behaviors are found in normal people to a lesser degree.
(D) A and B
(E) A and C

43. A neurosis is generally characterized by which of the following?

(A) bizarre behavior
(B) delusions
(C) defensiveness
(D) antisocial behavior
(E) manic-depression reactions

44. Which of the following defines phobia?

(A) massive repression
(B) urges to act
(C) persistent unwanted thoughts
(D) unwarranted fears
(E) none of the above

45. Which of the following therapies is used only in the most extreme cases?

(A) drug therapy
(B) psychosurgery
(C) psychodrama
(D) Gestalt
(E) group therapy

ANSWERS:

42. (E) Both (A) and (C) are correct. Statement (B) is false. Abnormal behavior can have more than one symptom.

43. (C) A neurosis is frequently characterized by defensive behavior. Bizarre behavior, delusions and manic-depressive reactions are characteristics of psychoses. Antisocial behavior is a symptom of a character disorder.

44. (D) A phobia is an unwarranted fear. Dissociation is massive repression, compulsion is the urge to carry out certain acts and obsession is persistent unwanted thoughts.

45. (B) Psychosurgery, such as frontal lobotomy, is used only in extreme cases.

GLOSSARY OF PSYCHOLOGY TERMS

Androgens: the male sex hormones responsible for the development of male characteristics.

Catharsis: an explosive release of feelings.

Compensation: behavior through which a person makes up his feelings of inferiority by substituting one goal for another which seems unrealistic or unreachable.

Cones: parts of the retina responsible for receiving color vision and patterns.

Construct: a concept or idea.

Denial: a defense mechanism in which the person refuses to accept a threatening situation as real.

Drug Dependence: habitual use of drugs to relax or sleep.

Encounter Groups: groups of people who, with a leader, meet to learn how to relate to others openly.

Enuresis: bed-wetting.

Epilepsy: a malfunction of the nervous system.

Estrogens: female sex hormones released by the ovaries.

Extroversion: the quality of being out-going.

Genetics: the study of traits inherited biologically.

Gerontology: the study of aging.

Habituation: the reduction of sensitivity to a stimulus which is repeated.

Homeostasis: the process which keeps body systems balanced.

Hormone: a chemical secreted into the bloodstream which can affect behavior.

Hypoglycemia: low blood sugar, a condition which can affect behavior.

Infantile Autism: a condition of extreme withdrawal in a child.

Mnemonics: techniques to improve memory.

Precognition: knowledge of an event before it occurs.

Psyche: the psychological self; in Greek the word means "soul or mind."

Psychiatrist: medical doctor who can treat the mentally ill through therapy, prescription drugs and other medical procedures.

Psychologist: a specialist who has studied human behavior and emotions.

REM (Rapid Eye Movement) Sleep: the fifth stage of sleep during which the eyes move rapidly and dreaming occurs.

Rods:	parts of the retina responsible for seeing in dim light.
Role:	the expected set of behaviors of a person in a specific position.
Self-fulfilling Prophecy:	a situation in which a person's expectations of a group (such as a teacher and the students) influences the group so that performance meets the expectations.
Sensory Deprivation:	a condition in which the person's sensory organs receive no outside stimulation.
Sex Role Stereotyping:	behaviors expected by society for members of each sex.
Socialization:	the process of learning the customs and behaviors of a culture.
Thyroid:	a gland located in the neck responsible for general metabolism.
Type A and B:	classifications for two personality patterns. Type A people generally smoke, are competitive and impatient, and are more likely to have heart attacks than Type B people. Type B's are much more relaxed and are less likely to develop heart disease.

Economics

Economics is the social science which studies the allocation of goods and services among the population. Generally, it is divided into two classifications, microeconomics and macroeconomics. Microeconomics (small-economics) includes the study of consumer theory (what we buy) and production theory (what we make).

Microeconomics looks at the individual in the market place, or as more recent theory states, it looks at the buying unit, the family. Production is the process of making goods and services available to consumers. Food, clothing and housing are goods. Bankers, doctors and repairmen provide services. In each case, the value of the goods or services is set by the quantity of other goods or services that can be exchanged for it. Since direct exchange (barter) is inefficient for complex exchange systems, money is used. Price of a good or service is the amount of money received for one unit of that good or service.

Macroeconomics (large-economics) examines business decisions, fiscal policy, monetary policy, money and banking, and the business cycle. The factors of production are land, labor and capital. The entrepreneur, or business organizer, makes business decisions. He examines the factors of production and decides how to allocate their use most efficiently. He considers technical knowledge, the division of labor, use of capital and financial opportunities in order to maximize profit.

Fiscal policy is the plan of financial organization and action determined by a government concerning the spending of public revenues. **Monetary policy** is the standards set by a government concerning currency. Deposit currency, money deposited in a bank, is today the main means of payment and supply of money. By writing a check, the depositor orders his bank to pay a certain amount of money to a person, a company or himself. The bank deducts this amount from the deposit and in turn pays the designated receiver either in cash or with credit to his account. The **business cycle** is short-run fluctuations in general prices occurring during periods of business prosperity, recession, depression and recovery. One of the most important problems in economics is the analysis and control of the business cycles, a feat which has not yet been accomplished.

Before going on with the review, try these sample CLEP questions:

1. Microeconomics includes which of the following features?

   I. fiscal policy
   II. business decisions
   III. consumer theory
   IV. family decisions
   V. money and banking

(A) II and III
(B) III and IV
(C) III, IV and V
(D) I and III
(E) all of the above

1. (B) The other items listed are factors of macroeconomics.

2. Which is an example of barter?

(A) depositing a paycheck in your account
(B) exchanging a personal check for a desired item
(C) using cash to purchase a desired item
(D) exchanging three eggs for two heads of lettuce
(E) none of the above

2. (D) Barter is direct exchange and does not involve cash or payment by check.

3. When a government determines a financial plan for spending revenues, it is setting

(A) monetary policy
(B) the business cycle
(C) deposit currency
(D) fiscal policy
(E) financial opportunities

3. (D) Monetary policy determines currency; the business cycle is short-run fluctuations in general prices; deposit currency is money deposited in a bank; businessmen use financial opportunities to maximize profits.

4. **The value of goods and services is set by**

(A) the quantity of other goods and services that can be exchanged for it

(B) the amount of money needed to buy one unit of the goods and services

(C) the amount of land, labor and capital needed to produce the goods and services

(D) the amount of profit the business man desires

(E) all of the above

5. **During the 1930's in the United States, which phase of the business cycle predominated?**

(A) business prosperity

(B) recession

(C) short-run fluctuation

(D) recovery

(E) depression

4. (A) (B) is the price of goods and services; (C) and (D) determine the cost, but if consumers do not want a particular good or service, the value of it will go down.

5. (E) This period in American history is known as the Great Depression.

HISTORY OF ECONOMIC ACTIVITY

Economics studies how scarce goods and services are allocated within a society. Early man simply gathered the food that he needed. As population increased and ready-to-pick food decreased, man became nomadic. His earliest tools were weapons useful in hunting—hatchets and bow and arrows. Eventually, he made tools useful in agriculture—plows and hoes.

As a food-gatherer, man was independent. But as he became involved in hunting, he needed the help of others. In agriculture his need for others grew. The basis of his economy changed from one where he could be totally self-sufficient to one where the group could be totally self-sufficient. Within agricultural society, a **division of labor** (tasks are assigned to members for increased efficiency) and **bartering** (the exchange of, e.g., grain for eggs) developed. This type of economy tended to be traditional. Even today we speak of jobs traditionally held by men (doctors) and women (nurses).

Traditional economics in many societies gave way to **command economics**. In this type there is a central authority which directs the activities of others. The feudal system of the Middle Ages is an example. In return for the protection the lord would give them, the serfs had to work in the fields and give military service. The Crusades and trade eventually broke up this system. It was, however, very efficient. An example of a command economy in the present day is the economic power a government assumes during wartime.

With increase in trade during the 14th century, European countries eventually developed a **market economy**. Competition among traders is the basis; supply (e.g., the amount of items available) and demand (e.g., the amount of items desired) regulate the market. Money became important and merchants united themselves into guilds in order to regulate trade by forming monopolies. Craftsmen later united also and made admittance into their guild more difficult by requiring several years of apprenticeship before becoming a master. Their aim was like that of the merchants, to reduce outside competition.

By the 16th century, these guilds were weakened by the **middleman**, one who would buy raw materials and tools, hire laborers, and then sell the product himself. This is known as the **domestic system**. The rise of nationalism further weakened the guilds and the towns. With the discovery of the New World and its wealth, many European nations, especially England, France, Spain and Portugal, adopted the principles of **mercantilism**. In order to increase national wealth, these nations encouraged colonization, increased military power and sought a favorable balance of trade. They also protected certain industries. Not only did they want gold and other precious metals for their coffers but also the products of the New World colonies (e.g., tobacco, furs and molasses).

The commercial class overseeing these operations became wealthy and began to see that their interests and those of the state were not always the same. In addition, the monarchs themselves were becoming wealthy and powerful, not the state. The response was a policy of **laissez faire**, "leave-them-alone," which held that the state should not interfere with individual activity. Just as the state had exercised close control over economic activity under mercantilism, now it would act only as an umpire to prevent abuses.

Adam Smith wrote *The Wealth of Nations* in 1776 in which he stated that the welfare of the state and the individual would be taken care of by free operation of the market. In other words, if everyone were allowed to follow his own self-interests, the greatest national good would result. The forces of supply and demand plus competition would regulate price to the point of **equilibrium** (supply meets demand at a good price) and everyone would benefit.

This is classical economic theory and, in practice, never completely materializes. Not everyone was free to act in his own self-interest. Governments still enforced laws and regulations and controlled monetary policy. There was no perfectly free market. Changes in the economy also contributed to this. A decrease in land for pasture and improvements in agricultural practices led to the rise of the country gentleman who purchased farmland and pushed out small farmers, many of whom found their way to factories of the Industrial Revolution.

The introduction of machines and use of mechanical power brought about the decline of the domestic system and the rise of the **Industrial Revolution**. Production no longer took place in the home because the machines were large and heavy and needed to be close to the source of their power (water and/or coal). Because England had great accumulated capital as a result of her colonies and foreign trade, her businessmen used these funds to finance industry. Laborers were available because of the changes in agriculture. Transportation increased; roads were improved, turnpikes and canals built, and the railway system begun.

The effects of the Industrial Revolution are many. Production and consumption increased greatly. However, since the laborer's skills were less important than the machine, he could easily be replaced by another laborer who, for example, would work for lower wages. Since laborers were in a poor bargaining position, they were exploited. To offset the laissez faire policy of industry, government stepped in with controls to protect the workers. Laws regulating hours of labor, working conditions and female and child labor resulted. Finally, as cities grew around the industries, so did urban problems. Housing was crowded and filthy, and the factories poured out pollution, all of which ruined the health of many city dwellers.

The ills which were brought about by capitalism were condemned by 19th and 20th century socialists and communists. **Socialism** and **communism** are often used interchangeably but differ in the degree to which the state owns the means of production and regulates economic activity. Under socialism, the state owns natural resources and the means of production in basic industries; they are operated for use by the people, not for profit. Small businesses and industries do exist and people can work for wages, but the government does direct the types of goods and services to be produced. Great Britain is a democratic-socialist state.

Communism is characterized by greater controls. The state owns both producer and consumer goods, and goods and services are allocated to the population according to need. The Soviet Union during the 1980's, owned all land and natural resources; farmers' cooperatives operated farms according to a government plan. There were few private businesses and no private hiring. Trade unions did represent workers but did not bargain as in the free enterprise system. There were restrictions on job choice and the types of products that could be made. Emphasis was on industrial output. The aim of communism is to create a classless, and eventually, a stateless society in which goods and services are distributed equally. Pure communist theory states that this will be achieved through revolution and authoritarian rule. Communism emphasizes the supremacy of the state (the people as a whole) and not the rights of the individual. With the demise of the Soviet Union, the various republics are struggling with privatization and a market economy. It will be years before the economies of these independent nations stabilize.

Before going on with the review, try these sample CLEP questions:

6. **An example of an autonomous, self-sufficient economic order would be**

(A) a man residing alone in a seashore villa
(B) a man residing alone on a deserted island
(C) a man residing alone on a tenant farm
(D) a man residing alone in a city apartment
(E) all of the above

ANSWERS:

6. (B) In (A), (C) and (D) it can be assumed that the man is buying goods (food, clothing, etc.) and services (a maid to clean the villa). Only in (B) is he totally self-sufficient.

7. All of the following are examples of a command economy EXCEPT

(A) government controls during wartime
(B) the feudal system
(C) a communist government
(D) a son learning his father's trade
(E) none of the above

7. (D) While the father is an authority figure, this type of father-to-son economy is based on tradition. A common economy has an authority directing the activities of many.

8. The domestic system depended upon

(A) a middleman who hired laborers and supplied raw materials
(B) a merchants' guild which formed monopolies
(C) a craftsmen's guild which required an apprenticeship
(D) a commercial class which conducted trade
(E) a powerful state which controlled economic policy

8. (A) The other organizations represent different regulating groups.

Questions 9 through 11 refer to the following:

I.   Domestic system
II. Mercantilism
III. Laissez faire
IV. Industrial Revolution
V.   Socialism

9. Which item would be characterized by the least amount of government regulation?

(A) I
(B) II
(C) III
(D) IV
(E) V

9. (C) Laissez faire is a hands-off policy on the part of government.

10. **Which item gave rise to the greatest exploitation of laborers?**

   (A) I
   (B) II
   (C) III
   (D) IV
   (E) V

10. (D) During the Industrial Revolution, many farmers were forced off their land and, therefore, became factory workers. Women and children, who in earlier times had done handicrafts and chores on the farm, were now also forced to work in the factories for a small wage.

11. **Which item was characterized by a strong growth in nationalism?**

   (A) I
   (B) II
   (C) III
   (D) IV
   (E) V

11. (B) As guilds and towns became less important, the nation and its wealth and prestige grew.

12. **One of the problems with classical economic theory is that**

   (A) governments do not enforce regulations
   (B) not everyone is free to act in his own self-interest
   (C) the market is free from restrictions
   (D) prices are determined by market conditions
   (E) individuals can always choose where they want to work

12. (B) In theory, everyone will be able to best serve his self-interest without regulation from governments. This is simply not the case. Governments do make restrictions which limit the freedom of the market, control price and restrict opportunities.

13. **Which system allows ownership of private property while the state owns natural resources and basic industries?**

   (A) Capitalism
   (B) Laissez faire
   (C) Free enterprise system
   (D) Communism
   (E) Socialism

13. (E) Capitalism is based on free enterprise, laissez faire is no government control, and communism does not allow for ownership of private property, only of consumer goods.

CONSUMER AND PRODUCTION THEORIES

Consumption is the using up of goods and services either directly by consumers or indirectly in the production of other goods and services. Consumption is difficult to measure, but rough estimates can be obtained. **Real wages** are one such measure, because they indicate the purchasing power of money wages. If you get a raise, but it just covers the rate of inflation, your real wages have not increased.

How you spend your wages is another measure. Generally speaking, those with higher wages will spend a smaller proportion on food and a higher proportion on clothes and luxuries than those with smaller incomes. Another measure is to compare the **Gross National Product (GNP)**, which is the dollar value of goods and services for a one-year period, to total consumer purchases.

In the market place, consumers let producers know what they want and how much they are willing to spend through prices. The producers who meet the needs of consumers are rewarded with increased sales and increased monetary gains. Consumers try to get the most for their money and producers lower production costs as much as possible.

Producers can also influence consumption through the type of product they offer and through marketing techniques, or sales promotion. Uninformed consumers can make foolish purchases of goods and services of inferior quality; price is not always a reliable indicator of quality. There are several government agencies to protect the consumer, such as the **Federal Trade Commission** and the **Food and Drug Administration**. The **Better Business Bureau** also helps consumers as does **Consumers' Report magazine**.

Maintaining a balance between consumption and production is very difficult. In order to offset losses caused by the consumers' not buying a product, producers maintain inflexible prices. Because these prices are high relative to production costs, people with smaller incomes are unable to buy. As a result, the unequal distribution of wealth and income is increased, and production tends to be greater than consumption. This is the weakness of capitalism.

The producer has two major factors to consider—where to locate and how to structure his organization. The availability of raw materials, power sources, labor, market for his product and the potential for growth help to determine location. Thus, a furniture manufacturer would be likely to locate near a forest with suitable trees, but close enough to a power source and a populated area to supply laborers. He must also have access to transportation so that his product can reach his market. He may form his business into an individual **proprietorship** (a one-man business), a **partnership** (two or more individuals who assume full responsibility for the business), or a **corporation** (a group of owners granted a charter making the group the legal entity, not the individual owners).

The producer in turn presents his product to the market; price for the product is determined in a free market by supply and demand. Consumers usually will purchase more of a product at a lower price, but only the amount that they can actually use (law of diminishing utility). An increase in demand means that consumers are willing to buy more of a product at the given price; a decrease means less. Sellers, on the other hand, usually will sell more of a product at a higher price because they gain more at a high price than a low price for the same quantity, and increased quantity eventually results in diminishing returns. Theoretically, the competitive **market price** can be found at the point of **equilibrium** of demand and supply.

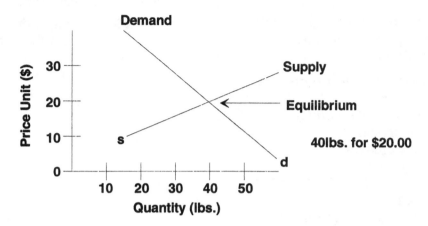

If costs are constant for an industry (that is, the cost of production, labor and material, remains the same), an increase in demand will temporarily raise the price. As new firms enter the industry (demand has increased), the price will eventually fall back to the original level.

If costs increase for an industry, an increase in demand will raise the price to a new level. As new firms enter the industry, the higher price will become permanent. The superior resources of the older firms will also have a higher value. Mining industries and agriculture usually produce in this fashion.

If costs decrease for an industry (improvement in machinery and production methods), an increase in demand will temporarily raise the price. As new firms enter the industry, and old firms expand operations, the price will eventually decrease. Manufacturing industries usually produce in this fashion.

Prices are usually semi-competitive because the pure competitive market exists only in theory. Products vary in style and quality; buyers may not be well-informed. For example, ball point pens vary in style and quality, even though they all serve the same purpose. Yet prices vary. The consumer may buy a certain type out of custom, or habit, because the price has not altered. A ball point pen used by a celebrity would increase in value, and therefore, price. The consumer may buy a certain type because it is available locally or because it is a brand name product.

The price of a monopolized commodity is set by the seller, or group of sellers acting as a unity, by regulating the supply. His profit depends upon the quantity sold and the difference between his costs and his price.

The government determines **fixed prices**, such as the rates a utility may charge. The minimum wage is also a fixed price. The fixing of prices is also done in time of emergency, e.g., war, excessive inflation. It is difficult to fix competitive prices, because some producers might store goods while others are forced out of business.

Before going on with the review, try these sample CLEP questions:

14. **Which of the following do NOT give a rough measure of consumption?**

    (A) real wages and proportion spent on food
    (B) money wages and GNP comparison
    (C) real wages and GNP comparison
    (D) money wages and inflexible prices
    (E) real wages and proportion spent on luxuries

15. **Which of the following statements is correct?**

    (A) Price is always a reliable indicator of quality.
    (B) The consumer is fully protected by the federal government against poor purchases.
    (C) Producers can influence consumption through the type of product they offer.
    (D) Producers maintain inflexible prices to greatly increase demand.
    (E) It is easy to maintain a balance between consumption and production.

16. **The weakness of capitalism is that**

    (A) inflexible prices prevent people with smaller incomes from buying
    (B) corporations remove personal liability from the individual members they represent
    (C) consumers will usually purchase more of a product at a lower price
    (D) sellers will usually sell more of a product at a lower price
    (E) none of the above

14. (D) Money wages do not reflect the effects of inflation. Inflexible prices are prices set by the producer to offset losses.

15. (C) Price is not always a reliable indicator of quality. While the government does have many regulations, a person may nonetheless buy a shirt that does not hold up as well as another might after several launderings. Producers maintain inflexible prices to be sure they stay in the black. It is difficult to maintain a balance between consumption and production.

16. (A) Unequal distribution of income and wealth and the ills that go with it mark the weakness of the capitalistic system.

17. Price for a product in a free market is determined by which of the following?

(A) supply and demand
(B) supply only
(C) demand only
(D) law of diminishing utility
(E) production costs alone

17. (A) Supply and demand go hand in hand in determining price. If people desire an item and it is in short supply, the price will surely go up. Production costs do contribute to price, but if few people want the item, the price will go down.

18. Compact disc players were introduced into the market a few years ago. Methods of production improved, and new firms entered the industry as demand for the sets rose. What has happened to their price?

(A) immediate increase
(B) gradual increase
(C) immediate decrease
(D) gradual decrease
(E) price has remained constant

18. (D) When first introduced, these sets were very costly. More efficient production methods and more competing firms have helped to lower the price.

19. The minimum wage is an example of which of the following?

(A) competitive price
(B) semi-competitive price
(C) monopoly price
(D) fixed price
(E) valuation price

19. (D) The minimum wage is fixed by the Federal Government. A valuation price is determined for goods which are not easy to reproduce and whose future income is expected to be greater than their present value.

20. Buying brand X soap detergent at Y price arises from

(A) custom
(B) uniqueness of the article
(C) location of the article
(D) advertised brand
(E) none of the above

20. (A) Buying this product is largely a matter of custom or habit. Its quality and price are known to the consumer. It is not unique; the buyer would look for it even if it were not seen on the shelf or advertised.

BUSINESS DECISIONS

In developing a business, the entrepreneur combines the factors of land, labor and capital in order to produce output. They can be combined in many ways, for example, more capital (more machines) and less labor. In any case, he is looking to arrive at a least-cost, or most profitable, combination of these factors.

The **cost** of a product is determined by the quantity and price paid for the factors contributing to it. If one of the factors is increased (amount of labor) while other factors remain the same (number of machines), the amount of output will first increase and, as more labor is added, decrease. If one man is in a factory, he will not be able to operate it to its full capacity; adding more laborers will increase its efficiency but only to the point where the **marginal product** (additional product of each laborer) is equal to the **average product** (the average output per worker). Eventually, more men will cause the marginal product to decline because each man is working with less and less equipment in the factory. This is know as the **Law of Diminishing Returns**.

The entrepreneur will also try to use less of the more expensive factors and more of the cheaper ones in order to get the lowest cost per unit. If machinery is expensive and labor is cheap, he will use more labor far into the stage of diminishing returns. If machinery is cheap and labor expensive, he will use less labor, which would be early in the stage of diminishing returns. However, the least-cost combination may not be the most profitable for a business; for example, an increase in demand may mean profits for a business which may have to increase production beyond the least-cost combination. The volume of sales will offset the increased cost. So long as the selling price of additional units (**marginal receipts**) is greater than the cost of added factors (**marginal cost**), the entrepreneur will realize a profit. These adjustments to the production factors in a business are called **factoral proportions**.

The entrepreneur may also seek to expand his business in order to lower the minimum cost of his factors through **specialization**. Each factor is increased and so does the total output. Larger plants can be more efficient, attract better staffs and buy raw materials and production goods in larger quantities. They do require, however, excellent managers. Because smaller firms are easier to manage, there are many.

Marketing is another business decision faced by the business man. **Wholesalers** (jobbers and brokers) buy from the manufacturer and sell to the retailer large quantities of goods. **Retailers** (department and chain stores), in turn, sell to the public above the wholesale price. The marketing agent must assemble goods, store them, classify, advertise and sell them, and finance them. In addition, he must assume the risk of their being destroyed, lost or stolen. To offset risks, he buys insurance. Transportation and its cost are another consideration. He must be able to get his goods to market. A rise in any of the costs of the factors listed above will usually affect the price of the goods.

Before going on with the review, try these sample CLEP questions:

21. The Law of Diminishing Returns states that

(A) the amount of output will first decrease, and then increase, as the variable factor increases

(B) the amount of output will first decrease slightly and then decrease rapidly, as the variable factor increases

(C) the amount of output will first increase slightly, and then increase rapidly, as the variable factor increases

(D) the amount of output will first increase, and then decrease, as the variable factor increases

(E) none of the above

21. (D) For example, as more farmers work on an acre of land, output will increase to that point where the marginal product meets the average product (and the farmers start to get in one another's way).

22. According to the least-cost combination rule of thumb, a business man would do which of the following if equipment were expensive and labor cheap?

(A) use more equipment and less labor

(B) use less equipment and more labor

(C) use equal amounts of labor and equipment

(D) use greater amounts of both labor and equipment

(E) use lesser amounts of both labor and equipment

22. (B) This would represent the least-cost combination.

23. Which of the following is not a feature of large-scale enterprise?

(A) ease of management

(B) greater utilization of waste material

(C) increased division of labor

(D) ability to buy in huge quantities

(E) more diverse staffs

23. (A) It is easier to manage a small-scale business. The remaining answer choices are advantages of large scale enterprise.

FISCAL POLICY

Fiscal policy, or public finance, examines the money that governments spend, the way this money is obtained, and the administration of these funds. **Government economy** is different from private economy in that the government can enforce contributions through taxes, and it is not always required to yield a profit.

Public expenditures have increased dramatically since the turn of the 19th century. Wars and defense, increasing numbers of governmental regulatory boards, and social welfare programs have been the leading causes of this increase. In order to manage this area more effectively, the steps have been taken to classify expenditures more carefully, to create an annual budget system, and to centralize the administration of expenditures.

There are several sources of **government income**, including commercial revenues, administrative revenues, tax revenues, public loans and bookkeeping transfers. **Commercial revenues** used to come largely from the sale of public lands; conservation measures have halted much of this. The United States Printing Office, the United States Post Office and the Tennessee Valley Administration are public industries. **Administrative revenues** include fines (parking tickets), fees (marriage licenses) and special assessments (property improvement).

Taxation raises a relatively large proportion of total revenue. In order to have a reliable tax system, the government must collect a variety of taxes to allow for differing incomes and fluctuations in the market. It must have a convenient collection system and clearly stated laws. This system must be designed to shift if necessary. This last point involves direct and indirect tax. In a **direct tax**, the person charged with it must pay it himself. An **indirect tax** may be shifted, for example, onto the consumer in the form of a higher price; payment of the tax is not coming out of the producer's pocket.

Equitable distribution of the tax burden is an additional test of reliability. Taxes are set according to both the taxing individuals benefits received from the government and his ability to pay. The poor would have to pay more taxes than the rich on a benefits basis, and the rich pay more on ability to pay. Equitable distribution is very difficult to administer fairly. Therefore, a combination of taxes is used. **Progressive taxes** increase in rate as the taxable amount increases (e.g., income tax). **Regressive taxes** decrease in rate as the taxable amount increases (e.g., excise tax). **Proportional taxes** are the same rate for all taxable amounts (e.g., property tax). Use of these taxes helps to reduce inequalities.

Taxes levied by the federal government include custom duties, excise tax (e.g., alcohol, gasoline), personal income tax, federal corporation income tax, and federal estate tax (inheritance tax). State and local taxes include property taxes, consumption taxes (e.g., sales tax), inheritance taxes, business (licenses) and income taxes.

Public borrowing is accomplished through the sale of bonds. The issuing of paper money has been done in times of emergency, but it is generally very risky.

A budget that remains unbalanced for a long period of time is risky because it can cause unstable prices and leaves the government unprepared for future emergencies. In order to promote stability, the general fiscal policy has been that there should be surplus funds in times of opportunity, a balanced budget in times of full employment and stability, and deficit spending in times of low employment. This flexibility is designed to carry the nation through difficult times as they occur in the business cycle. In recent years, deficit spending has increased substantially and attempts are being made to curb this.

Before going on with the review, try these sample CLEP questions:

ANSWERS:

24. **Public finance differs from private enterprise in that it does NOT have to do which of the following?**

    (A) classify expenditures
    (B) pay wages
    (C) maintain bookkeeping for audits
    (D) always yield a profit
    (E) abide by government hiring codes

24. (D) Government does have to classify and account for its spending, follow government guidelines concerning hiring practices and pay its employees. It does not necessarily have to yield a profit in its business organizations.

25. **Selling electricity from a federally owned power plant would provide which of the following?**

    (A) commercial revenue
    (B) administrative revenue
    (C) tax revenue
    (D) public loan
    (E) none of the above

25. (A) The Tennessee Valley Authority is a commercial operation and does yield revenue to the federal government.

26. **An example of a regressive tax would be which of the following?**

    (A) tax on items purchased while in Europe
    (B) tax on business property
    (C) tax on personal income
    (D) tax on corporate income
    (E) sales tax

26. (A) Custom duties are regressive taxes; the higher the taxable amount, the lower the tax rate.

27. **During times of economic growth and plentiful job opportunities, the government should seek to have which type of budget?**

    (A) a balanced budget
    (B) a budget with deficit spending
    (C) a budget with surplus
    (D) a budget with credits equaling debits
    (E) a budget running in the red

27. (C) When times are good, the government should have "extras" to tide the nation over in bad times. (D) is a balanced budget; (E) would require deficit spending.

MONETARY POLICY

Money is anything that can be readily exchanged for anything else as a means of payment. Wampum and tea have been used as money. Coins and bills (cash) are issued by governments. Checks (demand deposits) are most commonly used for payment in the United States.

Precious metals have been used through the years because they are portable, durable, easily recognized and limited in supply. Silver and gold, in particular, are also useful in the arts and in industry. Money functions as a storehouse of value and a medium of exchange. In the United States, gold and silver coins used to be the standard; this system is known as **bimetallism**. In 1934, because of a serious banking crisis, all monetary gold became United States Treasury property. **Fiduciary money** is paper money, the value of which is based on the trust of the people in their government. People sell goods and services to obtain it and can make purchases with it. **Federal Reserve Notes** are fiduciary money; these notes promise to pay standard money to the bearer without fiduciary because their metal value is less than their money value. For example, older silver coins now have a greater bullion (metal) value than a money value. Fiduciary money today is credit money.

The **gold standard** has gold as its standard metal; money value is on par with gold; gold is coined and is legal tender. The **silver standard** is the same, except that silver is the standard metal. A **gold bullion standard** uses gold to set the monetary unit and value of money, but does not allow gold coinage or redeeming of other money for gold. In **bimetallism,** the two metals are valued at a fixed weight which is proportionate to one another. These metals are coined and circulate as full legal tender. Should the market ratio change (e.g., gold's value increases over silver's), the **Gresham Law** comes into play: cheaper money drives more expensive money out of circulation.

When a country prints excessive amounts of paper money, as in times of emergency, purchasing power and confidence in it decline. It is called **fiat money**, or printing press money, even though it is expressed in terms of the specie standard that originally backed it. The **commodity standards** used an index derived from prices of commodities to help determine monetary and credit policy.

MONEY AND BANKING

Since money is made of cheap materials and checks require a banking organization, banking has assumed a major role in our money system. Banks can extend personal, bank or commercial credit, which is a loan of money to an individual, a bank or a businessman with a promise to pay in the future. A **check**, written by the depositor, tells the bank to transfer funds to the person or firm named on the check. The **promissory note** is a simple promise to pay signed by the person receiving the loan; **collateral** (stocks, bonds or other items of value used to guarantee a loan) may or may not be used. A **draft** is an order to pay, written by the agency giving the loan.

There are several types of banks. **Commercial banks** make loans to industry, although they also have services (checking, saving accounts) for private individuals. Loans can be secured by giving a promissory note; in addition to repayment of the principal, the borrower will have to pay interest. In some cases, the loan is discounted, that is, the interest is deducted from the principal at the time the loan is made. Since a depositor can demand his money from a bank, deposits are liabilities of the bank. **Primary deposits** are actual cash, checks and drafts. **Derivative deposits** are created by loans. **Reserves** are the actual cash supply that a bank has to pay depositors. **Securities** are secondary reserves. The rest of its assets are used to make loans; this is the fractional reserve system. A clearing house is a banking organization where the checks from the various banks can be exchanged and accounts balanced. Each bank receives only the net balance due it. Investment banks can offer long-term loans to industry. **Trust companies** act as commercial and investment banks and also perform the duties of a trustee administrator (e.g., hold funds in trust). **Savings banks** use the deposits made and invest them in long-term, low-risk securities. They, too, may offer loans, but usually for private individuals (e.g., mortgages, building loans).

The system of banking in the United States before and during the Civil War was too often unreliable. As a result, the **National Banking System** was instituted in 1864 by the federal government. The structure was weakened, however, by unsound methods of issuing notes and retaining reserves. The **Federal Reserve System** was adopted in 1913, and revised in 1933 and 1935. Its Board of Governors has many powers, including the ability to change reserve requirements, to determine discount rates, to issue or withhold supplies of Federal Reserve Notes, and to regulate interest on time and saving deposits by member banks. Thus, the decisions made by this board affect the availability of loans, interest rates for loans and savings accounts, and the amount of circulating money, which in turn affects the economy at large.

Other measures taken to insure banking stability have been the creation of the **Federal Deposit Insurance Corporation (FDIC)** which insures in part the deposits of member banks; the **Reconstruction Finance Corporation**, which lent money to industry in the 1930's and 1940's (it was terminated in 1954); the **Federal Home Loan Program** and the **Federal Housing Agency (FHA)**; and the **Farm Credit Administration**.

Before going on with the review, try these sample CLEP questions:

Questions 28-30 refer to the following list:

I. Gold Standard
II. Gold Bullion Standard
III. Silver Standard
IV. Bimetallism
V. Fiat

28. In which of the above is gold used as legal tender?

(A) II, III and V
(B) I, II and V
(C) I and II only
(D) I, II and IV
(E) I and IV only

ANSWERS:

28. (E) In the gold bullion standard, gold is used to determine money value, but it is not used as coin.

29. **In which of the above are the two metals valued at a fixed rate which is proportionate to one another?**

(A) I and III
(B) II and III
(C) III and V
(D) IV only
(E) V only

29. (D) In I, II and III, gold and silver are not used in relation to one another.

30. **Which of the above contains the greatest risk to the holder?**

(A) I
(B) II
(C) III
(D) IV
(E) V

30. (E) Fiat is printing press money. It is issued only in emergencies, and its circulation leads to high inflation.

31. **Credit is best defined as which of the following?**

(A) a loan of money to an individual or businessman with a promise to pay in the future
(B) a demand deposit
(C) funds discounted from his savings account if he fails to make the payment on his loan
(D) the loan minus the interest due
(E) none of the above

31. (A) (B) is a check; (C) is collateral; (D) is principal.

32. **The Board of Governors of the Federal Reserve System have the right to do all of the following EXCEPT**

(A) change reserve requirements
(B) determine discount rates
(C) issue supplies of Federal Reserve notes
(D) regulate interest on time accounts
(E) encourage high-risk speculation

32. (E) The Board does allow speculation but regulates it carefully; a high-risk speculative venture would probably not meet with the Board's approval.

154

BUSINESS CYCLE

Supply and demand causes the value of gold and money to fluctuate. This in turn affects the price of goods and services. Changes in price are indicated by **index numbers**, which are calculated to indicate the general price level compared with any base year (usually designated by 100). If prices rise by ten percent, the index would be 110.

It takes ten to twenty-five years to bring about general changes in the price level; these periods are known as **secular price trends**. Within these periods are short-term fluctuations; these changes are known as the **business cycle**. One theory that attempts to explain the changes in the business cycle is the **Quantity Theory of Money** which states that general prices vary directly with the amount of money in circulation and inversely with the volume of goods being sold. For example, if the amount of goods sold is reduced by half, prices will double.

Four phases characterize the business cycle: prosperity, recession, depression and recovery. **Prosperity** is marked by the amount of speculative buying, sales improvement, production increases, and employment for most workers.

When speculative buying reaches its limit and prices and profits reach their peak, a period of **recession** sets in. Security prices have fallen and some banks may have failed. Bank loans become difficult to obtain and prices for securities and commodities begin to decline.

As these prices decline further, **depression** sets in. It becomes even more difficult to get loans, and production is reduced resulting in unemployment for many. Many businesses go bankrupt and purchasing power drops. Rather than being invested in risky ventures, money is hoarded.

Recovery takes place when costs adjust to the lower price level. Banks will offer credit, and businessmen are encouraged to increase production because of lower prices. Unemployment decreases, purchasing power increases and profits and prices begin to rise.

Boom periods are marked by wasteful production methods and **bust periods** by market uncertainty. Periods of depression see waste in the form of idle men and machines.

Many factors contribute to the fluctuations of the business cycle; one is **profit motive**. Producers (financed by bankers) increase production and try to anticipate future markets. Over-production can occur, and competition to sell more to consumers, who already have what they need or cannot afford to buy more, results in falling prices. Early in a boom, the purchasing power of consumers leads production, which stimulates further investment and production. However, wage earners will eventually suffer from a lag in purchasing-power—their wages will not rise as quickly nor sufficiently to keep up with rising prices. Moreover, money is hoarded with the hopes that prices will decline and investment opportunities will become more favorable.

Remedies attempting to control severe fluctuations include control of credit and interest rates, changes in the tax structure, wage and price controls, increased tariffs on imports, unemployment and training programs, and increased educational opportunities for low-income groups.

Before going on with the review, try these sample CLEP questions:

33. The general price index does which of the following?

    (A) states average prices of goods and services for a one-year period

    (B) states average prices of goods and services for a ten-year period

    (C) states the general price level of goods and services as compared to a base year

    (D) states the general price level of goods and services for a ten-year period

    (E) none of the above

33. (C) The purpose of the general price index is to make comparison between the recent year's prices and the base year.

Questions 34 through 36 refer to the following list:

    I.   secular price trends
    II. prosperity
    III. recession
    IV. depression
    V. recovery

34. Which of the periods is characterized by a general rise in prices, peak employment and much speculative buying?

    (A) I
    (B) II
    (C) III
    (D) IV
    (E) V

34. (B) Prosperity is a period of expansion in business.

35. Which of the periods is characterized by wide fluctuations in the market?

    (A) I
    (B) II
    (C) III
    (D) IV
    (E) V

35. (A) Secular price trends will reflect many repetitions of the business cycle because they represent longer periods of time.

36. Which of the periods is characterized by an adjustment of costs to the lower price levels, an increase in credit from banks and a decrease in unemployment?

(A) I
(B) II
(C) III
(D) IV
(E) V

36. (E) The key point of recovery is the adjustment of costs to the lower price level. The use of fiscal policy and other controls have prevented severe depression in this country since the 1930's.

ROLE OF GOVERNMENT IN THE ECONOMY

The government today takes an active role in the economy, providing services such as military and police protection, highways, and education, as well as regulation to prevent fraud and unfair trade practices. In times of economic crisis, the government steps in and makes adjustments through money and credit controls, manufacturing and agricultural tariffs, subsidies to industries, and wage and price controls.

Key legislation through the years has demonstrated the government's role in the economy. The **Sherman Anti-Trust Act of 1890** stated that a contract drawn up to restrain trade was illegal. The **Clayton Act of 1914** specifically outlined unfair business practices referred to in the Sherman Act. In the same year the **Federal Trade Commission (FTC)** was established to report on business practices, to enforce the antitrust laws, and to prevent unfair competition. The **Robinson-Patman Act of 1936** prohibited discriminatory prices.

The rights of labor have been protected through the **Norris-LaGuardia Act of 1932** which provided more protection to strikers against injunction, and the **National Labor Relations Act of 1935**, also known as the **Wagner Act**, which requires an employer to bargain in good faith with a union.

Closed shops, that is, businesses which hire only union members, have been outlawed in most industries; construction is an exception. **Union shops** are allowed, for they permit non-union members to be hired; however, they must join the union. The majority of workers at a plant must vote in the union shop. **Check-off of dues**, whereby the employer deducts union dues from the employee's pay, is permitted only if the employee authorizes the deduction in writing. **Black listing** (names of union sympathizers circulated among employers who then would not hire them) and **yellow-dog contracts** (an agreement by an employee not to join the union as a condition of employment) are practices that have been outlawed. **Collective bargaining** (union-employee contract discussions), **mediation** (third-party assistance), voluntary and compulsory **arbitration** (third-party decision), **fact-finding** (third-party examination and recommendation) and **cooling-off** periods (time during which a strike is illegal) are all methods for labor dispute settlement provided for under the **National Labor Relations Board** guidelines.

Before going on with the review, try these sample CLEP questions:

37. **The Sherman Anti-Trust Act provided for which of the following?**

    (A)   declaration that a contract restraining free trade was illegal

    (B)   an outline of discriminatory prices

    (C)   an outline for female and child labor laws

    (D)   the establishment of the Federal Trade Commission

    (E)   all of the above

37. **(A)** (B) was provided for by the Robinson-Patman Act of 1936; the Federal Trade Commission was not established until 1914. The states have child-labor laws, and in 1938, the Fair Labor Standards Act had a child-labor clause. Women are protected in many industries; the Equal Rights Amendment, when passed, will protect women further.

38. **The main consideration of the Wagner Act was which of the following?**

    (A)   to provide child labor laws

    (B)   to establish the FTC

    (C)   to protect closed shops

    (D)   to require an employer to bargain in good faith

    (E)   to protect non-union members

38. **(D)** The Wagner Act, also called the National Labor Relations Act, concentrates on fair bargaining procedures.

39. **Which of the following practices have been outlawed?**

    (A)   closed shops

    (B)   automatic check-off dues

    (C)   yellow-dog contracts

    (D)   blacklisting

    (E)   all of the above

39. **(E)** All of these practices have been outlawed because they are not good for labor.

ECONOMISTS

In recent centuries, the economies of nations and the theories and principles that govern economies have been formulated. **Adam Smith**, who wrote *The Wealth of Nations* in 1776, is considered the father of classical economics. His principles regarding capitalism include the precept that a nation's wealth can be measured by its productivity. **Thomas Malthus** published an essay in 1798 in which he discussed theories of population growth and food supply. Population grows geometrically (2-4-8-16) while food grows arithmetically (2-4-6-8-10) according to his theory.

In the early nineteenth century, **David Ricardo** formulated the **Iron Law of Wages** theory, which stated that as demand increases and prices rose, population, especially in the working classes, would increase until wages fell to the level of subsistence. Thus, the force of wages would limit the working class. Ricardo also believed in free trade. **John Stuart Mill** at first opposed labor organizations but later stated that profits from an industry should be shared with the workers.

Friedrich Engels and **Karl Marx** were German social leaders and economists who formulated the theories of communism. In communism, the community as a whole (the state) owns all property. The country is classless, and eventually stateless, and goods are distributed equally. Achievement of these goals is brought about by revolution and dictatorship, not by gradual change. **Vladimir (Nikolai) Lenin** was the leader of the Communist Revolution in Russia in 1917.

In the twentieth century, **Wesley C. Mitchell** introduced extensive use of statistics to test economic theories. **Frank W. Taussig** proposed theories of international trade, and **John Maynard Keynes** proposed the concept of deficit spending and stated that the government plays a vital role in stimulating the economy through monetary and fiscal policy.

GLOSSARY OF ECONOMIC TERMS

Agency Shop: a business requiring all workers to pay union dues whether they are union members or not.

Amalgamation: the uniting or merger of two or more companies into one.

Amortization: the reduction of a debt over time, or the reduction of an asset's value over time.

Balance of Trade: the difference between exports and imports.

Bear: a person who estimates that prices will go down and sells his shares with the expectation of buying them at a lower price.

Bill of Exchange: a worksheet used by banks in foreign trade to balance out the debts between individuals in different countries.

Bond: an agreement to pay back a loan with interest.

Bull: a person who estimates that prices will go up and buys shares with the expectation of selling them at a profit.

Capital Asset: a resource that is held for use in production or as an investment.

Capital Gain: the profit from the sale of an asset which has increased in value while owned.

Capital Goods: manmade items used to produce other goods.

Cartel: an organization of raw material producers who agree to regulate output, prices and markets.

Caveat Emptor: Latin for "Let the buyer beware," suggesting that the consumer shop wisely.

Caveat Venditor: Latin for "Let the seller beware," suggesting that the seller is responsible for the quality of his merchandise.

Collectivism: an economic system that is controlled by the government, such as socialism or communism.

Consortium:	an agreement among nations to give aid to another nation by issuing loans.
Debasement:	the reduction of the amount of metal in a coin below its face value.
Deflation:	the reduction in the amount of money being circulated which causes prices to fall.
Econometrics:	the study and testing of economic theory through formulas and calculations.
Equity:	the net value of a business; the value of a property minus the claims against it.
Escalator Clause:	a condition stated in a union contract allowing for cost-of-living raises in wages.
Excess Profits Tax:	a tax charge assessed against excessive profits; also known as windfall profit tax.
Fair Trade Law:	a state law which allows producers to set minimum sales prices for their items.
Featherbedding:	the creation of unnecessary jobs.
Hedging:	the speculative buying and selling of goods to avoid or reduce losses.
Holding Company:	a parent corporation which owns most or all of the stock of other corporations in order to control those corporations.
Industrial Union:	regardless of skills, all the workers in an industry belong to the same union; also known as a vertical union.
Inflation:	the increase in the amount of money being circulated which causes prices to rise and devalues the money.
Interlocking Directorates:	corporations whose board of director members serve on several boards.
Margin:	the money deposited with a broker in order to insure him against losses on investments he makes for the buyers and sellers; if prices decline, the owner pays more of the purchasing price.
Marginal-Productivity Theory of Wages:	the principle that states that wages are determined by the productivity of the workers to the least productive member.
Marginal Utility:	the use or value of the last unit that is used to produce a good; price is based on value, which is determined by the item's relative scarcity.
Monopoly:	one seller of a good or service who controls the market.
Monopsony:	one buyer of a good or service.

Oligopoly:	having few sellers of a good or service; they in effect control the market.
Oligopsony:	having few buyers of a good or service.
Panic:	a widespread fear of financial collapse whereby people convert assets to cash and withdraw money from banks.
Pool:	a combination of businessmen who follow certain pricing policies or methods or production.
Preferential Shop:	a business which gives preference to union members.
Right of Work:	a guarantee by law to receive employment whether or not a person is a union member.
Scarcity:	the productive resources of land, labor and capital are available in limited amounts; this requires decisions about their use.
Short Sale:	a sale of borrowed goods which the seller expects to cover later.
Sinking Fund:	moneys set aside to be used to pay off debts.
Specific Tax:	tax set at a certain amount per unit, not as a percentage of the value.
Stock:	a unit indicating a percentage of ownership in a corporation. Common stock prices tend to fluctuate, so such stock is usually bought for speculative purposes. Preferred stocks are bought for long-term investment, for they always grant dividends. Their price tends to be stable.
Substitution:	by producing one type of good, another type is not produced because of the scarcity of resources.
Syndicate:	an association of banks which agree to a single financial plan.
Wages-Fund Theory:	the principle which states that wages can rise only if either workers are reduced in number or capital is increased.

Political Science

MAN AND SOCIETY

Political science is the study of the operations of government as designed by man. Man is a social creature even though he frequently acts as an individual. Governments today express man's desire to control large segments of society. But even in prehistoric times man resorted to forming and controlling groups. Such units resulted from two factors, **cooperation** and **competition**.

The need for basic necessities, such as food, clothing and shelter helped to promote cooperation among men; however, other needs not as necessary could be more easily obtained through cooperation. A more satisfactory home or a building to be used by all could be more readily constructed when men cooperated in the labor. In times of war, men have cooperated with one another to fight the common enemy.

This last point, fighting the common enemy, illustrates competition. When a man acts in his own self-interest, he may be affecting no one and acting independently. His actions may be benefiting others and he may in a sense be cooperating, but he may also be harming others. This is competition, and a group may form to control this behavior, that is, to form a governing body. If competitors fight it out for themselves without group control, it is called **anarchy**. If the onlookers establish rules to be used in settling the argument, or if they use these rules themselves to make a judgment concerning the conflict, we have the makings of government.

Competition divides men while cooperation unites them. Both are means to an end. If unchecked, however, competition destroys, for it seeks to destroy the opposition. Excessive cooperation is harmful, too, because it may hamper the human spirit and the creativity of the individual. Part of the role of governing bodies is to oversee the forces of cooperation and competition.

Groups form because of common interest, and the members tend to cooperate. Men may belong to several groups such as a church, a family, a business or a club. The purpose, membership, rules, institution and authority of each group differ as do the way the organization is financed, and the ideas that the group represents. Sometimes an individual may experience divided loyalties; the purpose or rules of one group may conflict with another. In this case, the individual may seek a compromise, reject one or both loyalties, or give more weight or credence to one loyalty at the expense of the other. He may choose these options voluntarily, be forced to choose or have an outside force make the choice. In any case, he will seek the highest degree of harmony possible.

It is the collection and interactions of groups that form society. Because the groups are diverse and may overlap and/or compete, the task of leading both cooperative and competitive forces to harmony results in the organization of the state.

Before going on with the review, try these sample CLEP questions:

1. **In seeking to construct walls around his cities, man probably sought which of the following?**

   (A) competition within his group
   (B) competition with outsiders
   (C) cooperation with outsiders
   (D) cooperation within his group
   (E) a combination of all of the above

2. **Which of the following would best represent anarchy?**

   (A) a mob rioting in the street
   (B) fighters in a boxing ring
   (C) town council debating an issue
   (D) town members debating an issue at the council meeting
   (E) inmates airing grievances with the warden

3. **Which of the following statements is NOT true?**

   (A) Cooperation and competition are essential factors in a society.
   (B) Cooperation is never ineffective while competition sometimes is.
   (C) Excessive cooperation can lead to lack of self-expression.
   (D) If left unchecked, competition can be excessively harmful.
   (E) Both competition and cooperation are useful means to an end.

4. **If faced with divided loyalties, an individual may do which of the following?**

   (A) seek a compromise
   (B) reject one loyalty
   (C) reject all loyalties
   (D) give more support to one loyalty
   (E) all of the above

ANSWERS:

1. (D) The most effective way of constructing a protective wall around the city would be to enlist the cooperation of those who would benefit from its erection. Outsiders would not be called upon, which eliminates answer (E).

2. (A) Compared to the other answers, a mob rioting in the street best exemplifies anarchy, the absence of a control group. The other answers all suggest elements of control, e.g., the referee, the town council and prison institution.

3. (B) Excessive cooperation can in fact be ineffective because it may stifle self-expression and creativity. Competition lends itself to generating new ideas. The key word in the statement is the word "never."

4. (E) The individual can choose any of the options and may even be forced to as in the case of a draft-age man, e.g., enter the service, resist as a conscientious objector or leave the country.

5. **The purpose of the state is best expressed in which of the following statements?**

(A) to identify and isolate groups
(B) to protect all the self-interests of each individual
(C) to coordinate the development of groups
(D) to lead cooperative and competitive forces of groups to harmony
(E) none of the above

5. (D) The state oversees the cooperative/competitive forces of individuals and groups. It cannot in every circumstance protect the self-interest of the individual, as in the case of an act harmful to others.

PURPOSE AND FUNCTIONS OF THE STATE

When man was a food-gatherer, and later a nomad moving from place to place in search of food, his weapons, wit and tribal cooperation were his only defense against invaders. As he shifted to an agricultural life, however, he needed more protection. The source of his food was stationary, and so he guarded the frontier and built a fortress in the center of the area for protection during an attack. This activity required the cooperation of all in the tribe or clan and benefited all. The organization to coordinate these activities was the **state**. Once protection has been secured for the society, other groups and institutions can survive and grow.

This protection does not pertain only to protection from outsiders; protection of the groups and individuals within the society is also necessary. This is **order**, a guarantee that interactions will take place in an orderly, regular way. To assure that this order is fair to all, a system of justice is developed in the form of **law**. To assure that it can promote the law, the state employs force. This force is concentrated in the state, which can use it both within and outside the society it protects. The officials of the society represent the community in the use of force. If the community consents to the force used by the officials, these officials also gain power. **Power** is the ability to "get things done." If the citizens recognize the power of the officials as rightful, then the officials have authority. Within the society there are three groups: the officials, those who support them and those who dissent. While it is lawful to oppose power, it is unlawful to resist authority, for authority implies the consent of the people and recognition of rightful use of power.

The means of the state are force, power and authority which work to bring about the ends, protection, order and justice. Once power is in the hands of the officials, it is hard to retrieve it, and so care must be taken by the community that force and power are not abused by the officials, for if they are, there may be a lesser or no degree of justice for the community.

States vary in the way they are organized, who is and is not considered a citizen, the source of authority and the purpose and methods of their interactions. By examining the differences and similarities, one can better understand the American Constitution and organization.

Throughout history it has been asked, "What makes a person a citizen?" Aristotle said that a **citizen** is a person who participates in authority, and that few are competent to do so. Others through history have made similar judgments with the result that most states have been elitist in nature. Only the few who meet certain criteria enjoy full citizenship and exercise authority in such states. This **rule of privilege** can revolve around race (racial superiority), ancestry (kingship to son), and sex (males usually rule). The rules of the elders and minimum age requirements for office are examples of age criteria. Monetary and military power have also been used. Religion, as in India, has also been a way to establish privilege. At any time there may be a combination of factors contributing to the rise of a privileged class.

The opposite of rule by the privileged is **equalitarianism**, equality for all. The reasoning behind this approach to rule is that as each looks after his own interests, the state may act in ways that affect him, and therefore, everyone has the right to participate in the direction of the state. Unlike Aristotle, the Stoics said that all men with the ability to reason, no matter to what degree, are equal. The Romans, too, established courts throughout the Empire to settle the disputes of the native people. The notion of equality was at the heart of the English, American and French Revolutions; these rebellions were directed against the rule of the privileged on the grounds that authority comes from the governed, that the people's authority had been stolen from them, and that they, therefore, had the right to rebel.

One way of determining the degree of equality in a state is to study its **franchise**, the right to vote. In England, the franchise broadened as the social power of the workers increased in the nineteenth century. Before that time, qualifications of wealth and sex allowed only a small minority to vote. In America, wealth, sex and race were barriers to the polls for many. As in England, ownership of property was a qualification to vote in many states, and women could not vote. African Americans were denied the right to vote. United States Constitutional Amendments made guarantees to these disenfranchised groups in America.

Before going on with the review, try these sample CLEP questions:

Questions 6 through 10 refer to the following list:

I.   Protection
II.   Order
III. Justice
IV.   Force
V.   Power
VI.   Authority

ANSWERS:

6. **Which of the above is the primary requisite for society?**

    (A) I
    (B) II
    (C) III
    (D) IV
    (E) V

6. (A) Protection is the basic need of society as a whole; once protection is established, other institutions and groups can emerge and be secure.

165

Questions 6 through 10 refer to the following list:

I. Protection
II. Order
III. Justice
IV. Force
V. Power
VI. Authority

7. Which of the above primarily assures that interactions within a society will be regular and fair?

(A) II
(B) III
(C) II and III
(D) IV
(E) III and IV

8. Which of the above can be legally resisted?

(A) II and III
(B) IV and V
(C) V and VI
(D) V only
(E) II and V

9. Which of the above is the consent of the community to the officials' use of force?

(A) III
(B) V
(C) V and VI
(D) V only
(E) VI only

10. Which of the above is expressed best in the laws of the state?

(A) II and III
(B) III only
(C) III and VI
(D) VI only
(E) none of the above

7. (C) Order assures an environment for orderly and regular interactions; justice establishes fair rules and applies to all.

8. (D) Only power can be legally resisted; when society confers authority upon the officials, it both gives consent and recognizes its rightful control.

9. (B) The power of the officials derives from the society's consent to their use of force. However, if this power is abused, society can legally resist.

10. (B) Justice is contained within the body of law.

11. **Aristotle's definition of a citizen would make his which of the following?**

(A) equalitarian
(B) anarchist
(C) elitist
(D) militarist
(E) none of the above

11. (C) Because he believed that not all were equally fit to rule, and these were, therefore, not citizens, Aristotle would be considered an elitist. An anarchist believes that there should be no government, only voluntary cooperation among people; some anarchists are terrorists against governments.

12. **Literacy test requirement for enfranchisement would be connected with rule by which of the following qualifications?**

(A) race
(B) age
(C) sex
(D) wealth
(E) knowledge

12. (E) Basically, this is a test of knowledge or intelligence; however, it can and has been used against certain groups, such as foreigners or racial minorities as a way to discriminate against them.

13. **Which of the following statements was the basis for equalitarianism during the American Revolution?**

(A) Men of the founding families have the right to vote.
(B) Women have the right to vote.
(C) Free Black men have the right to participate in the government.
(D) The people are the source of authority and, therefore, have the right to rebel.
(E) None of the above.

13. (D) This was the premise. The rights of Blacks and women were not issues of the Revolution. Men of founding families were not the only men seeking their rights; more recent immigrant men also opposed the British.

14. **At various times, which of the following have been barriers to the right to vote in the United States?**

(A) wealth, sex and race
(B) wealth, sex and age
(C) sex, race and knowledge
(D) sex, race and parentage
(E) all of the above

14. (E) Property ownership, sex, age, race, knowledge (literacy test) and parentage (slave, foreigner) have all been qualifications used to deprive people of their right to vote.

THE RELATION OF THE STATE TO SOCIETY

There are two basic ways of viewing the relation of the state to society. One looks for the highest good and gives one purpose to society and the state; the other states that since men have different goals, so, too, society and the state should reflect these many goals. In the first, the unifying factor may be religion, a tradition or a business, to name a few examples. A **theocracy** is rule of the state by religious officials; the purposes of the religion are the purposes of the state. The establishment of colonies is a business, but it also includes government, and so, the purposes of both are joined. A **pluralistic** society, on the other hand, has many purposes, and usually sets limits on the state.

The empires of Greece and Rome united the state with the people's religion and philosophy. The small size of the Greek city-states and the competition among them helped to foster the need for unity. The Roman Empire was immense, however, and so unity was achieved through the military, law and finance. When the Empire joined forces with the Christian Church, however, both church and state assumed power and authority, a condition called **dualism**. While the state was to handle earthly matters and the church heavenly ones, there was nonetheless much overlap and conflict in trying to keep the two separate. Moreover, the church itself was fragmented by the Protestant Reformation and other schisms, and so power and authority shifted back to the state during the fifteenth and sixteenth centuries. The theory of **sovereignty** developed, stating that the state was supreme and could exercise limitless power.

The rise of **nationalism** accompanied the growth of mercantilism. In order to increase national wealth, colonies were formed, national resources utilized and volume of production increased. **National wealth** was measured by the inflow of gold and silver which replaced the outflow of produced goods. Since economic decisions could affect this accumulation of wealth, the state intervened wherever it felt controls were necessary. The response from the economists was the theory of **laissez faire**, "leave them alone." This demand from economists and businessmen lasted throughout the Industrial Revolution in both England and the United States and presented limits to the states' powers. The results of this business expansion did not benefit everyone, particularly the workers, and unions developed to protect the interests of the workers. Socialism and communism were other responses. In the United States and other Western countries, the government eventually emerged to take on the roles as mediator between industry and labor and coordinator of social services. Thus, the power and authority of the states increased.

Before going on with the review, try these sample CLEP questions:

15. Which of the following would be the best example of a pluralistic group?

(A) a contractor's hiring hall
(B) a theological college
(C) a corporate law firm
(D) an electricians' union
(E) a liberal arts college

15. (E) In a liberal arts college, professors and students would be pursuing a variety of subjects with academic freedom; their purposes would be many. The other choices would tend to be more singular in purpose and function.

16. The formation of the Anglican Church did which of the following?

(A) increased the power of the state
(B) decreased the power and authority of the Roman Church
(C) decreased the authority of the state
(D) decreased the power of the king
(E) A and B combined

16. (E) When Henry VIII of England broke from the Roman Church to form the Anglican Church, the power and authority of the Roman Church necessarily decreased while the power of England increased, as he was head of state.

17. The theory of sovereignty states which of the following?

(A) The power of the state is supreme.
(B) The power of the state is limitless.
(C) The range of the state's control is limitless.
(D) The state's authority applies to all matters.
(E) all of the above

17. (E) All the statements describe the condition of sovereignty.

18. Which of the following was not a measure of national wealth during mercantilism?

(A) amount of goods produced and exported
(B) amount of gold and silver in the treasury
(C) amount of raw materials processed into exportable goods
(D) amount of imported goods
(E) amount of return on capital invested in the colonies

18. (D) In mercantilism, growth of national wealth was measured by the increase of gold and silver into the state treasury and by the factors that would contribute to this.

19. The policy calling for a "hand's-off" position by the government with regard to the economy is which of the following?

(A) laissez faire
(B) socialism
(C) communism
(D) capitalism
(E) mercantilism

19. (A) Laissez faire calls for no government interference in the economy, stating rather that the forces of supply and demand will regulate the market most efficiently.

20. Which of the following best exemplifies the United States' shift to a monistic state?

(A) wage and price controls
(B) governmental social services
(C) increased monetary controls
(D) anti-trust legislation
(E) all of the above

20. (E) Any control or service issued by the government tends to unify purpose and, therefore, create a move toward monism.

THE CONSTITUTION OF THE UNITED STATES

At the time the **Constitution** was being drafted, **Thomas Jefferson** asserted the principle that the consent of the people is the basis for the legitimacy of the government. Since it is impossible to have all people in agreement on all issues, it was decided that Congress, which represents the decisions of the people, should not be supreme, but that the Constitution should be. So too, the President and the Supreme Court are subordinate to this document. Public officials take an oath or affirmation to uphold it; procedures, such as impeachment, have been established to deal with betrayal of that oath. Amendments can be made to the text; and judicial review can test the constitutionality of laws passed by the Congress and approved by the President. By these measures, the Constitution has remained central to our government.

There is no specific provision for judicial review of legislation in the Constitution, but in the case of **Marbury versus Madison in 1803**, the right of the Supreme Court to determine the **constitutionality of laws** was first established. The merit of law can be assessed in a variety of ways such as custom, the law of nature or usefulness. Law can be the formalization of custom, or it can be judged by its appeal to reason or nature's laws. The usefulness of a law, for example, the number of people it will benefit, may indicate its worth. These measures can restrain a government from assuming inappropriate power. The writers of the Constitution were well aware of the need for **checks and balances** on power to protect the nation from the excesses of government. Thus, in addition to judicial review and other procedures, the President can veto acts of Congress. In turn, the Congress can override the veto by a two-thirds majority in both the House and the Senate.

The constitution begins with the words "We the People of the United States," stating that sovereignty lies with the citizenry. This **Preamble** also states several purposes: the establishment of justice, the insurance of domestic tranquillity, the provision for common defense and the promotion of the general welfare. Outlined broadly, these goals can be and have been interpreted in a variety of ways through the years. Seven Articles and Twenty-six Amendments follow the Preamble in the Constitution.

Article I vests legislative powers in the **Congress** of the United States, outlining the administrative plans for the **House and Senate**, establishing a **bicameral**, or two-house system. A basic outline for election, age, tenure and compensation of these representatives is given. This article lists several specific powers given to the Congress, including the laying and collection of taxes, the regulation of foreign and interstate commerce, the coining of money, the establishment of post offices, the right to declare war and the right to raise an army and navy. The last section limits the states by prohibiting them from entering into separate treaties with foreign nations; nor may states levy import/export duties without the consent of Congress.

Article II vests executive powers in the President, outlining the tenure, age, compensation and method of election through the **Electoral College**. Procedures are given for replacing the President for whatever reason. Article II names the **President** as Commander in Chief of the Army and Navy, gives him the power to grant pardons and allows him to make treaties with the advice and consent of the Senate. Also with Senate approval, he may appoint ambassadors, public ministers and judges of the Supreme Court. The President is also directed to give the Congress "from time to time" information regarding the state of the union, and he is given the power to convene and adjourn the Congress. Provision is also made for removal from office for impeachment and conviction of a crime of any civil official.

The **judicial power** of the United States, vested in the Supreme Court, is provided for in **Article III**; lower courts may also be established by this article. No limit is set on tenure, and provision for compensation is made. The article outlines the jurisdiction of the courts, which includes cases concerning laws and treaties of the United States, cases affecting ambassadors, public ministers, maritime jurisdiction, and controversies in which the United States is a party. Cases involving two or more states for their citizens and cases involving foreign states are also under the jurisdiction of the federal court system. The article also establishes the jury system for all criminal cases except impeachment. **Treason** is defined as levying war against the United States or giving aid and comfort to the enemy; conviction for this crime can result only from the testimony of two witnesses or confession in court.

Article IV provides for reciprocity of privileges to citizens from state to state and for extradition of persons charged with crimes to the state from which they fled. It also stipulates the admittance of new states to the Union and guarantees every state a republic form of government. **Article V** provides for amendments to the Constitution. **Article VI** states that the Constitution, laws and treaties of the United States are supreme law of the land, binding the judges of the states to adhere to this; furthermore, all federal and state legislative, executive and judicial officers are bound by oath or affirmation to support the Constitution. **Article VII** is the vehicle for ratification of the Constitution by the states.

Before going on with the review, try these sample CLEP questions:

ANSWERS:

21. **According to the Constitution, sovereignty of the United States lies with which of the following?**

    (A) the President
    (B) the House of Representatives
    (C) the Senate
    (D) the people
    (E) all of the above

21. (D) The American Constitution was the first to declare the sovereignty of the people. The wishes of the people are carried out through the acts of the President, the House of Representatives and the Senate.

22. **Which of the following provides checks to power?**

    (A) Presidential veto
    (B) Senate approval of ambassadors
    (C) judicial review of constitutionality
    (D) oath of allegiance to the Constitution
    (E) all of the above

22. (E) All the factors stated contribute a check of power. Presidential veto checks the power of Congress; Senate approval of ambassadors checks the power of the President; judicial review of constitutionality checks the powers of both the Congress and the President, and of the states; the oath of allegiance to the Constitution binds all officials to adherence to the document.

23. **Which of the following states the significance of the case of Marbury versus Madison, 1803?**

(A) the right of the House to instate appropriation of revenue bills

(B) the right of the federal court system to hear cases concerning maritime disputes

(C) the right of the Supreme Court to determine the constitutionality of laws

(D) the right of the legislature to insure domestic tranquillity

(E) the right of Congress to declare war

23. (C) Although judicial review is not stated specifically in the Constitution, the founding fathers intended it; this case provided clarification of this point.

24. **The Preamble of the Constitution contains which of the following?**

(A) the identification of sovereignty

(B) the amendments to the Constitution

(C) the Bill of Rights

(D) the Declaration of Independence

(E) the requirement of the oath of allegiance

24. (A) The Preamble identifies the sovereignty of the people and the purposes of the Constitution. The Bill of Rights is the first ten amendments to the Constitution. The Declaration of Independence, written in 1776, is a document which outlined the grievances of the states against England and declared the independence of the states from the mother country.

Questions 25 through 28 refer to the following list:

I.   Article I
II.   Article II
III. Article III
IV.   Article IV
V.   Article V

25. **Which of the above empowers the Congress to levy and collect taxes?**

(A) I

(B) II

(C) III

(D) IV

(E) V

25. (A) Article I outlines the election and duties of the Congress.

    I.   Article I
    II.   Article II
    III. Article III
    IV. Article IV
    V.   Article V

26. Which of the above stipulates the age of public officials?

(A) I
(B) II
(C) III
(D) I and II
(E) I, II and III

27. Which of the above provides for impeachment, conviction and removal from office of a public official?

(A) I
(B) II
(C) III
(D) I and II
(E) I, II and III

28. Which of the above provides for amendments to the Constitution?

(A) I
(B) II
(C) III
(D) IV
(E) V

26. (D) Article I stipulates the minimum ages for Congressmen, twenty-five years for Representatives and thirty years for Senators. Article II sets a minimum age for the President, thirty-five years. Article III establishes the judicial branch, but states no minimum age for judges.

27. (D) Article I states that "the Senate shall have the sole power to try all impeachments." Article II states that all civil officers shall be removed from office if impeached for and convicted of criminal acts.

28. (E) Article V provides for amendments to the Constitution. Amendments can be proposed either by two-thirds of both houses or if two-thirds of the state legislatures call for a convention for that purpose. Ratification requires approval by the legislatures of three-fourths of the states or three-fourths of the convention as represented by the states.

AMENDMENTS TO THE CONSTITUTION

The founding fathers who drafted the Constitution made provision for amendments to be made. To insure that proposed changes be scrutinized thoroughly and accepted by a clear majority, they stipulated that three-fourths of the states' legislatures pass the amendment before it can be attached to the Constitution.

The first ten amendments to the Constitution, known as the **Bill of Rights**, were adopted and in force in 1791. **Amendment I** prohibits Congress from making laws respecting the establishment of religion, making clearer the separation of church and state. It also guarantees the free exercise of religion. Amendment I also provides for freedom of speech, of the press, of peaceful assemblage and the right to petition the government.

Amendment II states that since a well-regulated militia is necessary for freedom, people have the right to keep and bear arms. **Amendment III** guarantees that in time of peace, owner's consent is required to quarter soldiers, and also in time of war except as prescribed by law. **Amendment IV** prohibits unreasonable search and seizure and requires probable cause supported by oath in order to conduct a search or seizure. **Amendment V** requires indictment by a grand jury, except in military cases, and prohibits double jeopardy and the compelling of a criminal to testify against himself. The amendment also guarantees due process of law. **Amendment VI** guarantees the right to a speedy and public trial by jury. Under this amendment the accused must be told the nature of the accusations, be able to confront witnesses testifying against him, as well as have witnesses in his defense.

Amendment VII states that re-examination of facts from a trial by jury shall be done according to the rules of the common law. **Amendment VIII** prohibits excessive bail, excessive fines and cruel and unusual punishments. **Amendment IX** makes clear that the rights listed in the Constitution are not to be construed to deny other rights retained by the people. **Amendment X** states that powers not delegated to the United States by the Constitution, nor prohibited to the states by it, belong to the states and the people.

Since the acceptance of these ten, there have been sixteen additional amendments approved. A summary of the contents of the amendments, Amendments XI through XXVI follows below:

- **Amendment XI**—Neither citizens of another state nor foreigners can sue a state in a federal court; this qualifies Article III.

- **Amendment XII**—Separate ballots are required for the President and Vice President; stipulations are made concerning the counting of the ballots and procedures for taking office. This revises Article II.

- **Amendment XIII**—Slavery is abolished, and Congress is empowered to enforce this amendment by legislation.

- **Amendment XIV**—Citizenship is guaranteed to all persons born or naturalized in the United States as is due process and equal rights under the law. This negates a portion of Article I. Amendment XIV also designates the number of Representatives to be apportioned according to the total population of each state.

- **Amendment XV**—Blacks are guaranteed the right to vote and Congress is empowered to enforce it by legislation.

- **Amendment XVI**—Congress is allowed to establish a federal income tax.

- **Amendment XVII**—The members of the Senate are to be elected by popular vote, not by the state legislatures as stated in Article I.

- **Amendment XVIII**—The manufacture and sale of liquor is prohibited; both the Congress and state legislatures are empowered to enforce it by legislation. (This is an example of concurrent power.)

- **Amendment XIX**—Women are guaranteed the right to vote.

- **Amendment XX**—The dates for federal terms of office to begin are stipulated.

- **Amendment XXI**—The eighteenth amendment is repealed.

- **Amendment XXII**—This amendment stipulates the length of the Presidential term of office; no person can be elected more than twice, and any person who takes over the office for more than two years can be elected only once.

- **Amendment XXIII**—Electors shall be appointed in the District of Columbia to insure the voting rights of the residents in Presidential elections.

- **Amendment XXIV**—Poll taxes are prohibited in elections for President, Vice President and Congressmen.

- **Amendment XXV**—The Presidential succession is outlined.

- **Amendment XXVI**—The right to vote is guaranteed to eighteen-year-olds.

Before going on with the review, try these sample CLEP questions:

Questions 29-32 refer to the following list:

I. First Amendment
II. Second Amendment
III. Fourth Amendment
IV. Fifth Amendment
V. Tenth Amendment

ANSWERS:

29. Which of the above amendments might an accused man evoke?

(A) I
(B) II
(C) III
(D) IV
(E) V

29. (D) An accused man might "plead the Fifth," which means that he is not compelled to testify against himself.

Questions 29-32 refer to the following list:

I.   First Amendment
II.   Second Amendment
III. Fourth Amendment
IV.   Fifth Amendment
V.   Tenth Amendment

30. Although the word privacy is not used in the Constitution, which of the above amendments is interpreted to guarantee this right?

(A) I
(B) II
(C) III
(D) IV
(E) V

30. (C) The Fourth Amendment prohibits unreasonable search and seizure which has been interpreted to include the right to privacy.

31. Which of the above amendments is frequently referred to by members of gun and hunting clubs?

(A) I
(B) II
(C) III
(D) IV
(E) V

31. (B) Amendment II guarantees the right to keep and bear arms; the wording is such that this right is connected to a militia. That is why there has been such debate over the interpretation.

32. Which of the above amendments is referred to as the "states' rights" amendments?

(A) I
(B) II
(C) III
(D) IV
(E) V

32. (E) Amendment X states that rights not reserved by the federal government are residual rights of the states.

33. **Which of the following amendments guarantees the right to vote to Blacks?**

(A) Thirteenth Amendment
(B) Fourteenth Amendment
(C) Fifteenth Amendment
(D) Twenty-third Amendment
(E) Twenty-fourth Amendment

33. (C) The Fifteenth Amendment guarantees Blacks the right to vote. The Thirteenth abolished slavery; the Fourteenth guarantees citizenship to all persons born or naturalized in the United States; the Twenty-third guarantees voting rights in Presidential elections for residents of the District of Columbia and the Twenty-fourth prohibits poll taxes.

34. **Which of the following amendments has been repealed?**

(A) Fourteenth Amendment
(B) Fifteenth Amendment
(C) Sixteenth Amendment
(D) Eighteenth Amendment
(E) Nineteenth Amendment

34. (D) The Eighteenth Amendment, which prohibits manufacture and sale of alcohol, was repealed in 1933 by the Twenty-first Amendment.

THE AMERICAN POLITICAL SYSTEM

When the **Articles of Confederation** were drafted in 1777, power was concentrated in the Congress, and the President was to act as the presiding officer at sessions of Congress. Since the United States was breaking away from Great Britain at the time, a strong central government was useful. After independence, however, it became clear that this type of power could be abused, and so the Constitution set forth the mechanism for separation of powers. This dispersion of power is reflected in the legislative, executive and judicial branches of the government. The **legislative branch**, Congress, is responsible for making the laws; the **executive branch**, headed by the President, is charged with enforcing the laws; and the **judicial branch**, notably the Supreme Court, interprets the laws. These branches do not operate in isolation but rather exercise overlapping power. Congress may or may not originate bills favored by the President; the President can reserve the right to veto legislation; the Supreme Court can declare legislation unconstitutional.

The exercise of these powers is known as our **system of checks and balances**. By distributing powers among the three branches, the authors of the Constitution attempted to keep the nation free from governmental excesses. Even if two branches try to overstep the boundaries outlined in the Constitution, the third can act to restrain them in order to restore balance.

There is a further dispersion of power, known as **federalism**, which is the distribution of power between the central government and the individual states. Some powers in the Constitution belong exclusively to the national government and are called **exclusive powers.** Examples are the powers to declare war, to coin money, to approve treaties and to regulate interstate commerce. Powers shared by the national and state governments are called **concurrent powers**, such as levying taxes and punishing criminals. The powers left to the state governments are called **residual powers**, e.g., divorce laws. Although this division of power seems clear, there is often dispute concerning which powers belong to the federal government and which belong to the state.

Before going on with the review, try these sample CLEP questions:

ANSWERS:

35. **A major difficulty with the Articles of Confederation was that it allowed which of the following?**

   (A) a standing army
   (B) a powerful Congress
   (C) a strong President
   (D) dispersion of power
   (E) concentration of power in the court system

35. (B) When the Articles of Confederation were in force, much power was concentrated in the central government. This was useful during the Revolutionary War; however, the Founding Fathers saw the possibilities for abuse, and so in drafting the Constitution they dispersed power.

36. **Which of the following statements is NOT true?**

   (A) The Constitution disperses power among the three branches of government.
   (B) The Congress enacts laws.
   (C) The President enforces laws.
   (D) The Supreme Court interprets laws.
   (E) These branches act in isolation.

36. (E) These branches do not operate in isolation; the nature of their division and the system of checks and balances provide for interaction.

37. **The term federalism means which of the following?**

   (A) All powers are concurrent.
   (B) Powers are dispersed between the central government and the states.
   (C) The power of Congress to set taxes is made clear.
   (D) Powers are concentrated in the executive branch.
   (E) none of the above

37. (B) A federal government has powers in both the central government and the states' governments.

POLITICAL PARTIES

When the Constitution was enacted and the nation was in its infancy, leaders such as George Washington disapproved of political parties. The general feeling was one of distrust of factions which would disrupt the unity of the nation; freedom had been won from Great Britain, and the United States had a Constitution with the people sovereign and the powers of the branches dispersed. It was thought that political parties would destroy the balance.

Nonetheless, political parties were formed by the followers of **Alexander Hamilton** and those of **Thomas Jefferson**. Hamilton's followers called themselves **Federalists**, emphasized order and stability and were strong in the Northeast and commercial centers. The followers of Jefferson were called **Republicans**, emphasized the importance of individual freedom and were strong in the South, West and rural areas. This rallying around central figures who espouse certain philosophies, beliefs and answers to key issues has continued in American history to this present day. The argument for political parties is a strong one. The opportunity to choose implies freedom; if a person can choose the political party that best expresses his own beliefs, then he has more freedom than if no parties existed. With a party system, the people of a nation can change the leaders without changing the structure of the government.

Thomas Jefferson favored a Republic form of government where most of the power would reside with the individual states. He was opposed by Alexander Hamilton who was an Federalist. He wanted a strong central government.

Various parties have existed in the United States. The **Antifederalists** originally opposed the Constitution and centralized power; some members eventually joined with Jefferson and the Republican Party. The Federalist Party, led by Hamilton, favored strong central government but faded from power by the 1820's.

The Republican Party of Jefferson by 1828 had split over a number of issues; some members formed the **Democratic-Republican Party**, which stood for personal liberty and became the party of farmers, workers and the poor. It eventually became the **Democratic Party**. The **Whig Party**, led by **Daniel Webster** and **Henry Clay**, was formed in 1834 mainly to oppose the Democrats; the party split and ended over the slavery issue. The **Liberty Party** formed in 1840 in its opposition to slavery. The **Barn-Burners** was a radical group of the Democratic Party formed in the 1840's to oppose the extension of slavery. This group eventually merged with the **Free-Soilers** of 1848 who opposed extension of slavery into the territory acquired from Mexico; this group favored homestead law, low tariffs and internal improvements. Eventually, the Free-Soil Party merged with the Republican Party of 1854. Democrats and Whigs who opposed the extension of slavery merged to form this new Republican Party which eventually came to represent conservative economic policies.

Also in the 1850's **Supreme Order of the Star-Spangled Banner** emerged as a secret organization opposed to Catholics and aliens holding public office. When asked about their organization, members would answer, "I know nothing." This gave rise to the name the **Know-Nothing Party**. The **American Party** had similar goals and eventually merged with the Know-Nothings. Prior to the 1860 Presidential election, the party called the **Constitutional Union** arose which favored the Union and the Constitution. Thus this election, which resulted in Abraham Lincoln's Presidency, saw four parties, the Republican, the Constitutional Union, and the Northern and the Southern Democrats who split and offered different nominees.

Formed in the 1870's, the **National Greenback Party** wanted an inflationary, easy-money policy; the legality of greenbacks eased the effects of the Panic of 1873. The **Populist Movement** of the 1890's known as the **People's Party**, united labor and farm workers who wanted free coinage of silver, direct election of senators, eight-hour work day and prohibition. This group eventually merged with the Democrats. The **Progressive Party**, also known as the **Bull Moose Party**, formed in 1912 to nominate Theodore Roosevelt for President; the platform included regulation of corporations, minimum wage, the elimination of child labor and other reforms. Many Republicans followed Roosevelt into this party. Others joined the **National Progressive Republican League** and supported Robert La Follette. The **Socialist Party**, active during the Progressive Era, also sought reforms for the working man.

Southern democrats who opposed Harry S. Truman for election to the Presidency formed the **States' Rights**, or **Dixiecrat Party** in 1948. The **Black Panther Party** was formed by extremist advocates of the Black Power movement of the 1960's; in 1968 they nominated Eldridge Cleaver for President.

Before going on with the review, try these sample CLEP questions:

ANSWERS:

38. **One of the earliest political parties, the Federalist, organized to promote which of the following?**

    (A) a strong central government
    (B) strong state legislatures
    (C) individual freedom
    (D) a strong executive branch
    (E) a strong Congress

38. (A) The Federalists favored a strong central government; the states exerted pressure and asserted their powers, and by the 1820's the Federalists faded.

39. **The Republican Party of Jefferson's day was the forerunner of which current political party?**

    (A) the Republican Party
    (B) the Democratic-Republican Party
    (C) the Democratic Party
    (D) the Socialist Party
    (E) none of the above

39. (C) Jefferson and the Republican Party favored the rights of the individual. Through the years there have been several changes and merges which produced what we today call the Democratic Party.

181

40. Teddy Roosevelt is associated with which of the following parties?

(A) the Bull Moose Party
(B) the People's Party
(C) the Greenback Party
(D) the Socialist Party
(E) none of the above

40. (A) Teddy Roosevelt was nominated for the Presidency by the Bull Moose Party in 1916. Also known as the Progressive Party, this group favored many social reforms.

41. The Dixiecrats of 1948 opposed which of the following positions?

(A) Civil Rights
(B) aid for Allies
(C) the rights of working men
(D) increased Presidential power
(E) all of the above

41. (A) The States' Rights Party was made up of Southern Democrats who opposed the then recently enacted Civil Rights Act of 1946.

COMPARATIVE GOVERNMENT

The right to vote in the United States has been extended to many more people than were eligible when the Constitution was formed. States have dropped their income and property requirements and Constitutional amendments have extended the vote to Blacks (15th), women (19th), and eighteen-year-olds (26th). The **Twenty-third Amendment** has increased voting rights for residents of the nation's capital and the **Twenty-fourth** eliminated the poll tax. Furthermore, the **Civil Rights Act of 1964** makes it a federal offense for anyone to interfere with another's right to vote; the **Voting Rights Act of 1965** gave the federal government the power to register voters, which in particular helped Southern Blacks. The Supreme Court in **Smith versus Alwright** ruled that Blacks can vote in primary elections (political parties are not private clubs); in **Baker versus Carr** the court ruled that state legislatures must be apportioned to reflect urban-rural population distribution.

The concept of the right to vote has its roots in Athenian democracy, which held that all power belonged to the people. (Women and slaves, however were NOT included.) The duties of the citizen included military service, jury work and attendance at the meetings of the Assembly in order to enact laws. Because Athens was relatively small, citizens could participate fully in government. The size of the Roman Empire prevented an Athenian democracy, although the Roman Republic did distribute and separate powers and permit citizens to elect officials and approve legislation. As the Empire grew and military power became more and more important, the Senate took control but eventually lost power to the Emperor. In this stage, power was concentrated in a central figure, authoritarian rule.

During the feudal times authoritarian rule was the standard; the serf was ruled by the lord. The Roman Catholic Church was also a source of authoritarian rule. As the nobles struggled against the kings, they found that by being united they could lessen the rulers' power. This gave rise to **Parliament**, a legislative body composed of the **House of Lords** (the higher nobility and clergy) and the **House of Commons** (lesser nobles and commoners). Originally designed to monitor the treasury and to air grievances, the power of Parliament grew as England grew both economically and socially. Unlike the United States where the Constitution is supreme, in England the Parliament has supremacy.

Despite their differences, the United States and England (and other countries) do afford their citizens a measure of equalitarianism. **Authoritarian states**, on the other hand, concentrate power in the rulers. The right to rule can be derived from Divine Right (the will of the god), military power, or heredity. An **aristocracy** is rule by the nobility or wealthy; a **monarchy** is rule by a king, queen, emperor, czar, etc.; an **oligarchy** is a corrupt aristocracy; a **tyranny** is rule by a corrupt monarchy; a **theocracy** is rule by leaders of the religion; an **autocracy** is rule by one person.

Most governments throughout history have been authoritarian in nature, and even the United States has some authoritarian features, e.g., enforced rationing in wartime. Authoritarians can maintain power through force, deception and propaganda. However, if the masses of people become too dissatisfied, revolution may be the result. V.I. Lenin led the **Bolsheviks** in overturning the Kerensky regime in Russia in 1917; this group was the forerunner of the **Communist Party** in the Soviet Union. **Communism** has as its theoretical goal a classless, stateless society; means of achieving this goal are state control of the economy, a one-party system, and the sacrifice of individual rights to the state. The **proletariat**, or working class, is directed by the officials of the government and the Communist Party.

The objectives of **fascism** differ from communism, but the methods are similar. In fascism there is a one-party dictatorship, private enterprise controlled by the government, intense nationalism and militarism. Power belongs to those able to mobilize these forces. **Nazism** under Adolph Hitler, as fascism under Benito Mussolini, required obedience to the state as well as rearmament and aggression. **Military dictatorships** have frequently arisen in third world countries, some of which may be progressive and modernize the country while others may be reactionary using the army to maintain the status quo. In a **democracy** leaders are chosen through free, periodic elections; in an **authoritarian government** new officials will be elected or appointed by the few (e.g., the party).

Before going on with the review, try a few sample CLEP questions:

42. In Smith versus Alwright the Supreme Court ruled which of the following?

(A) Literacy tests are illegal when used to determine voting eligibility.
(B) Political parties are not private clubs, which paved the way for Blacks to vote in primaries.
(C) Poll taxes are illegal.
(D) State legislatures must be apportioned to reflect urban-rural population distributions.
(E) It is a federal offense to hamper voter registration.

42. (B) This ruling made illegal the practice prevalent in the South of barring Blacks from political party meetings on the grounds that such groups are private clubs. The Supreme Court declared that political parties are not private clubs.

43. Which of the following nations has come closest to embodying the principles of democracy?

(A) the Roman Republic
(B) the Roman Empire in its later years
(C) the United States
(D) Athens of Greece
(E) Sparta of Greece

43. (D) Athens of Greece, because of its size, allowed adult free males to participate in the government.

44. Which of the following is an example of authoritarian rule?

(A) an autocracy
(B) a theocracy
(C) the Roman Catholic Church
(D) an oligarchy
(E) all of the above

44. (E) Each type of rule or group named is an example of authoritarian rule.

45. Which of the following statements is incorrect?

(A) Parliament is a unicameral system.
(B) Parliament maintains supremacy.
(C) Parliament gained more power as England grew economically.
(D) Parliament is led by the Prime Minister.
(E) None of the above.

46. V. I. Lenin led which of the following groups?

(A) the Mansheviks
(B) the Bolsheviks
(C) the Trotskyites
(D) the Nazis
(E) the Fascists

47. Communism and Nazism are similar in which of the following respects?

(A) one-party rule
(B) private enterprise controlled by the central government
(C) precedence of the state over the individual
(D) A and C
(E) A, B and C

45. (A) Parliament is a bicameral legislature composed of the House of Lords and the House of Commons.

46. (B) Lenin led the Bolsheviks; the Mansheviks were the more conservative members of the former Social Democratic Party of Russia which split into the two groups in 1903. The Bolsheviks were in the majority.

47. (D) Both communism and Nazism are founded on one-party rule and the subordination of individual freedoms to the state.

INTERNATIONAL RELATIONS

The relations among nations constitute international relations which can be peaceful or warlike, cooperative or competitive, or else neutral. Proximity to one another is a factor. Power to control is another. Rome attempted to unite the known world; the Middle Ages experimented with the Holy Roman Empire. Sea power allowed England, France, Spain and Portugal to acquire vast colonies. On the European continent, Spain, France, Germany and Austria tried at different times to reign supreme. In this century, Germany twice set out to subjugate the European continent. The United States and Russia have been successful in expanding their control over vast tracts of land.

For more than three centuries, men have detailed **international law**, an outline of rules of conduct that states should adhere to in dealing with one another. Without international government, these rules and laws have no bite and can be easily ignored. Nations have presented their disputes to third party panels. After World War I, three organizations were formed: the **International Labor Organization**, to aid governments, employers and laborers in raising standards for the working class; the **Permanent Court of International Justice**, to give advice on matters of international law; and the **League of Nations**, to provide an international forum to prevent future wars. The last group failed because of intense nationalism and lack of support by member nations.

World War II reinforced the need for a global forum, and the **United Nations** was established. Through the **Security Council**, the United Nations does have some provisions for enforcement which have been used in Korea, the Belgian Congo and the Suez Canal. The United Nations also has agencies for aiding in cooperative efforts among nations. Nations have also allied themselves for other reasons such as mutual defense (**North Atlantic Treaty Organization**), defense and cooperation (the **Organization of American States**), and economics (the **Common Market and Organization of Petroleum Exporting Countries [OPEC]**).

Before going on with the review, try these sample CLEP questions:

ANSWERS:

48. In order to be effective, international law would have to have which of the following?

(A) international legislatures
(B) international courts
(C) international police forces
(D) international jurisdiction
(E) none of the above

48. (D) While the other factors would assist in achieving international order, such a body would have to be given jurisdiction in order to settle a dispute.

49. The purpose of the International Labor Organization was which of the following?

(A) to police labor unions
(B) to force governments to accept unions
(C) to aid laborers to achieve higher standards
(D) to continue the fight for communism
(E) all of the above

49. (C) The International Labor Organization could give aid to countries which requested it. It did not have power of enforcement.

50. Nations have made treaties and pacts with one another for which of the following reasons?

(A) defense
(B) economic policy
(C) trade
(D) mutual cooperation
(E) all of the above

50. (E) Agreements have been made among nations for any or all of these reasons.

GLOSSARY OF POLITICAL SCIENCE TERMS

GENERAL TERMS

Common Law: those laws based upon tradition and custom, not through the acts of legislatures.

Conscription: compulsory registration and enrollment of men and resources into the military.

Diet: a legislative assembly.

Magna Carta: the document which King John of England was forced to sign that limited the king's power; this great charter was signed in 1215.

Parliamentary System: type of government in which the legislative body controls both lawmaking and administrative duties.

Plurality: in an election, the largest number of votes cast for a candidate; with three or more candidates, this may or may not be a majority.

Ratification: process by which government documents are approved by the voters or their representatives.

Republic: a type of government whereby the people elect representatives in order to govern themselves; it will be more democratic as more people have the right to vote.

Sedition: the advocating of government overthrow through action, speech or writing.

Soviet: the local, regional and national governing councils of the Soviet Union.

State: a unit of political power determined by its territory, government and sovereignty.

Suffrage: the right to vote.

Tariffs: taxes on goods imported from other countries in order to regulate trade.

Veto: the power of the President to reject legislation passed by Congress; a pocket veto occurs when the President keeps the bill unsigned until after the Congress adjourns; an item veto is the rejection of an individual item.

Vote of No Confidence: the forced resignation of cabinet members in a parliamentary system following the majority consensus of the legislature that these ministers are no longer trusted.

LEGAL TERMS

Bill of Attainder: legal document which deprives a person guilty of treason or a felony of his property.

Declaratory Judgment:	a court document which states the rights or status of an individual.
Eminent Domain:	the government's right to appropriate property for public use if accompanied by just compensation.
Ex Post Facto:	any law or document with an effect that is retroactive.
Injunction:	a court order prohibiting an act or ordering an action to be taken.
Writ of Habeas Corpus:	an order of the court requiring officials to show sufficient cause for detaining a person; if cause can not be given, the person must be set free.

AMERICAN GOVERNMENT TERMS

Bossism:	the control of the party organization by a politician within his district.
Caucus:	the planning committee of a political party which outlines policies and chooses candidates.
Cloture Rule:	a regulation which ends debate and puts the issue to an immediate vote.
Dark Horse:	a nominee for office who arises unexpectedly at a political convention.
Elastic Clause:	Section 8 of Article I of the Constitution which gives Congress the power to pass laws "necessary and proper" to enforce the Constitution.
Filibuster:	the use of long speeches or other measures to delay the legislative session.
Gerrymander:	the redistricting of a state giving unfair advantage to a political party.
Home Rule:	local self-government.
Impeachment:	the accusation of an official of wrong-doing; conviction or acquittal follows the proceedings. The House reserves the right to impeach, the Senate, to try the case.
Implied Powers:	powers not directly stated in the Constitution which the government maintains; delegated powers are directly stated.
Initiate:	the right of citizens to bypass the legislative body and originate laws themselves.
Jim Crow:	discrimination against Blacks.
Lame Duck:	a government official who has not been re-elected as he serves the remainder of his term.
Lobby:	a group which influences legislation, particularly for their cause.

Log Rolling:	the passing of bills favored by various officials who offer to approve each other's legislation.
Nullification:	the state's right to invalidate laws passed by the federal government.
Plank:	a principle of a political platform.
Platform:	the combined principles of a political party usually drafted at a convention.
President Pro Tem:	senator who presides over the Senate in the absence of the Vice President.
Recall:	the vote of the citizens removing a public official from office.
Referendum:	the procedure whereby citizens can either accept or reject measures passed by the legislature.
Short Ballot:	the election of a few officials while the rest are appointed to increase the accountability of those elected.
Solid South:	those states in the South which traditionally support the Democratic Party.
States' Rights:	the attempt to keep certain powers within the states, not the central government.
Spoils System:	the practice of awarding public positions to loyal party members; this is associated with President Andrew Jackson.
Third Parties:	political groups that arise to support temporary issues, other than the two major parties.

Anthropology

Anthropology is the study of man; in Greek, anthropos means "man." **Physical anthropology** studies mankind from a biological point of view. The various cultures that have occurred in the course of man's development are the subject of **cultural anthropology**.

Physical anthropologists study the biological nature of man in a number of ways. They study man as a member of the animal kingdom and compare his development to that of other creatures, in particular the primates. They also compare the biological evolution of man, and they make comparisons of people alive today and try to account for the physical differences present. **Cultural anthropology**, on the other hand, deals with the learned behavior of mankind. Here the scientist is concerned with the tools man has made, his customs and myths, his rituals and his language. The study of language is called **linguistics**.

Other studies are necessary for the anthropologist to complete his work. **Archaeology** is the study of the culture of ancient peoples through the digging up of cities and artifacts. By examining the finds of such excavations, the anthropologist can attempt to reconstruct the past. **Classical archaeology** is the study of these cultures through both ruins and written records of the people. **Prehistoric archaeology** relies on finding the material remains of a group. **Ethnology** is the study of the behavior of different groups of people. **Ethnography** is the study of a specific group of people at a particular time.

The physical anthropologist is aided by knowledge of **zoology** (the study of the animal kingdom), **anatomy** (the study of structure in animals), **heredity** (the study of genes and physical variation), and **physiology** (the study of function in animals). **Geology** (the study of the earth's history) and **paleontology** (the study of fossils) are also invaluable to the anthropologist. The cultural anthropologist who studies present day cultures needs to understand the religions, arts, family structure and codes, making it necessary for him to understand the principles of sociology and psychology.

Before going on with the review, try these sample CLEP questions:

1. **In studying Egyptian hieroglyphics, in what field would the anthropologist be concentrating?**

   (A) linguistics
   (B) classical archaeology
   (C) prehistoric archaeology
   (D) paleontology
   (E) physiology

1. (B) The study of hieroglyphics would be included in classical archaeology which studies both remains of buildings, artifacts, etc., and written records. Prehistoric archaeology does not include written records; this area goes much further back in man's history. Linguistics is the study of spoken language, some of which have been written. Paleontology is the study of fossils. Physiology is the study of the function of organisms.

2. **Cultural anthropology concentrates on which of the following?**

   (A) learned behavior
   (B) religion
   (C) kinship ties
   (D) linguistics
   (E) all of the above

2. (E) Cultural anthropology deals with all learned behaviors, which includes religion and myths, family structure and kinship ties, and linguistics.

3. **An anthropologist studying a present day African tribe would be involved in which study?**

   (A) ethnography
   (B) ethnology
   (C) heredity
   (D) prehistoric archaeology
   (E) psychology

3. (A) Ethnography is the study of a particular group in a particular time. Ethnology studies behaviors of groups of people. Heredity is a study of genetic structure and gene pools (the groups of genes present in a group). Prehistoric archaeology concentrates on prehistoric times. Psychology would be useful in studying this African tribe, but would not be the only consideration

4. **Which methods of study would an anthropologist be likely to use?**

(A) descriptive methods
(B) historical methods
(C) scientific methods
(D) A and B only
(E) all of the above

4. (E) The anthropologist uses descriptive methods when he describes the present conditions of a group and historical methods when he researches elements of that group's history. He is scientific both in describing observable facts accurately and in his use of scientific methods of dating and analyzing his finds.

CULTURE

Culture is the learned behavior of human society expressed in its ideas, knowledge, art, skills, customs and organizations. Anthropologists will frequently use the term civilization to refer to culture or to a specific group that has developed into a complex state. Ordinarily, civilization is a term of history which indicates that a group has developed to the point where they have written records, advanced agricultural and architectural techniques, and large cities. When an anthropologist refers to "a culture," he is referring to a specific group.

Learned behavior, or rather the degree to which man is motivated to act by learned behavior, is perhaps the most important condition that separates man from other animals. His linguistic ability is another feature that allows man so much further development. Because man can express and, in many cases, record his ideas, learned behaviors can be transmitted not only to members of the present group but also from generation to generation.

Lower animals are largely motivated by reflexes and instincts. A **reflex** is an automatic response to a stimulus, such as sneezing or grasping. An **instinct** is a behavior pattern with which an organism is born, such as nesting or migration. While man does possess some reflexes (sucking as an infant, knee-jerk reflex), he is largely motivated by drives. There are two kinds of **drives**, physical and acquired. **Physical drives** are bodily needs, such as the desire for food, water and sexual activity. For the most part, man fulfills these needs in the manner he has learned in his society. **Acquired drives** are needs for such items as money and power which can in turn satisfy bodily needs and provide personal satisfaction. These acquired drives are always learned.

The culture into which a person is born will in many ways dictate the direction of his development. He will learn the society's language, customs, mores, beliefs and rituals. He will be trained in order to take a place in that society from childhood, through adolescence and into adulthood. The roles assigned to the various ages and sex of the members will differ from culture to culture, but the society's culture will nonetheless have a profound effect on the person's development.

Modern technology has had a tremendous impact on cultures, causing them to change at a phenomenal rate. Advanced societies such as the United States have undergone remarkable changes in the past one hundred years. Television and telephones have changed communication to an instantaneous experience; jets and superhighways have changed transportation. Computer technology will soon be used in almost every facet of life. While it is easy to witness change in advanced countries, cultures without these developments also change even though the process may be very slow. Changes may be caused by a natural disaster, a drought, an invasion or a period of population growth or decline. Societies must adapt to these changes, and so parts of their culture must also adapt. There usually are forces present, however, to keep changes to a minimum, such as the religion or kinship rules of a group.

Acculturation is the process through which a culture changes because of extended contact with another culture. The impact of one culture upon the other may be equal, or one culture may have overriding influence upon the other. Many undeveloped nations in the world today are undergoing this process as the technology from advanced societies are brought to them. Some cultures, in many ways accept these advances while in other ways they resist, as in some Middle Eastern countries where automobiles and veiled women may be seen on the same street.

Through the centuries many groups have met and intermingled, sometimes in peace, sometimes in war, and the cultures of these groups have been brought to other lands. The feelings, however, that one's own culture, with its customs and beliefs, is superior to others is known as **ethnocentrism. Ethnic appreciation**, on the other hand, is an attitude of respect for other cultures while keeping intact one's own customs and beliefs.

Before going on with the review, try these sample CLEP questions:

ANSWERS:

5. **Man is most frequently motivated by which of the following?**

   (A)   acculturation
   (B)   drives
   (C)   instincts
   (D)   reflexes
   (E)   culture

5. (B)   Man is most frequently motivated by his drives, both physical and acquired. Reflexes are automatic responses, and instincts are inborn patterns of behavior. Acculturation is the process of change caused by another culture's influence. Culture is the learned behavior of mankind.

6. **A culture exerts control on the members of its society in which of the following ways?**

   (A)   laws regarding marriage
   (B)   social mores
   (C)   inheritance of leadership laws
   (D)   child-rearing guidelines
   (E)   all of the above

6. (E)   Marriage laws, social mores, inheritance of leadership laws and child-rearing guidelines are all ways that a culture can be preserved and can shape a society.

7. **Discrimination against minority groups can be viewed in one way as which of the following?**

   (A) ethnography
   (B) ethnology
   (C) ethnic appreciation
   (D) ethnocentric behavior
   (E) instinct

7. (D) Discrimination against minority groups in any society can stem in part from the majority's belief that its culture is superior. Ethnography is study of a particular time. Ethnology is the study of several cultures. Ethnic appreciation is an attitude of respect for other cultures. Instinct is an inborn pattern of behavior.

8. **Which of the following is generally considered one of the hallmarks of a civilization?**

   (A) small villages
   (B) oral tradition
   (C) basic hand tools for farming
   (D) folk art
   (E) none of the above

8. (E) The words culture and civilization can be used interchangeably in anthropology, but civilization is used more frequently to name large, powerful societies. Large cities and advanced methods of agriculture and art are signs, as is written language.

CROSS-CULTURAL COMPARISONS

Despite the individual characteristics that define a culture, the anthropologist nonetheless looks for common denominators so that he can make **cross-cultural comparisons**. Cultures frequently cross national boundaries and can not always be defined geographically. Therefore, the anthropologist will look for **cultural units**.

The most basic unit is the **household**, which may consist of father-mother-children or be extended to additional members. Households that are sedentary are next grouped into villages if the households number one hundred or so. Larger groupings are called **towns**, and still larger, **cities**. If the one hundred or so households are nomadic, they form a **band**. Bands that are united by the same culture are called **tribes**. Loosely united tribes are called **confederacies**.

A **society** is a group that shares a common culture and a common identity. Size of this group does not matter. A nation may have one society or several; the elements that distinguish a nation from other groups are the presence of a central government and set boundaries. Because a nation may have several societies present, anthropologists refer to the various cultures as **ethnic groups**. Such groups may be present in adjacent countries, and because of immigration, nations distant from one another.

Another approach useful to anthropologists in the comparison of cultures is to designate subdivisions of cultures with distinct characteristics as **subcultures**. Youth in America is an example of a subculture. **Culture traits**, behaviors or objects peculiar to a culture, are also useful classifications; a rickshaw is an Oriental trait.

Closely related culture traits form **trait-complexes**; customs and rituals surrounding a marriage ceremony would be an example. If these trait-complexes are shared by adjacent societies, anthropologists will classify the region a **culture area**.

Basic inventions are those discoveries that unlock or utilize basic principles, such as fire, the wheel or the steam engine. **Secondary inventions** use the principles of basic inventions, such as the cart or the steam boat. Through history, there have been inventions discovered in various parts of the world independent of one another. Written language is an example of an independent invention. **Diffusion** is the introduction of the inventions and other culture traits of a group to another. For example, gunpowder was brought from China to Europe.

In keeping a complete picture, some anthropologists study urban areas to learn of the impact of various ethnic groups on city life.

Before going on with the review, try these sample CLEP questions:

	ANSWERS:

9. **The most basic unit of a culture is which of the following?**

   (A)   husband-wife
   (B)   mother-father-children
   (C)   household
   (D)   related households
   (E)   village

9. (C)   The household is the basic unit, made-up of the people who live in one abode. A village is usually one hundred households.

10. **One hundred nomadic households would constitute which of the following?**

   (A)   league
   (B)   band
   (C)   confederacy
   (D)   village
   (E)   town

10. (B)   One hundred nomadic households would make up a band. Bands contribute to tribes, and loosely united tribes make up leagues, or confederacies. Villages and towns are stationary groups.

11. **The element that distinguishes a nation from a society is which of the following?**

   (A)   distinct territorial boundaries
   (B)   two or more diverse cultures
   (C)   a central government
   (D)   A and C
   (E)   all of the above

11. (D)   Central government and set boundaries distinguish a nation. A nation will usually, though not necessarily, have only one society. Two cultures means two societies, but not necessarily a nation.

12. **Those who attend rock concerts frequently would most likely be considered which of the following?**

(A) subculture
(B) culture
(C) society
(D) band
(E) ethnic group

12. (A) Rock concert followers comprise a subculture. Culture and society are terms that are too broad. Band means nomadic households. Ethnic group is used loosely to identify cultural and/or racial groups.

PHYSICAL ANTHROPOLOGY

In order to appreciate fully the development of man, an understanding of the theory concerning the origin of life is necessary. The earth is estimated to be five billion years old; scientists have guessed that the earliest life forms appeared about three billion years ago. The idea of **spontaneous generation**, which states that organisms spring from lifeless matter, was prevalent for centuries. When in the seventeenth century it was demonstrated that maggots are hatched from eggs and do not spontaneously generate from decaying meat, man began to look for other explanations concerning the origin of life.

The elements of hydrogen, oxygen, nitrogen and carbon are found in all living things. Combinations of these elements make up cells, the basic structural units of living matter. All living cells contain proteins, which are made up of chains of amino acids. Nucleic acids are found in the nuclei of cells and are responsible for directing the many activities of these cells. It is the variety of these cells that ultimately account for the variety of life forms.

Just how the basic elements of hydrogen, oxygen, nitrogen and carbon were transformed into living organisms is unclear, but an experiment first carried out in 1953 by **Stanley L. Miller** presents some startling evidence. In his experiment, Miller introduced four gases present in abundance in the primitive earth's atmosphere— water vapor, ammonia, methane and hydrogen—into a sealed chamber. For several days these gases were exposed to electrical charges, analogous to the electrical storms of primitive earth. When he analyzed the water solution in the container, he found that several amino acids, the building blocks of protein, had formed. Since at least two billion years elapsed between the earth's formation and the creation of earliest life forms, scientists consider it mathematically reasonable that the amino acids, proteins and nucleic acids formed by chance in the "soup" of the primeval seas. Since, however, these seas may have caused the compounds to dissolve, perhaps a molecule formed that could draw on its surroundings for survival and reproduce.

However the first life emerged, the millions of years that followed brought about amazing complexity and variation of life forms. It has been suggested, for example, that plant forms, which appeared first, may have transformed somehow into organisms with locomotion, early animal forms. This, of course, is not for certain. By studying present day animals, man has devised a system of classification. **Carolus Linnaeus (Karl von Linne)** devised a system in 1735 which has since been modified. Man belongs to the **chordates** (bilateral-two like sides) which have a notochord, a rod-like internal support structure in early development. In later development, man and other animals of this group develop vertebrae. Fish, amphibians, reptiles, birds and mammals all have vertebrae. Most mammals have hairy bodies, feed milk to their young from glands and have a system for maintaining body temperature. Modern man, **Homo sapiens**, belongs to the order of primates as do present day apes; however, man belongs to the family of hominids while the ape belongs to the family of pongids. In this nomenclature, homo is the genus, which means man, and sapiens, meaning wise, is the species.

The scientific work of two men, **Charles Darwin and Gregor Mendel**, made two most important contributions to man's understanding of evolution. Darwin's theory centered on the concept of **natural selection**. Nature allows for variations among organisms; no two are exactly alike. Organisms over-reproduce, which causes competition for food and space, a struggle for existence. Because of variation, some organisms will adapt better than others; the fittest survive. Those who survive reproduce and pass on the traits that aided survival. In time, this natural selection may give rise to a new species.

At about the same time, Mendel was recording observations of the variations of pea plants. His observations can be summarized as follows: **heredity** is based on the transmission of pairs of genes; each parent offers one gene for each separate trait; if the parents offer contrasting genes, the offspring is a hybrid, characterized by the dominant gene; genes assort randomly, but at a predictable rate. If the parents each offer a recessive gene, the offspring will be characterized by that recessive trait.

Since Mendel's time, it has been discovered that variations in organisms occur because of **mutations**, sudden changes in the genes of an organism. Genes are located on the chromosomes which are composed largely of proteins and deoxyribonucleic acid, DNA. The structure of DNA is a double helix and is found in cell nuclei. When a cell divides, the DNA splits and duplicates itself, a process called **replication**. If there is an error in this replication, a mutation will occur.

The workings of variation, mutation and natural selection have resulted in present day life forms. Anthropologists keep these concepts in mind as they view fossil remains. As they examine fossils, they are always using the earth's surface and subsurface layers to establish a time scale of the earth's history. Sediment is deposited by water and wind on the earth's surface; this is an ongoing process, and lower layers are under so much pressure that they eventually turn to rock. Fossils found at these various levels can thus be dated.

Geologists break down the earth's history into six eras, which are divided into periods, and subdivided again into epochs. Man and his closest ancestors appeared in the most recent era, the **Cenozoic**. In the **Tertiary period**, shrewlike ancestors of primates appeared. Primates appeared in the **Eocene epoch** of this period with characteristics that made it a special group. These primates developed binocular vision, increased cranial capacity (brain case), increased mobility of the feet and hands and more complex social behavior. In the **Miocene epoch** twenty-five million years ago, the ancestors of modern apes and man developed along separate lines. Features differentiating man from the apes include larger brains, smaller jaws, a decrease in the size of molars and lengthening of the lower limbs which eventually aided upright posture.

The smaller front teeth of **Ramapithecus**, found in Africa, indicate that this "man ape" may have used its forelimbs to grab vegetation and, therefore, may have been somewhat erect; since no pelvic bone has been found, this can not be said for certain. **Australopithecus africanus** did, however, move about on two limbs, which is called **bipedalism**, and used simple weapons. **Australopithecus robustus**, larger than the africanus, was also fairly upright. Ramapithecus is thirteen million years old; the australopithecines are between two to one-half a million years old. To date, scientists have not been able to state their exact relationship to man, except that the australopithecines had features which were closer to evolving into man than apes.

Other discoveries added more to the total picture. **Java man**, found in Indonesia and **Peking man**, found in China, are between 400,000 and 700,000 years old and have been classified as Homo erectus. While Peking man has a greater brain capacity, both walked upright and both probably used tools. Java man is the older of the two and existed when the australopithecines did; some anthropologists believed they may have even shared the same habitat, but this can not be proven. **Dr. Louis Leakey** and his wife Mary discovered fossils which were named **Homo habilis**. The Leakeys believe this group gave rise to modern man, not the australopithecines. Not all anthropologists agree, and this debate has not been settled.

Early varieties of Homo sapiens have been found around the globe. **Steinheim man**, found in Germany, is about 300,000 years old and has a cranial capacity larger than earlier fossils. **Swanscombe man**, found in England, has an even larger brain case, and stone axes and other tools were found nearby. **Neanderthal man** fossils (30,000 to 50,000 years old) have been found in Europe, Africa, the Middle East and Asia. The fossils of Europe indicate a powerfully built man with a large brain case and a capacity for mental processes and cultural expression. He made fine tools and buried his dead. Anthropologists believe, however, that modern man did not descend directly from this group, that another group appeared 35,000 years ago, the **Cro-Magnons**, who may have populated Europe, Africa, Asia and the Americas. This man looked like modern man except that he was larger. He was a skilled toolmaker, used fire, buried his dead and painted on the walls of his caves.

Just how these various groups interrelate is not known. Anthropologists do suspect, however, that the biological and cultural changes of these groups interacted. Man had to be bipedal in order to make and use tools. The more he needed tools, for defense for example, the greater his need to be upright. Those forms that developed larger brains were better able to make and use tools. Natural selection would have favored these forms. Larger brains would have contributed to other developments, greater manual dexterity, language and more complex social behavior. In turn, these developments favored increased brain development, a feedback system linked to natural selection.

Before going on with the review, try these sample CLEP questions:

13. Which of the following elements are found in all living things?

(A) hydrogen
(B) nitrogen
(C) carbon
(D) oxygen
(E) all of the above

14. Which of the following statements is true of spontaneous generation?

(A) It was proven to exist in the eighteenth century.
(B) It is another name for replication.
(C) It is the process of cell division under certain circumstances.
(D) It states that life forms from lifeless matter.
(E) None of the above.

15. The experiment conducted by Stanley L. Miller demonstrated which of the following?

(A) that certain gases were present in the primeval earth's atmosphere
(B) that certain gases present then are still present today
(C) that the gases then present may have formed certain compounds under particular conditions
(D) that electrical storms certainly were the life-creating forces
(E) all of the above

16. Which of the following groups do not have vertebrae?

(A) mammals
(B) insects
(C) reptiles
(D) fish
(E) amphibians

ANSWERS:

13. (E) Hydrogen, oxygen, nitrogen and carbon are found in all living things.

14. (D) Spontaneous generation states that life springs from lifeless matter. It was disproved in the seventeenth century. Replication is the division and reproduction of DNA.

15. (C) Miller's experiment demonstrated that gases in a sealed container exposed to electrical charges will produce several amino acids, the building blocks of protein. It does not prove exactly how life was created.

16. (B) Insects do not have vertebrae, internal support systems.

17. Gregor Mendel is remembered for which system or theory?

(A) nomenclature
(B) natural selection
(C) survival of the fittest
(D) variation through heredity
(E) all of the above

18. For geologists, the first time classification is which of the following?

(A) millennium
(B) period
(C) century
(D) era
(E) epoch

19. Variations that helped to make way for man include which of the following?

(A) binocular vision
(B) development of the thumb
(C) fewer offspring produced at one time
(D) increased life span
(E) all of the above

20. Which of the following is not classified Homo sapiens?

(A) Peking man
(B) Steinheim man
(C) Cro-Magnon man
(D) Swanscombe man
(E) Neanderthal man

17. (D) Mendel concentrated on variations determined by heredity. Nomenclature, or naming system, is associated with Linnaeus; natural selection and survival of the fittest are associated with Darwin.

18. (D) Geologists first classify time into eras, then periods, then epochs. A millennium is any thousand year period, and a century is an one hundred year period; these terms are not generally used by geologists.

19. (E) Binocular vision aids depth perception. Thumb development improves manual dexterity. Fewer offspring per pregnancy reduces care and increases the transmission of learning behavior. Increased life span aids overall survival.

20. (A) Peking man is classified Homo erectus.

PRIMATE BEHAVIOR

Because humans, monkeys and apes share a common ancestor and are closely related in the overall scheme of things, scientists have been interested in the behavior of monkeys and apes. Study of these creatures indicates some similarities in behavior shown by primates and man, and may offer clues about the behaviors of modern man's ancestors.

Most primates are social creatures, and the activities of foraging, grooming and sex are expressions of this social aspect in most species. Play, especially among the young, is another important feature, which may, in fact, prepare them for adult behaviors, including sex. Primates deprived of play activities in experiments do not develop normal adult behaviors. Since the various species have different behavior patterns, and since the same species in different locales develop differing behaviors, it can only be guessed that there is no one set of human behavior pattern, and that through his evolution, man has adapted to innumerable situations.

Of all the primates studied, chimpanzees display behaviors that are most like human behaviors. Chimpanzees get most of their food from trees and live in a very open society. Unlike some of the other primates, the rules of dominance are simple: grown males dominate females and young; among grown males, there is a flexible dominance order; grown females dominate all young. The only permanent bond observed is between a mother and her infants, which appears to continue into adolescence. Chimpanzees are promiscuous, however, and so the father cannot be ascertained. This behavior does not appear to arouse jealousy, and the animals tend to be very tolerant of one another. Chimpanzee babies are wholly dependent upon their mothers in the first six months of life. As they become independent, they play, but always within the mother's sight. Sexual maturity occurs at the ages of nine or ten, and life expectancy is thirty years or more.

Chimpanzees have been observed in the wilds standing, walking and running on their hind legs in special circumstances. This bipedal locomotion is used, for example, when the animal is carrying something or is fearful. Chimpanzees make and use tools, sometimes in ways that indicate foresight. One example is the "fishing rod," a carefully selected vine or twig used to catch termites. Chimpanzees in the wild have also been reported to hunt meat and to engage in cannibalism. However, there is no evidence thus far that the big cats prey on chimpanzees; one reason suggested is that the odor of the chimpanzee is a passive defense. Some anthropologists attribute man's survival in part to the same reason.

While chimpanzees do not have the capacity for speech as humans do, they have been observed to communicate through sounds and gestures. **Jane Goodall**, a foremost observer of this species, has even observed a type of "rain dance."

Before going on with the review, try these sample CLEP questions:

ANSWERS:

21. **One reason for studying primate behavior in the wild would be which of the following?**

   (A) to modify the behavior of the species
   (B) to study this pure behavior and apply the rules of primate society to human society
   (C) to make reasonable guesses about the behavior of man's ancestors
   (D) A and C
   (E) B and C

21. (C) Wild primates are studied in part to make conjecture about the behavior of man's ancestors. Scientists do not wish to modify the behavior of wild creatures and take precautions not to do so even in indirect ways. Scientists may make comparisons between the behavior of primates and man but do not attempt to change man's behavior.

22. **Which of the following statements is true of wild chimpanzees?**

(A) They are always bipedal.
(B) They are usually bipedal.
(C) They are bipedal only when angry.
(D) They are bipedal under certain circumstances.
(E) Their anatomical structure never permits bipedalism.

23. **As a rule, chimpanzees would be characterized as which of the following?**

(A) social
(B) fiercely aggressive
(C) apathetic
(D) neurotic
(E) none of the above

22. (D) Chimpanzees are bipedal under certain circumstances, such as when carrying something, looking around while in tall grass, or running in excitement or fear.

23. (A) Chimpanzees are very social creatures. They do show signs of aggression but only rarely.

Archaeology

Archaeology is the study of ancient cultures by excavation of ancient ruins. These excavations, or digs, involve the systematic removal of dirt and other debris which cover the site. Since archaeologists attempt to alter the site as little as possible, great care is taken in the removal of this debris. In the course of excavation, however, the original record of the site is destroyed, and so the archaeologist and his team carefully note the exact location of every bone, artifact and building that they unearth. Before any digging takes place, the area is mapped out and a point of reference is established; grids are used to pinpoint the location of each find. Picks and shovels of all sizes are used, the smallest ones around areas close to suspected finds. Measuring devices are needed, and so are paintbrushes, toothbrushes and air pumps to remove dirt. In many cases, dirt that has been moved is passed through a sieve to retrieve articles that have been overlooked.

Any number of factors may initiate interest in an area and spark an excavation. Natural disasters can unearth clues that ancient ruins lie beneath the surface. Sometimes, ordinary people stumble upon artifacts or other indications of ruins. Odd topographical features, such as mounds of dirt surrounded by plains, may yield finds. Construction sites of city buildings and highways, quarries or farming sometimes turn up evidence. Some sites have been chosen because of information contained in ancient documents; such texts and even legends have also led archaeologists to search for sunken treasure and other finds in the sea.

Once a general site has been chosen, the archaeologist will dig a test site, a series of trenches from which further digging originates. If the whole area is to be dug, square patches are excavated. As artifacts and bone fragments are found, their precise location is recorded before they are moved, noting also the depth at which they are found. Photography is a most useful tool here. Each piece is cleaned and numbered; a description of the piece, its location, number and finder are recorded. This information may later provide the archaeologist with clues when he conducts his analysis. Not only what is found, but also the relationship of the pieces to one another is important. The archaeologist may also examine the soil itself and plant and animal remains, therefore, knowledge of these areas is essential. He may also note carvings on walls, evidence of fire pits and other features indicating habitation. When the recording process is complete, the pieces are carefully packed and sent to museums or universities for study and storage.

Absolute chronology indicates specific ages of finds; **relative chronology** indicates age as older or younger than the age of other finds. **Crossdating** compares traits of sites with known ages with those sites of unknown age. **Dendrochronology** is a method of dating using the rings of trees. Study of soil and rock formation can also indicate age. **Carbon-14 testing** reveals age by measuring the amount of radioactive carbon-14 in organic matter; the content decreases at a regular rate. The **fluorine content** in bones increases with age, giving scientists another measure. The archaeologist also classifies his finds by material, shape, technique used to create the object, use and type of decoration, all of which yield clues about the culture. Much of his study takes place in the laboratory; only when the finds have been fully examined can he begin to make analysis and draw conclusions.

Before going on with the review, try these sample CLEP questions:

ANSWERS:

1. **In the course of uncovering ruins, which of the following may an archaeologist use?**

   (A) heavy machinery
   (B) toothbrush
   (C) ice pick
   (D) dentist's tools
   (E) all of the above

1. (E) Heavy earth-moving machinery may be called in to remove dirt, debris or other buildings, but only after tests have been conducted to be sure that valuable information will not be destroyed in trying to reach a site. Toothbrushes, ice picks and dentist's tools are all fine instruments with which to do delicate digging.

2. **Which of the following is dendochronology?**

   (A) use of dentist's tools at digs
   (B) radioactive dating
   (C) study of soil samples
   (D) tree-ring study
   (E) none of the above

2. (D) Dendochronology is the study of the rings of trees to determine age. Both the number of rings and their widths are considered when making comparisons.

3. **What is the first step an archaeologist would take at a site?**

   (A) dig trenches
   (B) map the area
   (C) dig square samples
   (D) call in a bulldozer
   (E) none of the above

3. (B) Before doing anything, the archaeologist maps the area and sets a point of reference for measurements. This work is frequently done by a trained surveyor.

4. **In addition to "home" sites, what other type of site is of interest to the archaeologist?**

   (A) burial grounds
   (B) garbage heaps
   (C) wrecked ships
   (D) A and C
   (E) all of the above

4. (E) Burial grounds frequently contain artifacts which were buried with the dead and reveal information about their culture. Garbage heaps may contain broken artifacts or seed samples useful to the archaeologist. Wrecked ships may contain treasures and everyday utensils.

PREHISTORY

Prehistory is the period of time before man started to record events; **written history** goes back only five or six thousand years, so there is a vast amount of time to be explored without the aid of written records. Generally, prehistory has been divided into three phases: the **Paleolithic (Old Stone) Age**, the **Mesolithic (Middle Stone) Age** and the **Neolithic (New Stone) Age**. By the end of the Neolithic Age, man started to use metals and to record events.

The **Paleolithic Age** is further subdivided into three periods. The Lower Paleolithic is the longest, running from 2,000,000 to about 150,000 years ago, during which time man made simple pebble tools by a technique called flaking. Flaking in general is the removal from the core of the stone, thin layers of flake to shape the tool. Some specific methods involved striking the stone with another object, while others involved pressuring the flake off the core. Toward the end of this period man developed the hand axe, a most useful tool. Man, during most of the Paleolithic Age, was a nomadic hunter living in relatively small groups and rounding out his diet with nuts, berries and fruits. By the Middle period, he had increased the types of tools to include spears and a variety of scrapers. There is also evidence that this **Neanderthal man** used fire and buried his dead.

The Upper period begins about 40,000 years ago and ends about 10,000 B.C. Most of the artifacts found are associated with **Cro-Magnon man** and reflect his full mental capacities and other cultural advancements. Not only did he invent useful tools, but he was also an excellent hunter. There is also evidence of a growing religious awareness as well as artistic development. Some of his tools had ornate carvings, and he sculpted figures out of stone. His artwork, found deep in the caves of southern France and northern Spain, includes depictions of animals painted on cave walls and probably had a magical purpose. By painting successful hunting scenes, man may have been wishing for success in the future; this imitating of desired results is called imitative magic.

Toward the end of the Upper Paleolithic, glaciers receded in Europe and the earth's temperature rose resulting in more vegetation. Man was able to shift from hunting large game to gathering wild food and catching small game during the following age, the **Mesolithic**. The tools of this age include the **microlith**, a small blade tool, and greater use of the bow and arrow. During this age man started to form small farming communities, especially in the Middle East. This tradition grew in the **Neolithic Age**. Archeologists have found ruins in the Middle East suggesting that man used grinding tools and sickles to harvest wild grain, some of which was stored. The step that followed was the cultivation of these seeds, agriculture, in areas with water supplies. The ancient cities of **Jarmo** in Iraq, **Jerich** in Israel and **Catal Hyuk** in Turkey have been excavated and have yielded information about this period.

The ability to raise and store food and the domestication of animals gave rise to cities. Because of the time cultivation requires, the nomadic tradition was abandoned by those with farms. Agricultural improvements occurred, including irrigation; proximity to a water source was essential, which is why so many cities sprung up near the Tigris-Euphrates river system. One of the most important cities to emerge was the city of **Ur**, a Sumerian city-state in what is today called Iraq. This city had temples, palaces and public projects such as irrigation canals. The king, priests, warriors, artisans, and peasants helped to make up classes. In the later part of this period, pure metals were used, followed by the development of alloys. Tin and copper were joined to form bronze. The **Bronze Age** not only saw the development of artwork and weapons from this material, but also the beginnings of written records.

Those humans who 30,000 years ago crossed the strip of land joining Asia with North America (today's Bering Strait) were the initiators of population growth and expansion throughout North, Middle and South America. One of the earliest known cultures centered on the hunting of large game, known as the **Big-Game Hunting tradition**, which dates back to at least 10,000 B.C. When the glaciers receded (about 8,000 B.C.), some groups in the western and eastern sections of North America turned to greater collection and eventually cultivation of seeds, while the Hunting tradition continued in the Great Plains for another 4,000 years. The most advanced tradition to develop in all the Americas, however, was the **Mesoamerican tradition** of Central America.

In what is today Mexico and Honduras, a number of civilizations arose. The ruins of one, **Teotihucan**, are thirty miles northeast of Mexico City, including the **Pyramid of the Sun**. After this ceremonial center was destroyed, another arose at **Tula**, north of Mexico City. This, too, fell and eventually the **Aztecs** emerged and built an empire. The center of this empire, **Tenachtitlan**, lies beneath today's Mexico City. Its society was divided into classes ranging from royalty to warriors, priests, merchants, freemen and slaves. Aztec art was closely related to its religion (which required sacrifice of human hearts); temples and stone figures were elaborately adorned. Spanish domination brought about the end of this empire. **Maya civilization** also had ceremonial centers, but the people were scattered in the area, convening for religious ceremonies. The Mayas achieved much, including an accurate calendar and prediction of solar eclipses, a symbol for and use of the concept of zero and hieroglyphic writing. The cause of this empire's collapse is not known, but it may have been connected to wide-spread crop failure or to population pressures.

Before going on with the review, try these sample CLEP questions:

5. Which of the following is the correct order of the Stone Age subdivisions?

(A) Paleolithic, Mesolithic, Neolithic

(B) Paleolithic, Neolithic, Mesolithic

(C) Mesolithic, Paleolithic, Neolithic

(D) Neolithic, Paleolithic, Mesolithic

(E) Mesolithic, Neolithic, Paleolithic

ANSWERS:

5. (A) "Paleo-" means "old," "Meso-" means "middle," and "Neo-" means "new"; the root "lith" means "stone."

6. Pebble-tools of the Stone Age were made by which of the following processes?

(A) firing
(B) flaking
(C) coring
(D) only stones with natural shapes were used
(E) none of the above

6. (B) Pebble-tools were made by a process called flaking. Flaking could be achieved by striking the stone or applying pressure to it. These thin flakes were removed from the core; these tools were not fired. Some were hafted, attached to shafts of wood or bone, in later ages. Some pebble-tools did occur naturally, but anthropologists believe that many were handmade.

7. Cro-Magnon man is associated with which period appearing below?

(A) Lower Paleolithic
(B) Middle Paleolithic
(C) Upper Paleolithic
(D) A and B
(E) none of the above

7. (C) Cro-Magnon man is associated with the Upper Paleolithic, ranging from about 40,000 to 12,000 years ago.

8. All of the following factors gave rise to cities except which one?

(A) seed cultivation
(B) domestication of animals
(C) improved agricultural techniques
(D) hunting large game
(E) water sources

8. (D) When man learned cultivation of seeds, he turned away from the hunting of large game as the mainstay of his diet. Agriculture requires time and care. It is also a safer way to obtain food. Man domesticated animals for food, clothing needs and as beasts of burden. Water sources and irrigation systems improved the prospects for agriculture, which in turn gave rise to the cities.

9. The Big-Game Hunting tradition lasted longest in which region?

(A) eastern North America
(B) western North America
(C) the Great Plains
(D) Middle America
(E) South America

9. (C) The Big-Game Hunting tradition lasted longest on the American Great Plains. To the east and west of this area, humans turned to collection of food and eventually agriculture.

10. Which civilization has ruins beneath the center of present-day Mexico City?

    (A) Maya
    (B) Inca
    (C) Tula
    (D) Toltec
    (E) Aztec

10. (E) Aztec ruins lie beneath Mexico City. Maya civilization extended from southern Mexico to the Yucatan to the Honduras. The Inca civilization was located in Peru. Tula was a ceremonial center founded by the Toltecs, warlike invaders from the north. This center was located north of today's Mexico City.

COMPARATIVE SOCIAL INSTITUTIONS

Early in man's evolution, the period of time between birth and maturity began to lengthen. Human infants and children still are dependent for longer periods of time than any other animal. Since the child depended upon the mother, the mother could not carry out all the survival behaviors and so depended upon the father. This cooperation in the raising of children most likely gave rise to the father-mother-child (children) relationship, called the **nuclear family** today. This relationship provides training for the young and companionship, emotional support and sexual expression for the parents. The children also experience emotional support and upon maturation initiate their own nuclear families. Most modern societies practice **monogamy**, the union of one man and one woman approved by the society. Some societies, however, approve **polygamy**, a union with more than one husband or wife. Usually, it is the husband who has several wives; in most societies where this occurs, he must look out for the welfare of each wife and of any offspring. This restriction tends to limit the number of polygamous unions.

An **extended family** is usually based on a nuclear family to which are added grandparents, aunts, uncles or other near relatives. In America's past, extended families occurred frequently, but the trend today is toward nuclear families. **Kinship** is relationship to another and can be established by blood (consanguinity) or marriage (affinity). The kinship relationship can vary from society to society; for example, those who would be called first cousins in American society would be called brothers and sisters in traditional Hawaiian society. The kinship scheme used by a society shows the ties that are important to that society and regulates the type of behavior required in each relationship. If descent of the individual is traced through the father, the line of descent is termed patrilineal; if traced through the mother, it is called matrilineal. Related lineages form a clan, and marriage between lineages is required or encouraged to keep the bonds of the clan firm.

The guidelines for marriage established by a society are referred to as **rules for preferential mating**; all societies influence marriage partner selection to some degree. All societies have incest taboos which prohibit marriage between certain close relatives. One exception was in Egypt where the sons and daughters of the king could intermarry. The rules regarding the incest taboo vary from culture to culture, and the decision to marry is not made solely by the couple, but rather the families are involved. **Dowries** are required in some cultures, whereby the bride's family may give money or goods to help the couple establish their household; this practice is still observed by some European societies. In several African societies, money or property is given to the bride's family by the groom; this is called a **bride-price**. Divorce is not encouraged by any society, although most set up guidelines to dissolve marriages in some circumstances.

Societal classification can be based on a number of factors. Association by sex, age or both is a common way of grouping people in a society. These groupings can also be useful in assigning roles and duties. Social class is another way of organizing a society; classless societies do exist, but they are exceptions. Eskimo society is an example. Class distinction can be based on heredity, property ownership, conquest or tradition. Class distinction in the United States is based largely on economic level. **Status** is the rank a person holds in relation to others within a society. **Achieved status** is won by the individual; **ascribed status** comes automatically to the individual by birth. Behavior associated with any single status is a **role**. Most times the individual must assume several different roles as he finds himself in different situations. In some societies there is movement of individuals among the social classes; however, a **caste system,** such as found in Hindu civilization in India, does not permit change of membership in a class. Class of the individual is hereditary. The highest class is the **Brahmans** (priests and scholars), followed by the **Kshatriyas** (rulers and warriors), **Vaisyas** (merchants and farmers) and the **Sudras** (landless peasants). There exist many subdivisions. The **untouchables** are those completely outside this system, and they are avoided. The Indian government abolished untouchability, but the tradition still exists in some parts of India.

Religion is another institution that is found in all societies. Several theories have been offered to explain the origin of religion, ranging from early man's concept of a soul to his desire to understand, and even control, his environment. Both Neanderthal and Cro-Magnon man are thought to have developed a religious consciousness by the careful burial of their dead and the inclusion of objects and tools in their graves. There are also similarities between religion and the magic found in simple cultures. **White magic** benefits people; **black magic** harms them. **Imitative magic**, such as Cro-Magnon may have been performing with his cave paintings, is based on the belief that an action will produce a like action. **Contagious magic** is based on the belief that objects which were once in contact with one another can exert influence over one another when separated; for example, burning a piece of cloth belonging to another may bring him harm.

Shamans, or medicine men, are practitioners of magic whose purpose is to cure others. They may lay hands on the ill to bring about a cure or pretend to remove an object from the body associated with the illness. While this may be trickery, it can afford the patient psychological relief. **Oracles**, such as the oracle of Apollo at Delphi in ancient Greece, practice divination, or foretelling the future. **Witchcraft** is another type of magic. It is inherited, not learned as the other practices are.

Many religious practices include offerings and rituals. Human sacrifice was part of Aztec and Egyptian religion. Ancestor worship was common in China. Rituals also add stability to a society and are frequently used to mark key events in the life of an individual, such as birth, maturity, marriage or death. Religions in some societies, particularly the more complex ones, develop ethical codes to guide behavior.

Before going on with the review, try these sample CLEP questions.

11. Most societies approve of which of the following?

(A) monogamy
(B) polygamy
(C) polyandry
(D) polygyny
(E) none of the above

11. (A) Most societies approve of monogamy, the union of one man and one woman. Polygamy is a union with more than one spouse; polyandry is the union of one woman and several husbands; polygyny is the union of one husband and several wives.

12. All the statements concerning kinship are true except which of the following?

(A) Ties can be established by blood.
(B) Ties can be established by marriage.
(C) These ties can regulate behavior.
(D) Descent can be traced through the father.
(E) Ties and relationships remain the same from society to society.

12. (E) Kinship ties and relationships vary from society to society; cousins in one society may be called siblings in another.

Questions 13 through 17 refer to the following list:

    I.   preferential mating
    II. role
    III. incest taboo
    IV. bride-price
    V.   shaman

13. Which of the above is behavior associated with a particular status within society?

(A) I
(B) II
(C) III
(D) IV
(E) V

13. (B) Role is behavior associated with a particular status in a society. An individual may hold several positions in a society and therefore display several roles.

I.   preferential mating
II. role
III. incest taboo
IV. bride-price
V.   shaman

14. Which is the name of a role, the purpose of which is to cure others?

(A) I
(B) II
(C) III
(D) IV
(E) V

14. (E)   A shaman is a medicine man.

15. Which are the guidelines established for mating within a society?

(A) I
(B) II
(C) III
(D) IV
(E) V

15. (A)   Preferential mating is the establishment of guidelines for marriage within a society.

16. Which is the practice of gift giving to the bride's parents from the groom?

(A) I
(B) II
(C) III
(D) IV
(E) V

16. (D)   The bride-price is the gifts to the bride's parents by the groom to make up for the loss of the bride to her family.

17. Which is the prohibition of marriage between close relatives?

(A) I
(B) II
(C) III
(D) IV
(E) V

17. (C)   The incest taboo, which varies from society to society, prohibits marriage between close relatives.

CULTURAL RELATIVITY

Anthropologists study not only the cultures of ancient societies but also modern day groups. Cultural anthropologists study these societies from a variety of viewpoints, one of which is the development of personality. **Cultural behavior** is learned behavior, and children are greatly influenced by the rearing practices of their society. Since these practices vary from society to society, the personality traits from group to group differ. In addition, the way in which a society views the world (its world view) influences the way in which the people respond to their environment.

Increases in communication, transportation and technology have brought about changes in many of the world's cultures. Some of these changes have taken place readily while others have not. A society may resist change or reject it because it differs from tradition and/or is not understood. An accepted innovation may have side effects that cause additional problems. Knowledge of the cultural perceptions and practices of a society aids all types of people who come into contact with foreigners, including humanitarians, business men and diplomats. Such differences occur not only among modern nations but also among developing nations. By studying these differences, the anthropologist can aid others in establishing successful foreign relations.

Before going on with the review, try these sample CLEP questions:

ANSWERS:

18. Which of the following describes cultural behavior?

(A) learned behavior
(B) inherited behavior
(C) behavior influenced by rearing
(D) A and B
(E) A and C

18. (E) Cultural behavior is learned behavior, influenced to a large extent by rearing. Inherited behavior is instinctive behavior.

19. Which of the following best describes the role of the anthropologist in world relations?

(A) to direct foreign aid programs
(B) to change the world view of developing nations
(C) to explain cultural practices to foreign businessmen
(D) A and C
(E) B and C

19. (E) Anthropologists through contact with leaders and educational programs may be able to alter the world view of the people of a developing nation. This may make them more willing to accept technologies that will benefit them. By explaining cultural practices of a society to foreign businessmen, the anthropologist helps to improve communication.

GLOSSARY OF ANTHROPOLOGY & ARCHAEOLOGY TERMS

Amerindian: relating to the American Indian.

Age-grade: the grouping of members of a society by sex and age.

Animism: a belief in the existence of spiritual beings.

Augury: the practice of prediction in ancient Rome; augurs would interpret the entrails of dead creatures.

Antiquities Act: a 1906 act of the United States Congress prohibiting the destruction of archaeological ruins on federal lands.

Brachiation: the use of the forelimbs to travel through trees by swinging from branch to branch.

Cephalic Index: the number expressing the ratio of head length to head width.

Cultural Ecology: the study of the influence of the environment upon the society.

Dialect: a form of a language peculiar to a region or social group.

Dryopithecus: a Miocene ape which shows manlike features of dentition.

Emergency Archaeology: excavation and recovery of ruins and artifacts threatened by modern construction.

Ethnomusicology: the branch of anthropology which studies the music of cultures, especially those of nonliterate people.

Folklore: the oral traditions, dances, beliefs and songs of a culture handed down from generation to generation.

Linguistic Topology: the grouping of languages according to the structure of the languages.

Local Race: a population which does not breed with others because of natural or social barriers.

Morpheme: the smallest meaningful unit in a language.

Nonliterate: lacking a writing system.

Peasantry: persons who till the soil as laborers or small landowners.

Phoneme: the smallest sound in a language.

Polytheism: belief in more than one god.

Primary Institution: a society's pattern of child treatment.

Proconsul: a Miocene ape thought to be the ancestor of modern gorillas and chimpanzees.

Rites of Passage: religious ceremonies which mark the person's transition from one position to another.

Secondary Institutions: the organizations and activities that characterize a society.

Sibling: a brother or sister

Subculture:	a cultural pattern different from the overall culture and grouped separately.
Vestigial Organ:	a body part which remains in an organism but which no longer serves a function.
Zinjanthropus:	a fossil discovered by Dr. and Mrs. Louis Leakey at Olduvai Gorge, Africa.

Geography, Climatology and Ecology

These topics will comprise approximately 10% of the questions on the CLEP Social Science and History test. The questions will deal with the human effects and affects of these topics, not on the specific scientific details of an issue.

GEOGRAPHY

Many of the geography questions could be classified in other areas, and in fact we have already covered many of them. It is important to note that while humans were in the hunter and gatherer phase of civilization they could live anywhere. Different types of land could support greater numbers of people, but those numbers were simply limited by the amount of food and shelter in the area.

When civilization moved on to the next phase, farming, people were now limited to areas with arable land. This is when you saw the early civilizations build up on the fertile river valleys. Today with food distribution systems, people are able to live everywhere, even Antarctica. One of the challenges of the 21st century will be to get food to all the people who need it. Many people are still starving due to wars and inadequate food distribution systems.

Geography also plays a major role in the development of civilizations. Questions will commonly ask why one civilization developed differently than another. For instance, "Why was the Egyptian Empire more stable and why did it last longer than its contemporaries along the Tigris and Euphrates valleys?" The Egyptian civilization was separated from the other civilizations by deserts and mountains, and these features prevented the invasions that the other civilizations suffered.

The final topic commonly found in geography type questions is the effect of different types of climate change on a given region. Human populations can be greatly affected by changes in geography. The change in the course of a river, the melting of a glacier, or the movement of the path of an ocean current can all have both beneficial or detrimental effects.

WEATHER

Changes in weather can have a tremendous effect on human societies. Local events like hurricanes, typhoons and tornadoes have devastating effects and leave survivors traumatized, but their effects tend to fade over time.

Of greater concern to social scientists is when weather is the cause for dramatic changes in human behavior. For instance, a change in the weather pattern can led to crop failures. Food is one of the basic human needs and lack of it has caused some of the most significant events in human history. The failure of the Irish potato crop led to massive numbers of Irish emigrating to the United States.

The CLEP Social Science test will often ask a question on climate change; its effect on weather, and how it will effect human populations in the future. The effects will not always be negative. An increase in rainfall in a desert could result in more arable land, or an overall increase in carbon dioxide in the atmosphere will increase overall crop yeilds.

HUMANITY'S EFFECT ON THE ENVIRONMENT AND ECOLOGY

Prior to the industrial revolution, the effects that humans had on the environment were minimal. Some land was cleared for growing crops, but this did not affect water soaking into the land. The feudal overlords controlled all growth.

With the onset of the industrial revolution, large numbers of people were concentrated into the cities. These great concentrations of people were able to make significant changes to the local environment. Coal, the first fossil fuel used in great quantities, produced a layer of soot that turned the cities black.

Human civilizations affect the environment in three major ways: water quality, air quality and simply by our sheer numbers.

WATER QUALITY

When cities developed, they needed to come up with a way to dispose of their wastes both human and industrial. The simplest solution was to simply dump it in a nearby river. Very quickly the local ecology was not able to process the waste stream and the rivers became polluted.

In the last half of the 20th century, the governments of developed countries realized that pollution was detrimental to the overall welfare of the populace and started to pass laws to prevent further pollution and to clean up existing pollution. In the United States two good examples of these types of legislation are the clean water act and the superfund cleanup act. Developing countries however are still battling with this problem. They are trying to control both growth and pollution at the same time. Unfortunately many of the waterways in developing nations contain very high levels of pollution.

AIR QUALITY

Air quality followed a pattern similar to water quality. Before the industrial revolution it was largely unaffected. With the onset of the industrial revolution, air quality soon became poor in the cities. Finally, government passed laws regulating air pollution in developed nations and the overall air quality improved. Air quality still remains a major problem in the developing world.

Of growing concern in the developed world is the issue of the release of carbon dioxide and its possible contribution to global warming. While not all scientists agree that the warming of surface temperatures is the result of human activity (the Earth has warmed and cooled many times in the past) rising temperatures will have significant effects on the environment.

Increases in temperature will cause an increase in the hydrologic cycle. This will mean both an increase in the amount of evaporation and the amount of precipitation. Many experts predict an expansion in both the tropical zones and in the size of the deserts. Others predict the melting of the polar ice caps, which will cause a corresponding rise in sea level. This would cause many coastal regions to flood.

POPULATION GROWTH

The last way that humanity is effecting the environment is simply by our sheer numbers. Humans put a great stress on the environment simply by going through our daily lives. People clear land for housing, businesses and roads. During the 1960's population growth experts were predicting the doubling of the Earth's population at an ever-increasing rate. High birthrates and an increase in longevity due to medical advances were fueling the overall growth.

However toward the end of the 20th century population experts noted a marked decrease in the birthrate in the developed world. This resulted in a dramatic decrease in the growth rate of these countries. The experts found that as the infant survival rate increased, parents tended to adjust the number of children they had.

Population experts hope that the developing world will follow a similar pattern. Medical advances are being used to increase the longevity and raise the infant survival rates throughout the world. Currently, there has not been a significant enough drop in the birthrate in the developing world to counteract this and the population in these areas is consequently exploding. This is one of the greatest challenges for the world in the 21st century.

Before moving on, try these sample questions.

1. **If the Earth's surface temperature increases as some scientists predict, which of the following would most likely be true about hurricanes.**

   (A) They would most likely be unaffected.
   (B) They would likely increase in number and severity.
   (C) They would likely decrease in number and severity.
   (D) They would likely only hit the state of Florida.
   (E) Insurers would stop issuing hurricane insurance.

Answers

1. (B) An increase in temperature would cause an increase in the amount of evaporation and precipitation. This would cause hurricanes to occur more frequently and for them to be more severe. Increasing temperature might have an effect on the path of an individual hurricane, but there would be no way to predict where they all would hit.

2. **If the developing world follows the pattern of the developed world over the next 50 years, which of the following will not happen?**

    (A) Population growth will continue unchecked.
    (B) Water pollution will be reduced.
    (C) Air quality will improve
    (D) The live span of the average person will increase.
    (E) The birthrate will decline.

2. (A) Over the last 50 years, the developed world has seen an overall improvement in air and water quality, the average life span has increased, and the birthrate has declined.

Reading Graphs And Charts

When taking CLEP tests, you will be given graphs and charts to examine and interpret. Usually at least two questions will follow the diagrams. It is important for you to know the basic graph and chart styles and how to approach them.

In all cases, read the question first. This will focus your attention on the specific information you need from the diagram. Then study the diagram to see the type of units used. Study the diagram by looking at the units and headings.

There are several types of graphs and charts, but the most commonly seen are the bar graph, the cumulative graph, the pie chart, and the line chart.

BAR GRAPH

To read a bar graph, study the units marked along the bottom (frequently years but not always), and along the side. Please note, however, that some bar graphs are vertical while others are horizontal. In the example given, each bar represents a year from 1977 to 1981. The units, 1 to 2.5, are in measures of .5; these measures, however, represent "millions of tons." It is necessary to know what the units stand for, as publishers will often abbreviate in this way rather than print out "1,000,000"-"1,500,000" on the graph or chart itself.

COAL PRODUCTION
(Millions of Tons)

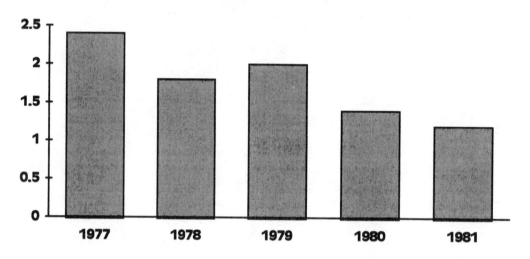

1. **How much coal was produced in the years 1978, 1979, and 1981?**

   (A) 50 million tons
   (B) 5,000,000 tons
   (C) .5 million tons
   (D) 5,300,000 tons
   (E) 6.0 million tons

2. **What was the average production for the years 1979, 1980, 1981?**

   (A) 2.0 million tons
   (B) 2.0 tons
   (C) 1.5 tons
   (D) 1.5 million tons
   (E) 1.1 million tons

ANSWERS:

1. **How much coal was produced in the years 1978, 1979, and 1981?**

   (A) 50 million tons
   (B) 5,000,000 tons
   (C) .5 million tons
   (D) 5,300,000 tons
   (E) 6.0 million tons

1. (B) 5 million tons were produced in the years 1978, 1979 and 1981. Be careful of decimal points in the units such as answer (C). In reading graphs you often have to approximate the intervals between units; use the side of your pencil as a guide by placing it sideways at the top of the bar you are reading and look over at the units on the left. The bar for 1978 is between the 1.5 and 2.0 marks, approximately 1.8; the bar for 1979 is even with the 2.0 mark; the bar for 1981 is between 1.0 and 1.5, approximately 1.2. These total to 5.0.

2. **What was the average production for the years 1979, 1980, 1981?**

   (A) 2.0 million tons
   (B) 2.0 tons
   (C) 1.5 tons
   (D) 1.5 million tons
   (E) 1.1 million tons

2. (D) Production for those years are as follows: 1979-2.0; 1980-1.4; 1981-1.2. These total to 4.6 million tons. To obtain the average, divide by 3, yielding 1.53 which can be rounded off to 1.5 million tons. Remember, the units represent millions of tons, not just tons as in answer (C).

CUMULATIVE GRAPH

Similar to the bar graph, the cumulative graph is read the same way except that each bar represents more than one quantity. Colors and/or markings are used to indicate the varying quantities. Again, look at the questions to see what is being asked and review the graph to see what the units are and what the differing markings stand for.

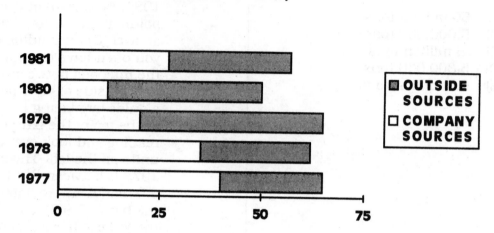

ZINC PRODUCTION
PRODUCTION BY SOURCE
(Thousands of Tons)

3. In which year was the greatest amount of zinc from an outside company produced?

    (A) 1977
    (B) 1978
    (C) 1979
    (D) 1980
    (E) 1981

4. What percentage of zinc came from outside sources in 1980?

    (A) 50%
    (B) 60%
    (C) 30%
    (D) 85%
    (E) 75%

ANSWERS:

3. In which year was the greatest amount of zinc from an outside company produced?

    (A) 1977
    (B) 1978
    (C) 1979
    (D) 1980
    (E) 1981

3. (C) By using the side of your pencil you can quickly measure the greatest amount of zinc represented on the graph produced by an outside company.

222

4. What percentage of zinc came from outside sources in 1980?

(A) 50%
(B) 60%
(C) 30%
(D) 85%
(E) 75%

4. (E) In this question, you need to look at the 1980 bar only. The entire bar represents 50 thousand tons—100%; the outside source produced more than 50%, eliminating answers A and C. By looking at the point where the two sources meet and then examining the unit scale below, you can see that the graph states that company sources produced approximately 12 thousand tons. 12/50 = .24 = 24%. 100% - 24% = 76%. Since this is an approximation, 75% is the correct answer.

PIE CHART

The pie chart (or circle graph) is so called because it looks like a pie with slices cut in it. The entire pie represents 100%; the slices represent percentages. These percentages will appear in the chart either within the slice or printed just outside. Sometimes colors or designs are used to distinguish the percents.

MINERALS PRODUCED - 1981

(Thousands of Tons)

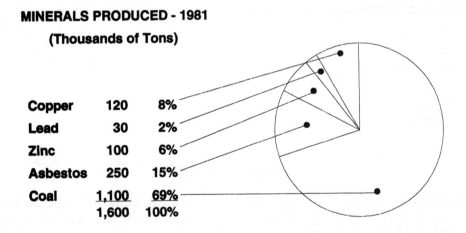

Copper	120	8%
Lead	30	2%
Zinc	100	6%
Asbestos	250	15%
Coal	1,100	69%
	1,600	100%

5. **The fraction of coal production for 1981 is approximately?**

    (A) 7/10
    (B) 3/5
    (C) 3/4
    (D) 1/2
    (E) none of the above

6. **In 1980, coal represented 60%, asbestos 14%, zinc 10%, lead 5% and copper 11%. Which mineral production increased the most in 1981?**

    (A) coal
    (B) asbestos
    (C) zinc
    (D) lead
    (E) copper

ANSWERS:

5. **The fraction of coal production for 1981 is approximately?**

    (A) 7/10
    (B) 3/5
    (C) 3/4
    (D) 1/2
    (E) none of the above

5. (A) This question requires that you convert percentage to fractions. In this case, the question states approximate conversion. 69% is almost 7/10. 60% = 3/5; 75% = 3/4; and 50% = 1/2.

6. **In 1980, coal represented 60%, asbestos 14%, zinc 10%, lead 5% and copper 11%. Which mineral production increased the most in 1981?**

    (A) coal
    (B) asbestos
    (C) zinc
    (D) lead
    (E) copper

6. (A) Coal increased from 60% in 1980 to 69% in 1981. The only other increase was in asbestos 14% in 1980, 15% in 1981.

LINE CHART

Like the bar graph, the line chart uses two sets of units; generally the units are placed along the bottom and along the left side. Line charts will use different markings or colors to differentiate the various lines plotted on the chart.

PRICE FOR COPPER, ZINC, and LEAD
(cents per pound)

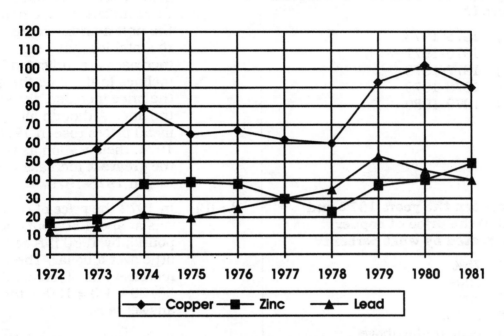

7. **What year saw the greatest upward trend for all three metals listed?**

   (A) 1975-1976
   (B) 1976-1977
   (C) 1977-1978
   (D) 1978-1979
   (E) 1979-1980

8. **Between the years 1972 and 1980 the price of copper increased by what percent?**

   (A) 75%
   (B) 100%
   (C) 50%
   (D) 200%
   (E) none of the above

7. **What year saw the greatest upward trend for all three metals listed?**

(A) 1975-1976
(B) 1976-1977
(C) 1977-1978
(D) 1978-1979
(E) 1979-1980

7. (D) The year 1978-1979 saw greater price increases for all three metals. Please note that the unit marking represents the total for that year. Increases are indicated by inclines in the line; the greater the price increase, the steeper the line. Although all three metal prices rose in 1973-1974, the question asks for the **greatest** increase which was in 1978-1979.

8. **Between the years 1972 and 1980 the price of copper increased by what percent?**

(A) 75%
(B) 100%
(C) 50%
(D) 200%
(E) none of the above

8. (B) In 1972 the price of copper was at about 50 cents per pound; by 1980 it rose to a little over a dollar. The increase was 50 cents. Since $50/50 = 1.0 = 100\%$, the answer is B.

Taking The CLEP Social Science/History Sample Examination

Now that you have completed the entire review section, you are ready to take a practice Social Science/History test. The test follows the format of the CLEP General Social Science/History Examination.

Take the practice examination now. It is important to practice working with a variety of questions in the specified amount of time.

For best results, it is recommended that you try to simulate the test situation as nearly as possible. That is:

1. **Find a quiet spot where you will not be disturbed.**

2. **Time yourself accurately. Work 45 minutes in both portions. DO NOT quit until the time is up!**

3. **Use the coding system for a systematic approach to the examination.**

After you finish the practice test:

1. **Check your answers.**

2. **Review the areas in which you had difficulty.**

CLEP GENERAL EXAMINATION IN SOCIAL SCIENCE AND HISTORY

PART I

TIME: 45 MINUTES   **65 QUESTIONS**

Directions: Each of the questions or incomplete statements below is followed by five suggested answers or completions. Select the one that is best in each case.

1. **Which of the following is the highest class in India's society?**

    (A)   Brahmans
    (B)   Kshatriyas
    (C)   Vaisyas
    (D)   Sudras
    (E)   none of the above

2. **A husband who has more than one wife is following which of the following patterns?**

    (A)   monogamy
    (B)   polyandry
    (C)   polygyny
    (D)   exogamy
    (E)   endogamy

3. **The purpose of a fair trade law is which of the following?**

    (A)   to allow producers to set minimum sales prices for their items
    (B)   to reduce the likelihood of price wars
    (C)   to increase foreign trade
    (D)   to decrease foreign trade
    (E)   A and B

4. **Cultural lag examines which of the following?**

    (A)   rates of change within a society
    (B)   population distribution
    (C)   social movements
    (D)   none of the above
    (E)   all of the above

5. The collective effort of environmentalists to influence society's values and actions concerning the physical world would be considered which of the following?

(A) social change
(B) social movement
(C) cultural lag
(D) deviant behavior
(E) none of the above

6. Which of the following statements concerning deviance is true?

(A) Deviance can have positive effects.
(B) Deviance is always punishable.
(C) Deviance always varies slightly from the norm.
(D) Deviance always varies greatly from the norm.
(E) The norm is always clearly established when discussing deviance.

7. In psychology, empirical studies would depend primarily on which of the following?

(A) the viewpoint of the classical Greek philosophers
(B) experimentation
(C) precise measurement of results
(D) direct observation and logical reasoning
(E) introspection

8. Merrill-Lynch is "bullish on America" suggests which of the following?

(A) The firm believes that prices will fall and sells.
(B) The firm believes that prices will rise and buys.
(C) The firm expects to sell at a profit in the future.
(D) The firm expects to buy at a lower price.
(E) A combination of B and C

9. Which of the following groups would be most likely to investigate physiological changes in an organism?

(A) the Greek philosophers
(B) the empiricists
(C) the behaviorists
(D) humanistic psychologists
(E) the functionalists

10. Which of the following is thought to be the ancestor of modern gorillas and chimpanzees?

(A) Proconsul
(B) *Zinjanthropus*
(C) *Dryopithecus*
(D) *Homo habilis*
(E) *Australopithecus*

11. **A morpheme is which of the following?**

   (A) the smallest sound in a language
   (B) a society lacking a system for writing
   (C) an oral tradition
   (D) the smallest meaningful unit in a language
   (E) none of the above

12. **Which of the following is an example of a vestigial organ?**

   (A) the appendix
   (B) human body hair
   (C) human finger nails
   (D) cecum
   (E) all of the above

Question 13 and 14 refer to the graph below:

SALES BY INDUSTRY

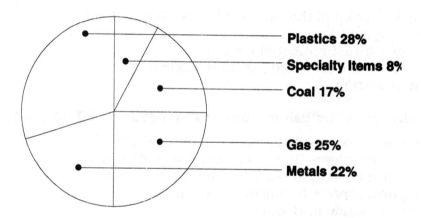

Plastics 28%

Specialty Items 8%

Coal 17%

Gas 25%

Metals 22%

13. **Which three items represent 50 percent of sales volume?**

   (A) plastics—specialty items—coal
   (B) coal—specialty items—metals
   (C) coal—specialty items—gas
   (D) gas—coal—metals
   (E) plastics—metals

14. **Which of the following items represents the largest percentage of sales excluding plastics?**

   (A) specialty items
   (B) gas
   (C) metals
   (D) coal
   (E) none of the above

15. **Those events which happened but which have left no physical or non-physical traces are known as**

(A) chronological warps
(B) actual history
(C) recorded history
(D) mythology
(E) legends

16. **The type of society which existed in Japan before that country was Westernized could best be characterized as**

(A) primitive
(B) fascist
(C) communist
(D) socialist
(E) feudal

17. **Which of the following is the best definition of the term "Industrial Revolution"?**

(A) the development of the factory system and production of goods through the use of machines
(B) the results of the use of steam power and the rise of organized labor
(C) the result of the development of factories and a nationwide market for the goods produced in factories
(D) the development of a democratic way of life and of production of goods in factories by machines
(E) the degradation of the worker in the factory system

18. **In 1789, which of the following had a revolution for "Liberty, Equality and Fraternity," which spread ideas of reform and democracy throughout Europe?**

(A) France
(B) United States
(C) England
(D) Germany
(E) Russia

19. **When a society or group is organized or set up with people and officials at different levels with each having certain powers and responsibilities, it is known as which of the following?**

(A) hierarchy
(B) anarchy
(C) bureaucracy
(D) monopoly
(E) totalitarian society

20. **Which of the following best describes a clan?**

(A) nuclear families
(B) extended families
(C) related lineages
(D) all members of the society
(E) none of the above

21. **Which of the following describes a dowry?**

(A) a gift from the bride's parents to the groom's parents
(B) a gift from the bride's parents to the groom and bride
(C) permission from the society to marry
(D) a bride-price
(E) a prohibition of marriage

22. **The Oracle of Apollo at Delphi practiced which of the following?**

(A) witchcraft
(B) divination
(C) white magic
(D) contagious magic
(E) none of the above

23. **The practice of not hiring persons whose names appear on lists of union sympathizers is called which of the following?**

(A) yellow-dog contract
(B) blacklisting
(C) check-off
(D) closed shop
(E) union shop

24. **A lag can best be described by which of the following?**

(A) Wages do not rise as quickly as rising prices.
(B) Money is hoarded.
(C) Workers earn wages at a faster rate than rising prices.
(D) Production increases and prices decline.
(E) Overproduction occurs.

25. **In the business cycle, which of the following is NOT a sign of recovery?**

(A) Costs adjust to the lower price level.
(B) Banks will offer credit.
(C) Unemployment decreases.
(D) Purchasing power increases.
(E) Profits remain at the same level or fall.

26. **Secular price trends are general changes in the price level witnessed within which of the following time spans?**

(A) 2-3 years
(B) 3-5 years
(C) 5-10 years
(D) 10-25 years
(E) 15-50 years

27. **Which of the following aids conformity?**

(A) sanctions
(B) interdependence among individuals
(C) identification with a group
(D) socialization
(E) all of the above

28. **Who of the following is credited with "The Looking Glass Self"?**

(A) Ferdinand Tonnies
(B) Emile Durkheim
(C) George Herbert Mead
(D) Charles Horton Cooley
(E) Robert E. Park

29. **Which of the following statements is NOT true?**

(A) Culture forms the basic personality of members of a group.
(B) Modern society produces individuals who are all alienated and lonely.
(C) The family is the most important contribution to socialization.
(D) A and B
(E) B and C

30. **Which of the following is an example of residual power?**

(A) declaring war
(B) levying taxes
(C) approving ministers
(D) enacting divorce laws
(E) coining money

31. **Which amendment gave eighteen-year-olds the right to vote?**

(A) 15th Amendment
(B) 16th Amendment
(C) 19th Amendment
(D) 24th Amendment
(E) 26th Amendment

32. **Of the following, which is the primary question a government must answer?**

   (A) Who shall rule?
   (B) Who shall vote?
   (C) What will the form of government be?
   (D) How much control and freedom shall there be?
   (E) How should revenue be collected?

33. **Which of the following is an example of a stereotype?**

   (A) a dedicated teacher
   (B) a devoted mother
   (C) a dumb blond
   (D) a dishonest politician
   (E) all of the above

34. **Which of the following statements is NOT true of culture?**

   (A) Cultures vary from group to group.
   (B) National boundaries determine cultural boundaries.
   (C) Cultures share some features in common such as marriage and child-rearing rules.
   (D) Cultures persist.
   (E) Subcultures may exist.

Questions 35 and 36 refer to the following graph:

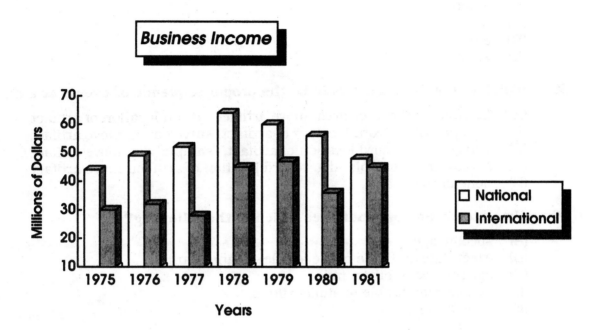

Business Income

35. **Which of the following years represents peak business income on the national level?**

(A) 1975
(B) 1976
(C) 1977
(D) 1978
(E) 1979

36. **What is the average international business income over the years 1975 through 1981?**

(A) $10 million-$20 million
(B) $20 million-$30 million
(C) $30 million-$40 million
(D) $40 million-$50 million
(E) $50 million-$60 million

37. **Which of the following is often called the "Cradle of Civilization"?**

(A) Ur
(B) Jericho
(C) Natuf
(D) Tigris-Euphrates
(E) Ubaid

38. **Written history goes back how many years?**

    (A) 10,000
    (B) 8,000
    (C) 5,000
    (D) 3,000
    (E) 2,000

39. **Which of the following would be the proper sequence of events at a dig?**

    (A) "sample" dig, survey area, move artifact, record location of artifact
    (B) "sample" dig, record location of artifact, survey area, move artifact
    (C) survey area, record location of artifact, "sample" dig, move artifact
    (D) survey area, "sample" dig, record location of artifact, move artifact
    (E) none of the above

40. **Absolute chronology indicates which of the following?**

    (A) specific ages
    (B) exact date and time of the article's manufacture
    (C) age relative to other finds
    (D) an age comparable to similar finds
    (E) none of the above

41. **In chimpanzee society which of the following is NOT a rule of dominance?**

    (A) Young males dominate grown females.
    (B) Older males dominate all.
    (C) Grown females dominate all the young males.
    (D) A flexible order of dominance exists among the grown males.
    (E) Grown females dominate young females.

42. **Baby chimpanzees are wholly dependent upon their mothers for how long?**

    (A) 1 week
    (B) 6 weeks
    (C) 3 months
    (D) 6 months
    (E) 2 years

43. **The most famous wagon train route to the Pacific Coast was known as the**

    (A) Wilderness Road
    (B) National Road
    (C) Natchez Trail
    (D) Oregon Trail
    (E) Jefferson Highway

44. **The main reason for the great Irish emigration to America in the middle of the 1800's was which of the following?**

   (A) religious tension between Ireland and England
   (B) unemployment, low wages, and high rents for land in Ireland
   (C) absentee landlords were selling the land for factories
   (D) the failure of the potato crop due to a blight
   (E) the lure of free land in America

45. **"The concept of 'black power' is not a recent or isolated phenomenon: It has grown out of the ferment of agitation and activity by different people and organizations in many black communities over the years. Where black men have a majority, they will attempt to use it to exercise control. This is what they seek: control. Where Negroes lack a majority, black power means proper representation and sharing of control.**

   The quote above reflects the viewpoint of whom of the following?

   (A) Martin Luther King
   (B) Booker T. Washington
   (C) W. E. B. DuBois
   (D) Stokely Carmichael
   (E) Marcus Garvey

46. **Which part of the body actually "sees" images?**

   (A) retina
   (B) rods
   (C) cones
   (D) optic nerve
   (E) cerebral cortex

47. **Railroad tracks which appear to converge in the distance is an example of which of the following?**

   (A) interposition
   (B) linear perspective
   (C) gradient texture
   (D) shadow
   (E) aerial perspective

48. **Development depends upon which of the following factors?**

   (A) environment
   (B) heredity
   (C) maturation
   (D) structure of the organism
   (E) all of the above

49. **At which point does a human embryo become a fetus?**

    (A) two weeks after conception
    (B) four weeks after conception
    (C) eight weeks after conception
    (D) three months after conception
    (E) one hundred and forty days after conception

50. **Which of the following situations would probably be the least stressful?**

    (A) starting a new job
    (B) meeting future in-laws
    (C) taking the CLEP test
    (D) moving to a new town
    (E) going window-shopping

51. **Which of the following best defines a hypothesis?**

    (A) a suspected relationship
    (B) a contributing factor
    (C) a proven truth
    (D) an expected result
    (E) an unexpected result

52. **The normal bell curve is which of the following?**

    (A) skewed positively
    (B) skewed negatively
    (C) all frequency distributions
    (D) all polygons
    (E) normal probability curve

53. **Which of the following is the mode?**

    (A) the number representing the common average
    (B) the number representing the score which appears most frequently
    (C) the number representing the middle score
    (D) the total of the scores
    (E) the total of the two extreme scores

54. **Which of the following societies is likely to undergo rapid change?**

    (A) folk
    (B) rural
    (C) *gemeinschaft*
    (D) sacred
    (E) none of the above

55. **Which of the following is NOT considered a concern of sociology?**

(A) objectivity
(B) proving all common sense observations about behavior
(C) finding solutions to social ills
(D) B and C
(E) all of the above

56. **According to the types of suicide outlined by Emile Durkheim, which of the following applies to suicide because of a failed love affair?**

(A) egoistic
(B) altruistic
(C) anomic
(D) ennui
(E) all of the above

Questions 57 through 61 refer to the following list:

   I. tropism
  II. reflex response
 III. instinctive behaviors
 IV. physiological drives
  V. acquired drives

57. **Migration is an example of which of the above responses?**

(A) I
(B) II
(C) III
(D) IV
(E) V

58. **The need for food is an example of which of the above responses?**

(A) I
(B) II
(C) III
(D) IV
(E) V

59. **A plant is most likely to display which of the above responses?**

(A) I
(B) II
(C) III
(D) IV
(E) V

60. **The desire for power is an example of which of the above responses?**

    (A) I
    (B) II
    (C) III
    (D) IV
    (E) V

61. **Blinking is an example of which of the above responses?**

    (A) I
    (B) II
    (C) III
    (D) IV
    (E) V

62. **A corrupt aristocracy is known as which of the following?**

    (A) autocracy
    (B) monarchy
    (C) tyranny
    (D) oligarchy
    (E) plurality

63. **The most likely explanation of modern man's arrival to the Americas is which of the following?**

    (A) by boat across the North Atlantic
    (B) by boat across the South Pacific
    (C) modern man developed independently in the Americas
    (D) crossing what is now the Bering Strait
    (E) none of the above

64. **Which of the following would be the correct order from earliest to latest?**

    (A) Neaderthal—Cro-Magnon—Peking man—Australopithecus
    (B) Peking man—Australopithecus—Neanderthal—Cro-Magnon
    (C) Cro-Magnon—Peking man—Australopithecus—Neanderthal
    (D) Australopithecus—Neanderthal—Cro-Magnon—Peking man
    (E) none of the above

65. **Which of the following fossils proved to be a hoax?**

    (A) Java man
    (B) Piltdown man
    (C) Swanscombe man
    (D) Steinheim man
    (E) none of the above

66. **In addition to the Spanish-American War, the United States has been accused of imperialism in which of the following wars?**

(A) Mexican War
(B) Civil War
(C) World War I
(D) World War II
(E) Vietnam War

Questions 67-69 refer to the following graph:

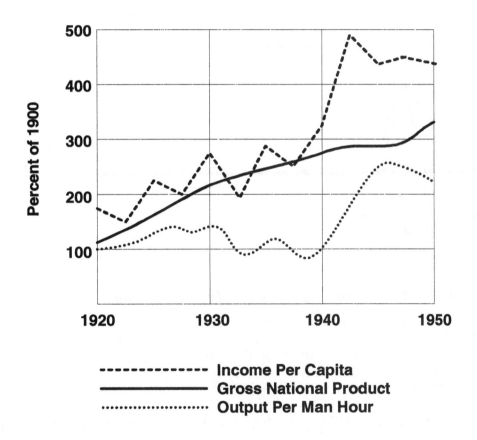

------------ **Income Per Capita**
———————— **Gross National Product**
·················· **Output Per Man Hour**

67. **According to the graph, which two factors show the greatest relationships?**

(A) GNP and output per man hour
(B) GNP and income per capita
(C) Income per capita and output per man hour
(D) All of the factors are equal.
(E) There is not enough information in the graph to determine this.

68. **At what point was production the lowest?**

   (A) 1921
   (B) 1932
   (C) 1933
   (D) 1935
   (E) 1938

69. **In the early 1930's, why did income per capita continue to rise, while both GNP and output per man hour declined?**

   (A) The decline was not enough to affect income per capita.
   (B) There is a time-lag between production and income.
   (C) The government, through New Deal policies, pumped money into the economy.
   (D) Income per capita is not related to GNP and output per man hour.
   (E) There is not enough information in the graph to determine this.

70. **What methods can scientists use to date their finds?**

   (A) geological studies
   (B) fluorine test
   (C) carbon-14 test
   (D) crossdating
   (E) all of the above

71. **Mutation is best described as which of the following?**

   (A) replication
   (B) phenotype-genotype
   (C) dominant gene
   (D) recessive gene
   (E) none of the above

72. **Diffusion occurs when which of the following happens?**

   (A) A society has no contact with other cultures.
   (B) The culture traits of one group are rejected by another.
   (C) The invention of a technique is made independently elsewhere.
   (D) The culture traits of two groups intermingle.
   (E) None of the above.

73. **Groups can be identified by which of the following factors?**

   (A) membership
   (B) purpose
   (C) function
   (D) structure
   (E) all of the above

74. **The primary purpose of government is to do which of the following?**

    (A) encourage cooperation
    (B) encourage competition
    (C) decide the form of government
    (D) decide the amount of control of competition and cooperation
    (E) decide who shall vote

75. **In which of the following offices must appropriations of money originate?**

    (A) the executive branch
    (B) the judicial branch
    (C) the Senate
    (D) The House of Representatives
    (E) all of the above

76. **Unlike the previous Confederation Government, the new Constitutional Government could do which of the following?**

    (A) act directly upon the people of the United States
    (B) issue money
    (C) require state officials to take an oath of allegiance to the *Constitution*
    (D) call up state militias
    (E) all of the above

77. **David Ricardo wrote about the Iron Law of Wages which states which of the following should occur?**

    (A) Wages should be kept at a low level in order to discourage population growth.
    (B) Wages should increase only if a profit is seen.
    (C) Wages should decrease in times of inflation.
    (D) Wages should be issued as an incentive to the worker to increase productivity.
    (E) Wages should reflect an equal distribution of company profit.

78. **Which of the following agencies have helped to insure banking stability?**

    (A) FDIC (Federal Deposit Insurance Corporation)
    (B) FHA (Federal Housing Authority)
    (C) Farm Credit Administration
    (D) Reconstruction Finance Corporation
    (E) all of the above

79. **Which of the following is the main purpose of an investment bank?**

    (A) to make short-term loans to private individuals
    (B) to act as a trustee administrator
    (C) to make long-term loans to industry
    (D) to offer checking and saving accounts
    (E) to compare checks of various member banks in order to counterbalance them

80. **The government borrows money for public projects through which of the following?**

   (A)   the sale of bonds
   (B)   increased taxes
   (C)   increased money supply from the central bank
   (D)   use of gold deposits
   (E)   custom duties

81. **Which of the following forms of taxation is currently considered to be the most equitable?**

   (A)   property tax
   (B)   placing the heaviest burden on those who are best able to pay
   (C)   placing the heaviest burden on those who benefit most from government projects
   (D)   even distribution of tax burden
   (E)   none of the above

82. **Which of the following provides an indication of the degree of deviation of each score from the mean?**

   (A)   the standard deviation
   (B)   measures of correlation
   (C)   random sampling
   (D)   standard error of the mean
   (E)   critical ratio

83. **Pavlov can be considered the father of which of the following?**

   (A)   psychoanalysis
   (B)   operant conditioning
   (C)   instrumental conditioning
   (D)   classical conditioning
   (E)   structuralism

84. **Which of the following is associated with the id?**

   (A)   thought processes
   (B)   area housing repressed thoughts
   (C)   area housing non-repressed thoughts
   (D)   biological urges
   (E)   the conscience

85. **Which of the following is the correct order of progression presented in the Three Stages developed by Auguste Comte?**

   (A)   theological—scientific—metaphysical
   (B)   metaphysical—scientific—theological
   (C)   scientific—theological—metaphysical
   (D)   theological—metaphysical—scientific
   (E)   metaphysical—theological—scientific

86. **By studying data such as occupation and income level, sociologists study stratification from which of the following approaches?**

(A) subjective
(B) objective
(C) reputational
(D) all of the above
(E) none of the above

87. **Which of the following would be an example of an indirect tax?**

(A) income tax
(B) sales tax
(C) custom duty
(D) higher price for an item
(E) all of the above

88. **Who of the following is best known for his theory concerning population growth and food supplies?**

(A) Adam Smith
(B) John Stuart Mill
(C) Milton Friedman
(D) John Maynard Keynes
(E) none of the above

89. **Which of the following statements best describes the Law of Diminishing Returns?**

(A) As more labor is added, productivity will continue to rise indefinitely.
(B) As more labor is added, productivity will continue to rise to the point where the marginal product is less than the average product.
(C) As more labor is added, productivity will at first decline and then rise indefinitely.
(D) As more labor is added, productivity will increase to the point where the marginal product is equal to the average product.
(E) None of the above.

90. **In order to avoid excessive business fluctuations, which approach needs to be adopted?**

(A) proper monetary policy
(B) proper fiscal policy
(C) governmental regulation
(D) A and B only
(E) A, B and C

Questions 91 through 95 refer to the following list:

    I. cooperation
   II. competition
  III. conflict
  IV. accommodation
   V. assimilation

91. Which can be, but is not always, destructive?

    (A) I
    (B) II
    (C) III
    (D) IV
    (E) V

92. Which is an example of mediation?

    (A) I
    (B) II
    (C) III
    (D) IV
    (E) V

93. As ethnic groups reside in one area, intermarry and share cultural traditions, which process is taking place?

    (A) I
    (B) II
    (C) III
    (D) IV
    (E) V

94. When two distinct groups join forces to petition the town council for a recreational facility in their area, they are using which process?

    (A) I
    (B) II
    (C) III
    (D) IV
    (E) V

95. If one company sabotages the operations of another in order to gain a larger share of the market, which process is being employed?

    (A) I
    (B) II
    (C) III
    (D) IV
    (E) V

96. **The Know-Nothing Party opposed which of the following groups?**

   (A) unions
   (B) carpetbaggers
   (C) Catholics
   (D) blacks
   (E) women

97. **Under *The United States Constitution* the House must originate which of the following bills?**

   (A) declaration of war
   (B) interstate commerce
   (C) revenue appropriation
   (D) bankruptcy
   (E) foreign commerce

98. **People of a state may demonstrate their approval or rejection of legislation through which of the following?**

   (A) referendum
   (B) short ballot
   (C) recall
   (D) cloture rule
   (E) initiative

99. **Mayors Richard Daly of Chicago and Frank Hague of Jersey City can be associated with which of the following?**

   (A) gerrymandering
   (B) bossism
   (C) dark horse
   (D) log rolling
   (E) Jim Crow

Question 100 refers to the following graph:

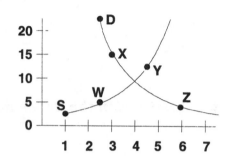

100. **In a competitive market, which point represents equilibrium?**

    (A) W
    (B) X
    (C) Y
    (D) Z
    (E) none of the above

101. **Which of the following institutions has the power to control the supply of money in the economy?**

    (A) savings banks
    (B) the Congress
    (C) the Federal Reserve System
    (D) the President
    (E) the Federal Trade Commission

102. **A check can be defined best as which of the following?**

    (A) bond
    (B) liability
    (C) paper currency
    (D) demand deposit
    (E) fiat

103. **Which of the following is NOT an advantage of the "corporation" as a form of business organization?**

    (A) It can obtain larger amounts of money through the sales of shares of stock on the corporation than other forms can raise.
    (B) The corporation has "perpetual life" and thus avoids interruptions to business.
    (C) Shares can be bought and sold easily by their owners if they wish to get out or invest more fully in the business.
    (D) It is a less complicated form of business organization to set up than the individual ownership or partnership type of business.
    (E) Stockholders are legally responsible for only the amount of money they invested in the corporation and not for all of its debts (limited liability).

104. **The demand for African independence after World War II was NOT influenced by which of the following?**

(A) newly independent states in Asia
(B) Allied war propaganda
(C) a money economy
(D) the collapse of the colonial system in Asia
(E) the defeat of Germany, which lost the German colonies in Africa

105. **The principle of mercantilism and Adam Smith's theory of economics differ most sharply on which of the following points?**

(A) Smith stated that a nation's wealth was based on its ability to produce, not its precious metals.
(B) Smith stated that there should be tight government control; mercantilism believes in laissez faire.
(C) The market place is found only in mercantilism.
(D) Mercantilism needed colonies but Smith's theory did not.
(E) none of the above.

106. **The type of economic system which depended upon the exploration of colonies to benefit the mother country was which of the following?**

(A) traditional
(B) market
(C) guild
(D) feudal
(E) mercantilism

107. **A wife who locks herself in the bedroom and cries after a long unsettled argument with her husband would be displaying which of the following responses?**

(A) aggression
(B) hostility
(C) withdrawal
(D) repression
(E) regression

108. **Mesomorph is a term belonging to a study of personality developed by whom of the following?**

(A) Hippocrates
(B) Sheldon
(C) Oedipus
(D) Rorschach
(E) none of the above

109. **A statistical approach to defining abnormality is based on which of the following?**

   (A) Behavior is abnormal if it differs sufficiently from the norm.
   (B) Quality of adjustment determines normality/abnormality.
   (C) symptoms of abnormality
   (D) all of the above
   (E) none of the above

110. **Which of the following is mnemonics?**

   (A) reduction of sensitivity
   (B) quality of being outgoing
   (C) memory improvement devices
   (D) stage of sleep when dreams occur
   (E) Greek word for "soul" or "mind"

111. **Which of the following collections of people would constitute a group?**

   (A) a church choir
   (B) riders on a subway
   (C) all Vermont high school graduates
   (D) all workers in a downtown office building
   (E) draft-age males

112. **The discovery of fire was most likely which of the following?**

   (A) basic invention
   (B) secondary invention
   (C) an independent invention
   (D) an example of diffusion
   (E) A, C and D

113. **Physical anthropologists concentrate on which of the following areas?**

   (A) comparison of man to the primates
   (B) evolution
   (C) learned behavior
   (D) A and B
   (E) all of the above

114. **The introduction of new farming techniques to a third world nation would be an example of which of the following?**

   (A) acculturation
   (B) ethnocentricism
   (C) civilization
   (D) ethnic appreciation
   (E) all of the above

115. **Which of the following elements is not found in all living things?**

(A) calcium
(B) hydrogen
(C) nitrogen
(D) phosphorus
(E) A and D

116. **Reinforcement is best defined by which of the following?**

(A) desensitization
(B) conditioned response
(C) increased likelihood that a response will occur
(D) unconditioned response
(E) extinction

117. **According to the structuralist approach to learning, conjunctive rules require which of the following?**

(A) the stating of all the relative attributes
(B) the stating of all the important relative attributes
(C) the stating of some of the relative attributes
(D) the stating of one relative attribute
(E) none of the above

118. **Eli Whitney's greatest contribution to the American Industrial Revolution was his application and demonstration of the value of which of the following?**

(A) the cotton gin
(B) interchangeable parts
(C) steam power
(D) dynamite
(E) steel in construction

119. **Which of the following was NOT a consequence of World War I?**

(A) the League of Nations
(B) the fall of European aristocracies
(C) the displacement of millions of people
(D) the collapse of the British Empire
(E) the rise of communism is Russia

120. **The famous founder and leader of the American Federation of Labor was who?**

(A) William Sylvis
(B) Uriah S. Stephens
(C) Samuel Gompers
(D) Terence V. Powderly
(E) Samuel Slater

121. **The "Great Compromise" during the Constitution Convention refers to which of the following?**

    (A) addition of the Bill of Rights to the *Constitution*
    (B) separation of power among the three branches
    (C) how Congress would be represented—the Senate by two from each state, the House by the population of each state
    (D) how much slavery would be allowed
    (E) how the war debts would be paid

122. **Which of the following was NOT a benefit that the Cold War brought to the African nations?**

    (A) military assistance
    (B) economic aid
    (C) both the United States and the Soviet Union voted in the United Nations for the independence of an African state.
    (D) Intertribal rivalry was encouraged.
    (E) the Peace Corps

123. **Which of the following statements is the most accurate regarding the relationship between the middle class and the absolute monarchs of Europe (1500 to 1800)?**

    (A) The bourgeoisie rallied to support the monarchs because of mercantilist policies.
    (B) The bourgeoisie supported the monarchs in order to withstand the demands of the working classes.
    (C) The bourgeoisie turned against the monarchs when they adopted anti-middle class policies.
    (D) The bourgeoisie at first supported the feudal lords but later supported the monarchs during the time of the Industrial Revolution.
    (E) The bourgeoisie turned against the monarchs when the monarchs supported legislation favoring the working class.

Questions 124 and 125 refer to the following list:

    I. Carrie Nation
    II. Nellie Bly
    III. Elizabeth Cady Stanton
    IV. Jane Addams
    V. Victoria Woodhull

124. **Who was the woman whose settlement house, Hull House, in the slums of Chicago did much social good?**

    (A) I
    (B) II
    (C) III
    (D) IV
    (E) V

125. **Who was the first woman stockbroker on Wall Street and the first woman to run for President?**

    (A)   I
    (B)   II
    (C)   III
    (D)   IV
    (E)   V

Answers And Explanations

1. **Which of the following is the highest class in India's society?**

   (A) Brahmans
   (B) Kshatriyas
   (C) Vaisyas
   (D) Sudras
   (E) none of the above

1. (A) The Brahmans are the priests and scholars and are the highest class. Next are the Kshatriyas, the rulers and warriors, followed by the Vaisyas, or merchants and farmers. The Sudras, laborers and landless peasants, are the lowest class. The "untouchables" have no place in the caste system.

2. **A husband who has more than one wife is following which of the following patterns?**

   (A) monogamy
   (B) polyandry
   (C) polygyny
   (D) exogamy
   (E) endogamy

2. (C) Polygyny is the pattern of one husband and several wives; polyandry is the opposite pattern. Monogamy is one husband and one wife. Exogamy is marriage outside the clan or group. Endogamy is marriage within the clan or group.

3. **The purpose of a fair trade law is which of the following?**

   (A) to allow producers to set minimum sales prices for their items
   (B) to reduce the likelihood of price wars
   (C) to increase foreign trade
   (D) to decrease foreign trade
   (E) A and B

3. (E) A and B. Many appliance prices, for example, are covered by fair trade laws.

4. **Cultural lag examines which of the following?**

   (A) rates of change within a society
   (B) population distribution
   (C) social movements
   (D) none of the above
   (E) all of the above

4. (A) Cultural lag examines rates of change within society.

5. **The collective effort of environmentalists to influence society's values and actions concerning the physical world would be considered which of the following?**

(A) social change
(B) social movement
(C) cultural lag
(D) deviant behavior
(E) none of the above

5. (B) The efforts of environmentalists to bring about social change make up a social movement. While cultural lag and deviant behavior are involved, the work of such a group is called a social movement.

6. **Which of the following statements concerning deviance is true?**

(A) Deviance can have positive effects.
(B) Deviance is always punishable.
(C) Deviance always varies slightly from the norm.
(D) Deviance always varies greatly from the norm.
(E) The norm is always clearly established when discussing deviance.

6. (A) Deviance can have positive effects; for example, it can solidify a group. Some deviant behavior is approved of by society. Not only can degree of deviance from the norm vary, but it can also be difficult to define the norm.

7. **In psychology, empirical studies would depend primarily on which of the following?**

(A) the viewpoint of the classical Greek philosophers
(B) experimentation
(C) precise measurement of results
(D) direct observation and logical reasoning
(E) introspection

7. (D) An empirical approach would rely on direct observation and logical reasoning. This is more scientific than the Greeks, but less scientific than the structuralists and behaviorists.

8. **Merrill-Lynch is "bullish on America" suggests which of the following?**

   (A) The firm believes that prices will fall and sells.
   (B) The firm believes that prices will rise and buys.
   (C) The firm expects to sell at a profit in the future.
   (D) The firm expects to buy at a lower price.
   (E) A combination of B and C

8. (E) A bull is a person who expects that prices will rise and so buys with the hopes of selling at a future date to make a profit.

9. **Which of the following groups would be most likely to investigate physiological changes in an organism?**

   (A) the Greek philosophers
   (B) the empiricists
   (C) the behaviorists
   (D) humanistic psychologists
   (E) the functionalists

9. (C) Only the behaviorists would be concerned primarily with physiological changes in organisms. The Greeks and the empiricists would be more philosophical in their approach. Functionalists would concentrate on the workings of the mind. Humanistic psychologists are concerned with helping people adopt healthy behavior patterns.

10. **Which of the following is thought to be the ancestor of modern gorillas and chimpanzees?**

    (A) Proconsul
    (B) *Zinjanthropus*
    (C) *Dryopithecus*
    (D) *Homo habilis*
    (E) Australopithecus

10. (A) The Proconsul group is thought to be the ancestor of modern gorillas and apes.

11. **A morpheme is which of the following?**

    (A) the smallest sound in a language
    (B) a society lacking a system for writing
    (C) an oral tradition
    (D) the smallest meaningful unit in a language
    (E) none of the above

11. (D) A morpheme is the smallest meaningful unit in a language. A phoneme is the smallest sound in a language. A nonliterate society lacks a system for writing.

12. **Which of the following is an example of a vestigial organ?**

(A) the appendix
(B) human body hair
(C) human finger nails
(D) cecum
(E) all of the above

12. (E) The human appendix, hair, fingernails and cecum are all vestigial organs which once served specific purposes.

Question 13 and 14 refer to the graph below:

SALES BY INDUSTRY

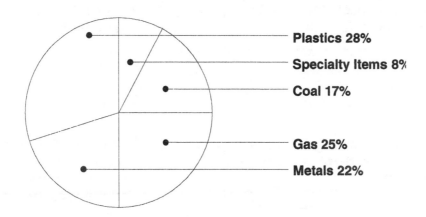

Plastics 28%

Specialty Items 8%

Coal 17%

Gas 25%

Metals 22%

13. **Which three items represent 50 percent of sales volume?**

(A) plastics—specialty items—coal
(B) coal—specialty items—metals
(C) coal—specialty items—gas
(D) gas—coal—metals
(E) plastics—metals

13. (C) Specialty items, coal and gas represent 50%. Plastics and metals also represent 50%, but the question stated three items, not two.

14. **Which of the following items represents the largest percentage of sales excluding plastics?**

(A) specialty items
(B) gas
(C) metals
(D) coal
(E) none of the above

14. (B) Gas represents the largest percentage at 25. Plastics, at 28, was excluded in the question.

15. Those events which happened but which have left no physical or non-physical traces are known as

(A) chronological warps
(B) actual history
(C) recorded history
(D) mythology
(E) legends

15. (B) Those events which actually happened comprise actual history.

16. The type of society which existed in Japan before that country was Westernized could best be characterized as

(A) primitive
(B) fascist
(C) communist
(D) socialist
(E) feudal

16. (E) Although feudalism is a term usually associated with Europe, it can be applied to Japan as well.

17. Which of the following is the best definition of the term "Industrial Revolution"?

(A) the development of the factory system and production of goods through the use of machines
(B) the results of the use of steam power and the rise of organized labor
(C) the result of the development of factories and a nationwide market for the goods produced in factories
(D) the development of a democratic way of life and of production of goods in factories by machines
(E) the degradation of the worker in the factory system

17. (A) The other choices may be by-products of industrialization in some societies, but not the definition of the term.

18. **In 1789, which of the following had a revolution for "Liberty, Equality and Fraternity," which spread ideas of reform and democracy throughout Europe?**

(A) France
(B) United States
(C) England
(D) Germany
(E) Russia

19. **When a society or group is organized or set up with people and officials at different levels with each having certain powers and responsibilities, it is known as which of the following?**

(A) hierarchy
(B) anarchy
(C) bureaucracy
(D) monopoly
(E) totalitarian society

20. **Which of the following best describes a clan?**

(A) nuclear families
(B) extended families
(C) related lineages
(D) all members of the society
(E) none of the above

21. **Which of the following describes a dowry?**

(A) a gift from the bride's parents to the groom's parents
(B) a gift from the bride's parents to the groom and bride
(C) permission from the society to marry
(D) a bride-price
(E) a prohibition of marriage

18. (A) France

19. (A) A bureaucracy is a hierarchy, but a hierarchy is not necessarily a bureaucracy.

20. (C) Clans are composed of people with related lineages. Several nuclear and/or extended families must be related to one another in order to be considered a clan. While a small society may be a clan, societies usually are larger and contain several clans.

21. (B) A dowry is a gift from the bride's parents to the bride and groom to help them set up housekeeping.

22. **The Oracle of Apollo at Delphi practiced which of the following?**

(A) witchcraft
(B) divination
(C) white magic
(D) contagious magic
(E) none of the above

22. (B) Oracles practice divination, or prediction of the future. Witchcraft is a type of magic that is inherited. White magic, which benefits people, and contagious magic, which used materials which were once in contact to exert influence over one another, are learned.

23. **The practice of not hiring persons whose names appear on lists of union sympathizers is called which of the following?**

(A) yellow-dog contract
(B) blacklisting
(C) check-off
(D) closed shop
(E) union shop

23. (B) Blacklisting

24. **A lag can best be described by which of the following?**

(A) Wages do not rise as quickly as rising prices.
(B) Money is hoarded.
(C) Workers earn wages at a faster rate than rising prices.
(D) Production increases and prices decline.
(E) Overproduction occurs.

24. (A) Lags contribute to fluctuations in the business cycle.

25. **In the business cycle, which of the following is NOT a sign of recovery?**

(A) Costs adjust to the lower price level.
(B) Banks will offer credit.
(C) Unemployment decreases.
(D) Purchasing power increases.
(E) Profits remain at the same level or fall.

25. (E) Another sign of recovery is that profits begin to increase.

26. **Secular price trends are general changes in the price level witnessed within which of the following time spans?**

(A) 2-3 years
(B) 3-5 years
(C) 5-10 years
(D) 10-25 years
(E) 15-50 years

27. **Which of the following aids conformity?**

(A) sanctions
(B) interdependence among individuals
(C) identification with a group
(D) socialization
(E) all of the above

28. **Who of the following is credited with "The Looking Glass Self"?**

(A) Ferdinand Tonnies
(B) Emile Durkheim
(C) George Herbert Mead
(D) Charles Horton Cooley
(E) Robert E. Park

29. **Which of the following statements is NOT true?**

(A) Culture forms the basic personality of members of a group.
(B) Modern society produces individuals who are all alienated and lonely.
(C) The family is the most important contribution to socialization.
(D) A and B
(E) B and C

26. (D) General pricing trends can be seen within 10 to 25 years. Within these time periods are short-term fluctuations, known as the business cycle.

27. (E) Conformity to social norms is aided by sanctions (rewards and punishments), interdependence among individuals, identification with a group, and socialization.

28. (D) Cooley is the originator of "The Looking-Glass Self." Tonnies divided society into *gemeinschaft* and *gellenschaft*. Durkheim emphasized the importance of the group. Mead is associated with the "I"-"Me" aspects of the self. Park also emphasized the group.

29. (D) There is no proof that all cultures form the basic personality of members of the group, nor that all members of modern society are anomic. The family remains the most important factor in socialization. Schools are in some cases assuming this role more and more.

30. **Which of the following is an example of residual power?**

(A) declaring war
(B) levying taxes
(C) approving ministers
(D) enacting divorce laws
(E) coining money

31. **Which amendment gave eighteen-year-olds the right to vote?**

(A) 15th Amendment
(B) 16th Amendment
(C) 19th Amendment
(D) 24th Amendment
(E) 26th Amendment

32. **Of the following, which is the primary question a government must answer?**

(A) Who shall rule?
(B) Who shall vote?
(C) What will the form of government be?
(D) How much control and freedom shall there be?
(E) How should revenue be collected?

33. **Which of the following is an example of a stereotype?**

(A) a dedicated teacher
(B) a devoted mother
(C) a dumb blond
(D) a dishonest politician
(E) all of the above

---

30. (D) States are allowed to enact divorce laws. Declaring war, approving ministers and coining money are exclusive powers of the national government. Levying taxes is a concurrent power, that is, shared by national and state governments.

31. (E) The twenty-sixth amendment guarantees this right; it is the most recent amendment to the *Constitution.*

32. (D) While all the questions are important factors, the amount of control and freedom outlined by a government is most influential in determining the welfare and happiness of a people.

33. (E) The dedicated teacher and the devoted mother are positive stereotypes; the dumb blond and the dishonest politician are negative stereotypes. All stereotypes are false to some degree; for example, not all teachers are dedicated.

34. **Which of the following statements is NOT true of culture?**

(A) Cultures vary from group to group.
(B) National boundaries determine cultural boundaries.
(C) Cultures share some features in common such as marriage and child-rearing rules.
(D) Cultures persist.
(E) Subcultures may exist.

34. **(B)** National boundaries do not always indicate cultural boundaries. Immigrants, for example, transplant their culture in their new country. Cultures do vary but often share common features. They tend to persist and may contain subcultures.

Questions 35 and 36 refer to the following graph:

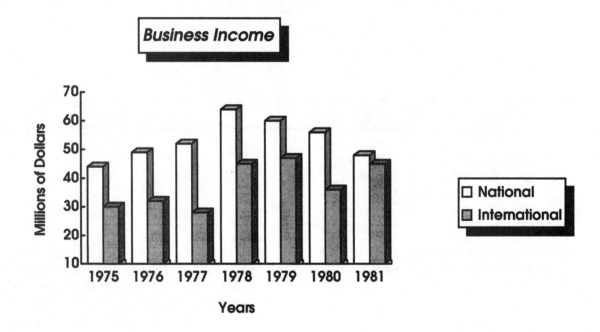

35. **Which of the following years represents peak business income on the national level?**

(A) 1975
(B) 1976
(C) 1977
(D) 1978
(E) 1979

35. **(D)** 1978—the national income was approximately $64 million.

263

Business Income

Millions of Dollars

Years

☐ National
▨ International

---

36. **What is the average international business income over the years 1975 through 1981?**

(A) $10 million-$20 million
(B) $20 million-$30 million
(C) $30 million-$40 million
(D) $40 million-$50 million
(E) $50 million-$60 million

37. **Which of the following is often called the "Cradle of Civilization"?**

(A) Ur
(B) Jericho
(C) Natuf
(D) Tigris-Euphrates
(E) Ubaid

36. (C) The international business income is in the $30 million to $40 million range.

37. (D) The Tigris-Euphrates river system is often called the "Cradle of Civilization" because so many cities, including Ur, Ubaid and Jarmo, were on the shores. During the Neolithic Age (in Israel), Natuf was a preagricultural city of people who collected and stored seeds. Jericho, also in Israel, was a Neolithic city.

38. Written history goes back how many years?

(A) 10,000
(B) 8,000
(C) 5,000
(D) 3,000
(E) 2,000

39. Which of the following would be the proper sequence of events at a dig?

(A) "sample" dig, survey area, move artifact, record location of artifact
(B) "sample" dig, record location of artifact, survey area, move artifact
(C) survey area, record location of artifact, "sample" dig, move artifact
(D) survey area, "sample" dig, record location of artifact, move artifact
(E) none of the above

40. Absolute chronology indicates which of the following?

(A) specific ages
(B) exact date and time of the article's manufacture
(C) age relative to other finds
(D) an age comparable to similar finds
(E) none of the above

38. (C) Written history goes back between five and six thousand years.

39. (D) The area is surveyed; "sample" or "test" digs are then made. When found, the location of an artifact is recorded before it is moved.

40. (A) Absolute, or direct, chronology indicates specific age. It does not indicate exact date and time. Relative, or indirect, chronology indicates age as either younger or older than the age of other finds. Crossdating is the comparison of traits, when the age of one is known, to indicate age.

41. **In chimpanzee society which of the following is NOT a rule of dominance?**

(A) Young males dominate grown females.
(B) Older males dominate all.
(C) Grown females dominate all the young males.
(D) A flexible order of dominance exists among the grown males.
(E) Grown females dominate young females.

41. (A) Grown female chimpanzees dominate the young of both sexes.

42. **Baby chimpanzees are wholly dependent upon their mothers for how long?**

(A) 1 week
(B) 6 weeks
(C) 3 months
(D) 6 months
(E) 2 years

42. (D) Baby chimpanzees are fully dependent upon their mothers for about six months.

43. **The most famous wagon train route to the Pacific Coast was known as the**

(A) Wilderness Road
(B) National Road
(C) Natchez Trail
(D) Oregon Trail
(E) Jefferson Highway

43. (D) So named for the territory it led to.

44. **The main reason for the great Irish emigration to America in the middle of the 1800's was which of the following?**

(A) religious tension between Ireland and England
(B) unemployment, low wages, and high rents for land in Ireland
(C) absentee landlords were selling the land for factories
(D) the failure of the potato crop due to a blight
(E) the lure of free land in America

44. (D) The other conditions may have contributed, but the potato blight was the chief reason.

45. "The concept of 'black power' is not a recent or isolated phenomenon: It has grown out of the ferment of agitation and activity by different people and organizations in many black communities over the years. Where black men have a majority, they will attempt to use it to exercise control. This is what they seek: control. Where Negroes lack a majority, black power means proper representation and sharing of control.

The quote above reflects the viewpoint of whom of the following?

(A) Martin Luther King
(B) Booker T. Washington
(C) W. E. B. DuBois
(D) Stokely Carmichael
(E) Marcus Garvey

45. (D) The call for black power occurred in the 1960's; therefore, Washington, DuBois, and Garvey were too early; King tended to avoid use of the term.

46. Which part of the body actually "sees" images?

(A) retina
(B) rods
(C) cones
(D) optic nerve
(E) cerebral cortex

46. (E) It is the cerebral cortex, a part of the brain, that interprets stimuli and "sees." The retina and its rods and cones receive stimuli, and the optic nerve carries these impulses to the cerebral cortex.

47. Railroad tracks which appear to converge in the distance is an example of which of the following?

(A) interposition
(B) linear perspective
(C) gradient texture
(D) shadow
(E) aerial perspective

47. (B) "Converging" railroad tracks is an example of linear perspective. Broken contours of distant objects by nearer objects is interposition. The smooth appearance of distant objects is an example of gradients of texture. Shadows are patterns of dark and light. Distant objects appearing less clear is an example of aerial perspective.

48. Development depends upon which of the following factors?

(A) environment
(B) heredity
(C) maturation
(D) structure of the organism
(E) all of the above

48. (E) Individual development depends upon the structures present as well as heredity which determines structure and maturation. The environment also influences development.

49. At which point does a human embryo become a fetus?

(A) two weeks after conception
(B) four weeks after conception
(C) eight weeks after conception
(D) three months after conception
(E) one hundred and forty days after conception

49. (C) A human embryo becomes a fetus eight weeks after conception. At this point the fetus will respond to stimuli in a head-to-tail fashion.

50. Which of the following situations would probably be the least stressful?

(A) starting a new job
(B) meeting future in-laws
(C) taking the CLEP test
(D) moving to a new town
(E) going window-shopping

50. (E) Window-shopping would probably be the least stressful because it is done primarily for relaxation and enjoyment; there is no pressure to buy. New situations or ones that involve change tend to be stress-producing.

51. Which of the following best defines a hypothesis?

(A) a suspected relationship
(B) a contributing factor
(C) a proven truth
(D) an expected result
(E) an unexpected result

51. (A) A hypothesis is a suspected relationship. An axiom is a proven truth. A result is an effect. A theory is a principle backed by considerable evidence but not yet proven absolutely.

52. The normal bell curve is which of the following?

(A) skewed positively
(B) skewed negatively
(C) all frequency distributions
(D) all polygons
(E) normal probability curve

52. (E) The normal bell curve is the normal probability curve. Positively skewed curves have more scores at the low end; negatively skewed curves have more scores at the high end. Frequency distributions are not always normal curves, nor are polygons (a type of frequency distribution).

53. Which of the following is the mode?

(A) the number representing the common average
(B) the number representing the score which appears most frequently
(C) the number representing the middle score
(D) the total of the scores
(E) the total of the two extreme scores

53. (B) The mode is the number representing the score appearing most frequently. The mean is the common average; the median is the middle score.

54. Which of the following societies is likely to undergo rapid change?

(A) folk
(B) rural
(C) *gemeinschaft*
(D) sacred
(E) none of the above

54. (E) All the types mentioned—folk, rural, *gemeinschaft* and sacred—are centered on the family and kinship ties and depend upon an agricultural way of life; these tend to change less rapidly than modern, urban societies.

55. Which of the following is NOT considered a concern of sociology?

(A) objectivity
(B) proving all common sense observations about behavior
(C) finding solutions to social ills
(D) B and C
(E) all of the above

55. (D) Sociology does not seek to prove common sense notions; in fact, some of these ideas have been "disproven." The sociologist concentrates on generalizing human behavior objectively; he does not concentrate on solving social problems.

56. According to the types of suicide outlined by Emile Durkheim, which of the following applies to suicide because of a failed love affair?

(A) egoistic
(B) altruistic
(C) anomic
(D) ennui
(E) all of the above

56. (A) According to Durkheim, suicide is egoistic if prompted by the individual's weakening belief in the group. It is altruistic if he is thoroughly committed to the group's goals and anomic if his goals are threatened by rapid social change. Ennui simply means boredom.

Questions 57 through 61 refer to the following list:

I. tropism
II. reflex response
III. instinctive behaviors
IV. physiological drives
V. acquired drives

57. Migration is an example of which of the above responses?

(A) I
(B) II
(C) III
(D) IV
(E) V

57. (C) Migration is instinctive behavior. It is a pattern of action with which the organism is born.

58. The need for food is an example of which of the above responses?

(A) I
(B) II
(C) III
(D) IV
(E) V

58. (D) The need for food is a physiological drive. It is an arousal caused by physical need satisfied by a learned pattern of behavior.

59. A plant is most likely to display which of the above responses?

(A) I
(B) II
(C) III
(D) IV
(E) V

59. (A) A plant's response to light is phototropism, the movement toward light.

60. The desire for power is an example of which of the above responses?

(A) I
(B) II
(C) III
(D) IV
(E) V

60. (E) The desire for power is an acquired drive, a behavior guided by learned habits and values.

61. Blinking is an example of which of the above responses?

(A) I
(B) II
(C) III
(D) IV
(E) V

61. (B) Blinking is a reflex response, the automatic reaction of muscles if, for example, a piece of lint gets in a person's eye.

62. A corrupt aristocracy is known as which of the following?

(A) autocracy
(B) monarchy
(C) tyranny
(D) oligarchy
(E) plurality

62. (D) An oligarchy is rule by a few which has become corrupt.

63. The most likely explanation of modern man's arrival to the Americas is which of the following?

(A) by boat across the North Atlantic
(B) by boat across the South Pacific
(C) modern man developed independently in the Americas
(D) crossing what is now the Bering Strait
(E) none of the above

63. (D) The most likely explanation is that man arrived in America by crossing what is now the Bering Strait but what was an almost continuous strip of land about 30,000 years ago.

64. Which of the following would be the correct order from earliest to latest?

(A) Neaderthal—Cro-Magnon—Peking man—Australopithecus
(B) Peking man—Australopithecus—Neanderthal—Cro-Magnon
(C) Cro-Magnon—Peking man—Australopithecus—Neanderthal
(D) Australopithecus—Neanderthal—Cro-Magnon—Peking man
(E) none of the above

64. (D) *Australopithecus* is the oldest species listed; Peking man, *homo erectus*, comes next, then Neanderthal followed by Cro-Magnon, both *Homo sapiens*.

65. Which of the following fossils proved to be a hoax?

(A) Java man
(B) Piltdown man
(C) Swanscombe man
(D) Steinheim man
(E) none of the above

65. (B) Piltdown man was discovered in the early 1900's by Charles Dawson. Fluorine testing in 1953 proved the fossil to be a hoax. Other tests proved the upper skull to be human and the jaw to be a modern ape's.

66. In addition to the Spanish-American War, the United States has been accused of imperialism in which of the following wars?

(A) Mexican War
(B) Civil War
(C) World War I
(D) World War II
(E) Vietnam War

66. (A) The United States gained California and the Southwest Territory as a result of the Mexican War.

Questions 67-69 refer to the following graph:

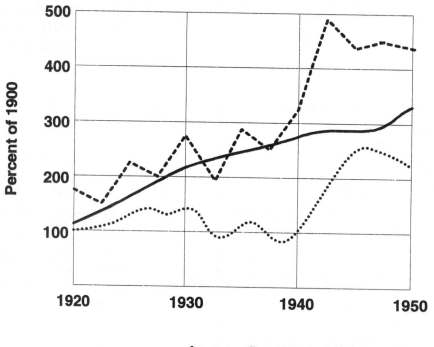

```
------------- Income Per Capita
———————————— Gross National Product
·················· Output Per Man Hour
```

67. According to the graph, which two factors show the greatest relationships?

(A) GNP and output per man hour
(B) GNP and income per capita
(C) Income per capita and output per man hour
(D) All of the factors are equal.
(E) There is not enough information in the graph to determine this.

67. (C) As workers are more productive and produce more goods, they tend to earn more money.

68. **At what point was production the lowest?**

(A) 1921
(B) 1932
(C) 1933
(D) 1935
(E) 1938

68. (A) The GNP was the lowest about 1921.

69. **In the early 1930's, why did income per capita continue to rise, while both GNP and output per man hour declined?**

(A) The decline was not enough to affect income per capita.
(B) There is a time-lag between production and income.
(C) The government, through New Deal policies, pumped money into the economy.
(D) Income per capita is not related to GNP and output per man hour.
(E) There is not enough information in the graph to determine this.

69. (E) The graph does not contain enough information to determine WHY the income per capita rose.

70. **What methods can scientists use to date their finds?**

(A) geological studies
(B) fluorine test
(C) carbon-14 test
(D) crossdating
(E) all of the above

70. (E) Scientists can study rock formations to get accurate estimates of time. The fluorine test is based on the fact that bones increase in fluorine with time. The carbon-14 test indicates age because the content of radioactive carbon 14 decreases with age. Comparison of finds at a site of unknown age with those of determined age is useful.

71. **Mutation is best described as which of the following?**

(A) replication
(B) phenotype-genotype
(C) dominant gene
(D) recessive gene
(E) none of the above

71. (E) Mutation is a sudden change in the genes of an organism which will cause variation. Replication is the DNA's processes of splitting and reproducing itself. Phenotype is the observable traits; recessive genes are hidden unless there are two, which make the trait observable.

72. **Diffusion occurs when which of the following happens?**

(A) A society has no contact with other cultures.
(B) The culture traits of one group are rejected by another.
(C) The invention of a technique is made independently elsewhere.
(D) The culture traits of two groups intermingle.
(E) None of the above

73. **Groups can be identified by which of the following factors?**

(A) membership
(B) purpose
(C) function
(D) structure
(E) all of the above

74. **The primary purpose of government is to do which of the following?**

(A) encourage cooperation
(B) encourage competition
(C) decide the form of government
(D) decide the amount of control of competition and cooperation
(E) decide who shall vote

75. **In which of the following offices must appropriations of money originate?**

(A) the executive branch
(B) the judicial branch
(C) the Senate
(D) The House of Representatives
(E) all of the above

72. (D) When culture traits intermingle, or those of one group are accepted by another, diffusion occurs. Inventions made independently are conveniently called independent inventions.

73. (E) All of the items listed are ways to identify a group.

74. (D) The primary purpose of government is to control both cooperation and competition. In doing so, a government sets a relationship between amounts of control and freedom.

75. (D) Article I of the *Constitution* stipulates that all bills appropriating funds originate in the House of Representatives.

76. Unlike the previous Confederation Government, the new Constitutional Government could do which of the following?

(A) act directly upon the people of the United States
(B) issue money
(C) require state officials to take an oath of allegiance to the *Constitution*
(D) call up state militias
(E) all of the above

76. (E) All of these powers were delegated to the central government under the new *Constitution*

77. David Ricardo wrote about the Iron Law of Wages which states which of the following should occur?

(A) Wages should be kept at a low level in order to discourage population growth.
(B) Wages should increase only if a profit is seen.
(C) Wages should decrease in times of inflation.
(D) Wages should be issued as an incentive to the worker to increase productivity.
(E) Wages should reflect an equal distribution of company profit.

77. (A) By keeping wages low, the worker would be discouraged from having more children than he himself could afford to rear.

78. Which of the following agencies have helped to insure banking stability?

(A) FDIC (Federal Deposit Insurance Corporation)
(B) FHA (Federal Housing Authority)
(C) Farm Credit Administration
(D) Reconstruction Finance Corporation
(E) all of the above

78. (E) All of the above.

79. **Which of the following is the main purpose of an investment bank?**

(A) to make short-term loans to private individuals
(B) to act as a trustee administrator
(C) to make long-term loans to industry
(D) to offer checking and saving accounts
(E) to compare checks of various member banks in order to counterbalance them

79. (C) Investment banks operate primarily for the benefit of industry.

80. **The government borrows money for public projects through which of the following?**

(A) the sale of bonds
(B) increased taxes
(C) increased money supply from the central bank
(D) use of gold deposits
(E) custom duties

80. (A) Through the sale of government bonds many public projects are financed. These bonds do return the price of the bond and interest to the buyer.

81. **Which of the following forms of taxation is currently considered to be the most equitable?**

(A) property tax
(B) placing the heaviest burden on those who are best able to pay
(C) placing the heaviest burden on those who benefit most from government projects
(D) even distribution of tax burden
(E) none of the above

81. (B) This is known as the graduated income tax; it is based on income, assets and liabilities.

82. **Which of the following provides an indication of the degree of deviation of each score from the mean?**

(A) the standard deviation
(B) measures of correlation
(C) random sampling
(D) standard error of the mean
(E) critical ratio

82. **(A)** The standard deviation measures degree of deviation of each score from the mean. Correlations describe the relationship between sets of measures. Random sampling is selecting a study group by chance. Standard error of the mean is used to be certain that the sample's characteristics do not vary too greatly from the whole. Critical ratio tells significance of difference between sample means.

83. **Pavlov can be considered the father of which of the following?**

(A) psychoanalysis
(B) operant conditioning
(C) instrumental conditioning
(D) classical conditioning
(E) structuralism

83. **(D)** Pavlov is associated with classical conditioning. Operant, or instrumental, conditioning is associated with Skinner. Psychoanalysis is associated with Freud. Structuralism is associated with Kelly and the cognitive approach.

84. **Which of the following is associated with the id?**

(A) thought processes
(B) area housing repressed thoughts
(C) area housing non-repressed thoughts
(D) biological urges
(E) the conscience

84. **(D)** The id is associated with biological urges, the ego with rational thought, and the superego with the conscience; the unconscious holds repressed thoughts, the conscious and preconscious, non-repressed thoughts.

85. Which of the following is the correct order of progression presented in the Three Stages developed by Auguste Comte?

(A) theological—scientific—metaphysical
(B) metaphysical—scientific—theological
(C) scientific—theological—metaphysical
(D) theological—metaphysical—scientific
(E) metaphysical—theological—scientific

85. (D) In Comte's "Law of the Three Stages," the theological, a supernatural explanation of events, comes first. Next comes the metaphysical, unsubstantiated conjecture to explain events; the scientific, rational study follows.

86. By studying data such as occupation and income level, sociologists study stratification from which of the following approaches?

(A) subjective
(B) objective
(C) reputational
(D) all of the above
(E) none of the above

86. (B) The objective approach studies data. The subjective approach asks participants in the study to rank themselves. The reputational approach asks participants to rank others in their society.

87. Which of the following would be an example of an indirect tax?

(A) income tax
(B) sales tax
(C) custom duty
(D) higher price for an item
(E) all of the above

87. (D) The higher price paid by the consumer may in part offset taxes the producer had to pay for raw materials. Income tax, sales tax and custom duty are all examples of direct tax.

88. Who of the following is best known for his theory concerning population growth and food supplies?

(A) Adam Smith
(B) John Stuart Mill
(C) Milton Friedman
(D) John Maynard Keynes
(E) none of the above

88. (E) In the 18th century, Thomas Malthus wrote about population explosion and food shortages. Smith is the father of Classical Economics; Mill stated that profits should be shared with workers; Friedman is a modern economist; Keynes wrote about inflation and deficit spending.

89. **Which of the following statements best describes the Law of Diminishing Returns?**

(A) As more labor is added, productivity will continue to rise indefinitely.

(B) As more labor is added, productivity will continue to rise to the point where the marginal product is less than the average product.

(C) As more labor is added, productivity will at first decline and then rise indefinitely.

(D) As more labor is added, productivity will increase to the point where the marginal product is equal to the average product.

(E) None of the above.

89. (D) Remember the marginal product is the additional output of each worker; the average output is the average for ALL workers. If one more man reduces AVERAGE output, he is reducing productivity.

90. **In order to avoid excessive business fluctuations, which approach needs to be adopted?**

(A) proper monetary policy
(B) proper fiscal policy
(C) governmental regulation
(D) A and B only
(E) A, B and C

90. (E) Post-Depression economic theory stated that successful regulation of business fluctuations requires sound monetary and fiscal policy along with additional government regulation. Truth be known, this is debatable.

Questions 91 through 95 refer to the following list:

I. cooperation
II. competition
III. conflict
IV. accommodation
V. assimilation

91. **Which can be, but is not always, destructive?**

(A) I
(B) II
(C) III
(D) IV
(E) V

91. (B) Competition can produce hostile feelings among players and can be destructive. However, competition can be healthy because it brings out the best in some people.

Questions 91 through 95 refer to the following list:

I.   cooperation
II.   competition
III.   conflict
IV.   accommodation
V.   assimilation

92. Which is an example of mediation?

(A) I
(B) II
(C) III
(D) IV
(E) V

92. (D) Mediation is a compromise solution offered by a third party which the conflicting parties may or may not accept. It is a form of accommodation.

93. As ethnic groups reside in one area, intermarry and share cultural traditions, which process is taking place?

(A) I
(B) II
(C) III
(D) IV
(E) V

93. (E) Assimilation occurs when two cultures interact, exchange ideas and blend together.

94. When two distinct groups join forces to petition the town council for a recreational facility in their area, they are using which process?

(A) I
(B) II
(C) III
(D) IV
(E) V

94. (A) Joining forces for a common goal is an example of cooperation.

95. If one company sabotages the operations of another in order to gain a larger share of the market, which process is being employed?

(A) I
(B) II
(C) III
(D) IV
(E) V

95. (C) Conflict is competing for scarce goods and harming those who are also competing. Companies normally compete for markets, but sabotage may be ethically and/or criminally wrong.

96. **The Know-Nothing Party opposed which of the following groups?**

(A) unions
(B) carpetbaggers
(C) Catholics
(D) blacks
(E) women

96. (C) The Know-Nothings opposed Catholics and aliens holding public office; they desired stricter naturalization laws and literacy tests for voting.

97. **Under *The United States Constitution* the House must originate which of the following bills?**

(A) declaration of war
(B) interstate commerce
(C) revenue appropriation
(D) bankruptcy
(E) foreign commerce

97. (C) All bills appropriating revenue must originate in the House, Article I, section 7 of the *Constitution.*

98. **People of a state may demonstrate their approval or rejection of legislation through which of the following?**

(A) referendum
(B) short ballot
(C) recall
(D) cloture rule
(E) initiative

98. (A) Citizens can approve or reject passed legislation through a referendum. Through initiative, citizens can originate legislation they desire.

99. **Mayors Richard Daly of Chicago and Frank Hague of Jersey City can be associated with which of the following?**

(A) gerrymandering
(B) bossism
(C) dark horse
(D) log rolling
(E) Jim Crow

99. (B) Both mayors were heads of strong political machinery in their respective towns.

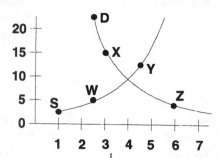

100. In a competitive market, which point represents equilibrium?

(A)   W
(B)   X
(C)   Y
(D)   Z
(E)   none of the above

100. (E)   None of the above. The point of equilibrium is the point where the demand curve meets the supply curve, in other words where supply meets demand.

101. Which of the following institutions has the power to control the supply of money in the economy?

(A)   savings banks
(B)   the Congress
(C)   the Federal Reserve System
(D)   the President
(E)   the Federal Trade Commission

101. (C)   One of the functions of the central bank is to control the amount of money in circulation.

102. A check can be defined best as which of the following?

(A)   bond
(B)   liability
(C)   paper currency
(D)   demand deposit
(E)   fiat

102. (D)   A check is a demand deposit; upon demand, money can be withdrawn from an account.

103. **Which of the following is NOT an advantage of the "corporation" as a form of business organization?**

(A) It can obtain larger amounts of money through the sales of shares of stock on the corporation than other forms can raise.

(B) The corporation has "perpetual life" and thus avoids interruptions to business.

(C) Shares can be bought and sold easily by their owners if they wish to get out or invest more fully in the business.

(D) It is a less complicated form of business organization to set up than the individual ownership or partnership type of business.

(E) Stockholders are legally responsible for only the amount of money they invested in the corporation and not for all of its debts (limited liability).

103. (D) The corporation is a much more complicated form of business organization.

104. **The demand for African independence after World War II was NOT influenced by which of the following?**

(A) newly independent states in Asia

(B) Allied war propaganda

(C) a money economy

(D) the collapse of the colonial system in Asia

(E) the defeat of Germany, which lost the German colonies in Africa

104. (E) Germany lost the African colonies after World War I, not after World War II.

105. **The principle of mercantilism and Adam Smith's theory of economics differ most sharply on which of the following points?**

    (A) Smith stated that a nation's wealth was based on its ability to produce, not its precious metals.

    (B) Smith stated that there should be tight government control; mercantilism believes in laissez faire.

    (C) The market place is found only in mercantilism.

    (D) Mercantilism needed colonies but Smith's theory did not.

    (E) none of the above.

105. (A) Adam Smith stated that a nation's wealth lies in its ability to produce.

106. **The type of economic system which depended upon the exploration of colonies to benefit the mother country was which of the following?**

    (A) traditional
    (B) market
    (C) guild
    (D) feudal
    (E) mercantilism

106. (E) Mercantilism needed colonies for, among other things, their natural resources.

107. **A wife who locks herself in the bedroom and cries after a long unsettled argument with her husband would be displaying which of the following responses?**

    (A) aggression
    (B) hostility
    (C) withdrawal
    (D) repression
    (E) regression

107. (C) Because the argument is described as long and unsettled, the wife is withdrawing from the source of frustration, the argument. Some might choose regression, the turning to coping behaviors of childhood, but crying is a legitimate adult response to relieve tension. Withdrawal does not have to be permanent.

108. Mesomorph is a term belonging to a study of personality developed by whom of the following?

(A) Hippocrates
(B) Sheldon
(C) Oedipus
(D) Rorschach
(E) none of the above

108. (B) W. H. Sheldon developed a system based on body types—endomorphs, ectomorphs and mesomorphs. Hippocrates' body type system was based on the "humors." Oedipus is a Greek figure whose name is used in labeling a complex in Freudian analysis. The Rorschach Inkblot Test is a projective test.

109. A statistical approach to defining abnormality is based on which of the following?

(A) Behavior is abnormal if it differs sufficiently from the norm.
(B) Quality of adjustment determines normality/abnormality.
(C) symptoms of abnormality
(D) all of the above
(E) none of the above

109. (A) A statistical approach defines abnormality as sufficient deviation from the norm. A theoretical approach looks for symptoms of abnormality.

110. Which of the following is mnemonics?

(A) reduction of sensitivity
(B) quality of being outgoing
(C) memory improvement devices
(D) stage of sleep when dreams occur
(E) Greek word for "soul" or "mind"

110. (C) Mnemonics are techniques to aid memory. Habituation is reduction of sensitivity to recurring stimuli. REM (Rapid Eye Movement) is the stage of sleep when dreams occur. Psyche is the Greek word for "soul" or "mind." Mnemonics comes from the Greek word for memory.

111. **Which of the following collections of people would constitute a group?**

    (A) a church choir
    (B) riders on a subway
    (C) all Vermont high school graduates
    (D) all workers in a downtown office building
    (E) draft-age males

111. (A) A church choir is a group. They are known to one another, interact and communicate. Vermont high school graduates and draft-age males form categories; they share characteristics but do not communicate. Riders in a subway and office workers in a large building form aggregates; they are in close proximity but do not have on-going communication.

112. **The discovery of fire was most likely which of the following?**

    (A) basic invention
    (B) secondary invention
    (C) an independent invention
    (D) an example of diffusion
    (E) A, C and D

112. (E) Fire is a basic invention. It is likely that it was discovered independently in various locations and passed from one member of a group to another.

113. **Physical anthropologists concentrate on which of the following areas?**

    (A) comparison of man to the primates
    (B) evolution
    (C) learned behavior
    (D) A and B
    (E) all of the above

113. (D) Physical anthropologists concentrate on man/primate comparisons and man's biological evolution. The cultural anthropologist is more concerned with man's learned behavior.

114. **The introduction of new farming techniques to a third world nation would be an example of which of the following?**

    (A) acculturation
    (B) ethnocentricism
    (C) civilization
    (D) ethnic appreciation
    (E) all of the above

114. (A) Introduction of modern farming techniques to a third world nation is an example of acculturation. This nation will not necessarily turn overnight into a civilization. This is not an example of ethnocentrism (love of own culture, distrust of others) or necessarily of ethnic appreciation.

115. **Which of the following elements is not found in all living things?**

(A) calcium
(B) hydrogen
(C) nitrogen
(D) phosphorus
(E) A and D

116. **Reinforcement is best defined by which of the following?**

(A) desensitization
(B) conditioned response
(C) increased likelihood that a response will occur
(D) unconditioned response
(E) extinction

117. **According to the structuralist approach to learning, conjunctive rules require which of the following?**

(A) the stating of all the relative attributes
(B) the stating of all the important relative attributes
(C) the stating of some of the relative attributes
(D) the stating of one relative attribute
(E) none of the above

118. **Eli Whitney's greatest contribution to the American Industrial Revolution was his application and demonstration of the value of which of the following?**

(A) the cotton gin
(B) interchangeable parts
(C) steam power
(D) dynamite
(E) steel in construction

115. (E) Hydrogen and nitrogen are found in all living things. Calcium and phosphorus are not always present.

116. (C) Reinforcement is a principle which states that a response followed by a reinforcing (encouraging) stimulus is more likely to occur again. An unconditioned response is untrained; a trained response is conditioned. The stimulus associated with response comes before the response. Desensitization eases and extinction eliminates the conditioned response.

117. (A) Conjunctive rules describe a concept by stating all the relative attributes (shared characteristics). Inclusive disjunctive rules do not require the stating of all shared characteristics.

118. (B) Whitney may be famous for his cotton gin, but interchangeable parts made the Industrial Revolution possible.

119. **Which of the following was NOT a consequence of World War I?**

    (A)   the League of Nations
    (B)   the fall of European aristocracies
    (C)   the displacement of millions of people
    (D)   the collapse of the British Empire
    (E)   the rise of communism is Russia

119. (D) The Empire may have been weakened but did not break up until after World War II.

120. **The famous founder and leader of the American Federation of Labor was who?**

    (A)   William Sylvis
    (B)   Uriah S. Stephens
    (C)   Samuel Gompers
    (D)   Terence V. Powderly
    (E)   Samuel Slater

120. (C) Samuel Gompers

121. **The "Great Compromise" during the Constitution Convention refers to which of the following?**

    (A)   addition of the Bill of Rights to the *Constitution*
    (B)   separation of power among the three branches
    (C)   how Congress would be represented—the Senate by two from each state, the House by the population of each state
    (D)   how much slavery would be allowed
    (E)   how the war debts would be paid

121. (C) This is also known as the Connecticut Compromise.

122. **Which of the following was NOT a benefit that the Cold War brought to the African nations?**

(A) military assistance
(B) economic aid
(C) both the United States and the Soviet Union voted in the United Nations for the independence of an African state.
(D) Intertribal rivalry was encouraged.
(E) the Peace Corps

122. (D) Intertribal rivalry tended to be detrimental not beneficial.

123. **Which of the following statements is the most accurate regarding the relationship between the middle class and the absolute monarchs of Europe (1500 to 1800)?**

(A) The bourgeoisie rallied to support the monarchs because of mercantilist policies.
(B) The bourgeoisie supported the monarchs in order to withstand the demands of the working classes.
(C) The bourgeoisie turned against the monarchs when they adopted anti-middle class policies.
(D) The bourgeoisie at first supported the feudal lords but later supported the monarchs during the time of the Industrial Revolution.
(E) The bourgeoisie turned against the monarchs when the monarchs supported legislation favoring the working class.

123. (C) The bourgeoisie were strong supporters of the monarchy until the monarchs, through the mercantile policies, tended to undermine the middle-class interests.

Questions 124 and 125 refer to the following list:

    I.   Carrie Nation
    II.   Nellie Bly
    III.   Elizabeth Cady Stanton
    IV.   Jane Addams
    V.   Victoria Woodhull

124. Who was the woman whose settlement house, Hull House, in the slums of Chicago did much social good?

(A) I
(B) II
(C) III
(D) IV
(E) V

124. (D)   Jane Addams

125. Who was the first woman stockbroker on Wall Street and the first woman to run for President?

(A) I
(B) II
(C) III
(D) IV
(E) V

125. (E)   Victoria Woodhull

Notes

Notes